The Governance of British Higher Education

Praise for *The Governance of British Higher Education*

'A superb overview of higher education across the four UK nations: broader, clearer and more coherent in its core argument than other recent works. It also creates a compelling picture of the global landscape in which the UK institutions sit, and focuses our attention on the curiously partial nature of their connection to that landscape.

Without being at all strident or ideological, Shattock and Horvath have destroyed the premises on which contemporary UK policy is based – the assumptions that tighter state control, consumer markets and easy entry to commercial providers will somehow usher in a new flowering of quality, access, university autonomy and academic creativity.'

Simon Marginson, Professor of Higher Education, University of Oxford, UK, and Editor of the Bloomsbury Higher Education Research series

'*An admirable assessment of the changes in system and institutional governance during a critical period. It updates Shattock's own previous work with new empirical evidence, razor sharp analysis and wise conclusions.'*

William Locke, Professor and Director of the Melbourne Centre for the Study of Higher Education, University of Melbourne, Australia

'*This book provides a sophisticated and comprehensive analysis of how British universities have been transformed, not always for the better, by government-led funding and management initiatives in recent decades. The comparison of the different countries of the United Kingdom and the discussion of the global environment are especially useful.'*

Philip G. Altbach, Research Professor and Founding Director, Center for International Higher Education, Boston College, USA

Bloomsbury Higher Education Research

Series editor: Simon Marginson

Bloomsbury's Higher Education Research Series provides the evidence-based academic output of the world's leading research centre on higher education, the ESRC/Higher Education Funding Council for England (HEFCE) Centre for Global Higher Education (CGHE) in the UK. CGHE, with its central office at University College London, is a consortium of five British and eight international universities. It currently includes sixteen research projects and thirty-eight individual researchers, and is financed by £6.7 million in funding from the UK Economic and Social Research Council, partner universities and other sources. The core focus of CGHE's work and of the Bloomsbury Higher Education Research Series is higher education, especially *the future of higher education in the changing global landscape*. The emergence of CGHE reflects the remarkable growth in the role and importance of universities and other higher education institutions, and research and science, across the world. National higher education systems now take in almost 40 per cent of all young people on the global scale (in fifty-six countries, more than half of all young people) and have become engine rooms for technological and social innovation. In addition to Europe/UK and North America, higher education and science are now growing especially rapidly in China and East Asia, Southeast Asia, India and Latin America, with diverse new ideas about best practice coming forward all the time. Corresponding to CGHE's projects, monographs in the series will consist of social science research on global, international, national and local aspects of higher education, drawing on methodologies in education, learning theory, sociology, economics, political science and policy studies. Monographs will be prepared so as to maximize worldwide readership and selected on the basis of their relevance to one or more of higher education policy, management, practice and theory. Topics will range from teaching and learning and technologies, to research and research impact in industry, national system design, the public good role of universities, social stratification and equity, institutional governance and management, and the cross-border mobility of people, institutions, programmes, ideas and knowledge. Much of CGHE's work is global and comparative in scale, drawing lessons from higher education in many different countries and from the skills and wisdom of researchers in the UK, USA, Australia, Ireland, China, Hong Kong, Japan, South Africa and the Netherlands, including a dozen postdoctoral and doctoral scholars who will be tomorrow's research leaders in this field. The Higher Education Research Series is at the cutting edge of world research on higher education.

Forthcoming in the series

The Future of Higher Education, edited by Claire Callender, William Locke and Simon Marginson

The Governance of British Higher Education

The Impact of Governmental, Financial and Market Pressures

Michael Shattock and Aniko Horvath

BLOOMSBURY ACADEMIC
LONDON • NEW YORK • OXFORD • NEW DELHI • SYDNEY

BLOOMSBURY ACADEMIC
Bloomsbury Publishing Plc
50 Bedford Square, London, WC1B 3DP, UK
1385 Broadway, New York, NY 10018, USA

BLOOMSBURY, BLOOMSBURY ACADEMIC and the Diana logo are trademarks
of Bloomsbury Publishing Plc

First published in Great Britain 2020

Series design by Adriana Brioso
Cover image © Setthasith Wansuksri/EyeEm/Getty Images

A catalogue record for this book is available from the British Library.

A catalog record for this book is available from the Library of Congress.

ISBN: HB: 978-1-3500-7402-6
ePDF: 978-1-3500-7403-3
eBook: 978-1-3500-7404-0

Series: Bloomsbury Higher Education Research

Typeset by Deanta Global Publishing Services, Chennai, India

To find out more about our authors and books visit www.bloomsbury.com
and sign up for our newsletters.

Contents

Series Editor's Foreword

The Governance of British Higher Education: The Impact of Governmental, Financial and Market Pressures is the first book to be published in the Bloomsbury Higher Education Research book series. This series brings to the public, government and universities across the world the new ideas and research evidence being generated by researchers from the ESRC/OFS/RE Centre for Global Higher Education.˙ The Centre for Global Higher Education (CGHE), a partnership of researchers from fifteen UK and international universities, is the world's largest concentration of expertise in relation to higher education and its social contributions. The core focus of the CGHE's work, and of the Bloomsbury Higher Education Research Series, is higher education, especially the future of higher education in the changing global landscape.

Each year this mega-topic of 'higher education' seems to take on greater importance for governments, business, civil organizations, students, families and the public at large. In higher education much is at stake. The role and impact of the sector is growing everywhere. More than 220 million students enrol at tertiary level across the world, four-fifths of them in degree programmes. Almost 40 per cent of school leavers now enter some kind of tertiary education each year, though resources and quality vary significantly. In North America and Europe that ratio rises to four young people in every five. Universities and colleges are seen as the primary medium for personal opportunity, social mobility and the development of whole communities. About 2.5 million new science papers are published worldwide each year and the role of research in industry and government continues to expand everywhere.

In short, there is much at stake in higher education. It has become central to social, economic and political life. One reason is that, even while serving local society and national policy, the higher education and research sectors are especially globalized in character. Each year six million students change countries in order to enrol in their chosen study programme, and a third of all

---

˙ The initials ESRC/OFS/RE stand for the Economic and Social Research Council/Office for Students and Research England. Part of the ESRC funding that supports the Centre for Global Higher Education's research work was sourced from the Higher Education Funding Council for England, the ancestor body to the OFS and RE.

published research papers involve joint authorship across national borders. In some countries fee-based international education is a major source of export revenues, while some other countries are losing talent in net terms each year. Routine cross-border movements of students, academics and researchers, knowledge, information and money help to shape not only nations but the international order itself.

At the same time, the global higher education landscape is changing with compelling speed, reflecting larger economic, political and cultural shifts in the geostrategic setting. Though research universities in the United States (especially) and United Kingdom remain strong in comparative terms, the worldwide map of power in higher education is becoming more diverse. A larger range of higher education practices, including models of teaching/ learning, delivery, institutional organization and system, will shape higher education in future. Anglo-American (and Western) norms and models will be less dominant and will themselves evolve. Rising universities and science in East Asia and Singapore are already reshaping the flow of knowledge and higher education. Latin America, South East Asia, India, Central Asia and the Arab nations have a growing global importance. The trajectories of education and research in sub-Saharan Africa are crucial to state-building and community development.

All of this has led to a more intensive focus on how higher education systems and institutions function as well as on their value, performance, effectiveness, openness and sustainability. This in turn has made research on higher education more significant – both because it provides us with insights into one important facet of the human condition, and because it informs evidenced-based government policies and professional practices.

The CGHE opened in late 2015. Its UK researchers are drawn from University College London (UCL) and the Universities of Oxford, Lancaster, Sheffield, Durham and Bath. UCL houses the largest number of researchers; however, the headquarters of the centre are located at Oxford. The international researchers are from Hiroshima University in Japan, Shanghai Jiao Tong University in China, Lingnan University in Hong Kong, the Australian National University and the University of Melbourne in Australia, Cape Town University in South Africa, the University of Michigan in the United States, Technological University Dublin in Ireland, and Leiden University in the Netherlands. The CGHE investigates higher education using a range of social science disciplines, including economics, sociology, political science and policy studies, psychology and anthropology, and a portfolio of quantitative, qualitative and synthetic-historical research techniques. It currently maintains sixteen research projects, variously of between eighteen months and four years' duration (though some are shorter) and involves forty active individual researchers. It is financed by £6.7 million in funding from the UK ESRC, partner universities and other sources.

The CGHE has a full agenda. The unprecedented growth of mass higher education, the striving for excellence and innovation in the research university sector, and the changing global landscape, pose many researchable questions for governments, societies and higher education institutions themselves. Some of these questions already figure in CGHE research projects. For example: What are the formative effects on societies and economies of the now much wider distribution of advanced levels of learning? How does it change individual graduates as people – and what does it mean when half or more of the workforce is higher educated and much more mobile; and when confident human agency has become widely distributed across civil and political society in nations with little state tradition, or where the main experience has been colonial or authoritarian rule? What does it mean when many more people are becoming steeped in the sciences, many others understand the world through the lenses of the social sciences or humanities, and a third group are engaged in neither? What happens to those parts of the population left outside the formative effects of higher education? What is the larger public role and contribution of higher education, as distinct from the private benefits for and private effects on individual graduates? What does it mean when large and growing higher education institutions have become the major employers in many locations and help to sustain community and cultural life, almost like branches of local government, while also being linked to global cities across the world? And what is the contribution of higher education, beyond helping to form the attributes of individual graduates, to the development of the emerging global society?

Likewise, the many practical problems associated with building higher education and science take on greater importance. How can scarce public budgets provide for the public role of higher education institutions, for a socially equitable system of individual access and for research excellence, all at the same time? What are the roles for and limits of family financing and tuition loans systems? What is the potential contribution of private institutions, including for-profit colleges? In national systems, what is the best balance between research-intensive and primarily teaching institutions, and between academic and vocational education? What are the potentials for technological delivery in extending access? What is happening in graduate labour markets, where returns to degrees are becoming more dispersed between families with differing levels of income, different kinds of universities and different fields of study? Do larger education systems provide better for social mobility and income equality? How does the internationalization of universities contribute to national policy and local societies? Does mobile international education expand opportunity or further stratify societies? What are the implications of new populist tensions between national and global goals, as manifest for example in the tensions over Brexit in the United Kingdom and the politics of the Trump era in the United States, for higher education and research? And always, what can national systems of higher education and science learn from each other, and how can they build stronger common ground?

In tackling these research challenges and bringing the research to all, we are very grateful to have the opportunity to work with such a high-quality publisher as Bloomsbury. In the book series, monographs are selected on the basis of their relevance to one or more of higher education policy, management, practice and theory. Topics range from teaching and learning and technologies, to research and its organization, the design parameters of national higher education systems, the public good role of higher education, social stratification and equity, institutional governance and management, and the cross-border mobility of people, programmes and ideas. Much of CGHE's work is global and comparative in scale, drawing lessons from higher education in many different countries, and the centre's cross-country and multi-project structure allows it to tap into the more plural higher education and research landscape that has emerged. The book series draws on authors from across the world and is prepared for relevance across the world.

The CGHE places special emphasis on the relevance of its research, on communicating its findings, and on maximizing the usefulness and impacts of those findings in higher education policy and practice. The CGHE has a relatively high public profile for an academic research centre and reaches out to engage higher education stakeholders, national and international organizations, policymakers, regulators and the broader public, in the United Kingdom and across the world. These objectives are also central to the book series. Recognizing that the translation from research outputs to high quality scholarly monographs is not always straightforward – while achieving impact in both academic and policy/practice circles is crucial – monographs in the book series are scrutinized critically before publication, for readability as well as quality. Texts are carefully written and edited to ensure that they have achieved the right combination of, on the one hand, intellectual depth and originality and, on the other hand, full accessibility for public, higher education and policy circles across the world.

Simon Marginson
Professor of Higher Education, University of Oxford
Director, ESRC/OFS/RE Centre for Global Higher Education

Acknowledgements

The authors express their gratitude to the institutions visited and to the individuals who gave their time to be interviewed. We hope that they will feel that the contents of this book make some recompense for the interview process that we engaged them in. We should also like to express our appreciation for the contribution to the project of Peter Scott, who was its initial project leader, and who wrote the first draft of its research plan. Our thanks are also due to Professor Ellen Hazelkorn and Andrew Gibson, members of the project team, who undertook the interviews for us in Northern Ireland, using the template developed for interviews in England, Wales and Scotland. We are grateful to David Warner, David Caldwell and Rosalind Pritchard for their helpful comments on the contents of Chapter 3. We would again wish to express our thanks to Professor Hazelkorn, drawing on her unique knowledge of the mechanisms for regulating and coordinating global higher education, for her contribution to Chapter 6, which was jointly written by her and Aniko Horvath. The research has been carried out under the auspices of the Centre for Global Higher Education (Director Simon Marginson). We would like to thank Simon for his constant support for the project. Lastly we would like to record our thanks to Caroline Steenman-Clark who undertook the preparation of the manuscript for delivery to the publishers. The funding support of the Economic and Social Research Council, the Office for Students and Research England (grant reference ES/MO10082/1) is gratefully acknowledged.

Abbreviations and Acronyms

AfriQAN	African Quality Assurance Network
AHELO	Assessment of Learning Outcomes in Higher Education
AQRF	ASEAN Qualifications Reference Framework
ARWU	*Academic Ranking of World Universities*
ASEAN	Association of South East Asian Nations
BEIS	Business, Energy and Industrial Strategy
BFUG	Bologna Follow-Up Group
BIS	[Department for] Business, Innovation and Skills
CAMES	*Le Conseil Africain et Malgache pour l'Enseignement Supérieur*
CAT	College of Advanced Technology
CDP	Committee of Directors of Polytechnics
CGHE	Centre for Global Higher Education
CHEA	Council for Higher Education Accreditation
CIQG	CHEA International Quality Group
CMA	Competition and Markets Authority
CSR	Comprehensive Spending Review
CUC	Committee of University Chairmen
CVCP	Committee of Vice Chancellors and Principals
DEQAR	Database of External Quality Assurance Reports
DES	Department of Education and Science
DfE	Department for Education

DIUS   Department for Innovation, Universities and Skills

DTI   Department of Trade and Industry

ECTS   European Credit Transfer System

EHEA   European Higher Education Area

ELIR   Enhancement-Led Institutional Review

ENQA   European Association for Quality Assurance in Higher Education

EQAR   European Quality Assurance Register for Higher Education

ERA   European Research Area

ERC   European Research Council

ESG   European Standards and Guidelines

ESRC   Economic and Social Research Council

ETER   European Tertiary Education Register

EU   European Union

EUA   European University Association

EURITO   EU Relevant, Inclusive, Timely, Trusted, and Open Research Innovation Indicators

FSSG   Financial Sustainability Strategy Group

GATS   General Agreement in Trade and Services

HEFC   Higher Education Funding Council

HEFCE   Higher Education Funding Council for England

HEFCW   Higher Education Funding Council for Wales

HEI   higher education institution

HERA   Higher Education and Research Act

IAU   International Association of Universities

IMF   International Monetary Fund

IMHE	Institutional Management of Higher Education
INES	International Indicators and Evaluation of Educational Systems
INQAAHE	International Network for Quality Assurance Agencies
ISCED	International Standard Classification of Education
JISC	Joint Information Systems Committee
KIS	Key Information Sets
NAB	National Advisory Body for Public Sector Higher Education
NAO	National Audit Office
NCH	New College of the Humanities
NSS	National Student Survey
NUS	National Union of Students
OA	Open Access
OECD	Organisation for Economic Co-operation and Development
OEEC	Organisation for European Economic Co-operation
Ofcom	Office of Communications
Ofgem	Office of Gas and Electricity Markets
OfS	Office for Students
Ofwat	Water Services Regulation Authority
PAC	Public Accounts Committee
PCFC	Polytechnic and Colleges Funding Council
PIAACC	Programme for the International Assessment of Adult Competencies
PISA	Programme for International Student Assessment
QAA	Quality Assurance Agency
QR	quality research

RAE	Research Assessment Exercise
REF	Research Excellence Framework
RIS3	Research and Innovation Strategies for Smart Specialisation
SBS	Skills Beyond School
SCOP	Standing Conference of Principals
SFC	Scottish Funding Council
SHEDL	Scottish Higher Education Digital Library
SHEFC	Scottish Higher Education Funding Council
SLC	Student Loans Company
SNP	Scottish National Party
STEM	science, technology, engineering and mathematics
TEF	Teaching Excellence Framework
THE	*Times Higher Education*
TRAC	Transparent Approach to Costing
TVET	Technical and Vocational Education and Training
UCAS	Universities and Colleges Admissions Service
UCCA	Universities Central Council for Admissions
UCL	University College London
UCU	Universities and Colleges Union
UFC	Universities Funding Council
UGC	University Grants Committee
UKRI	UK Research and Innovation
UMR	U-Multirank
UN	United Nations
UNESCO	United Nations Educational, Scientific and Cultural Organization

USTREAM   Universities for Strategic, Efficient and Autonomous
           Management

UUK   Universities UK

VET   Vocational Education and Training

WTO   World Trade Organization

A Timeline

1963 Publication of the Report of the Committee on Higher Education (the Robbins Report), which recommended a substantial expansion of higher education, primarily based in the universities. In its comments on institutional governance it supported a lay majority on university governing bodies but only 'when it recognises a proper division of labour between itself and the senate... . It is no part of its function to interfere in the business of internal academic organization still less in matters of syllabuses and curricula. The situation is likely to become intolerable if such attempts are made' (Robbins Report: para. 666).

1967 Secretary of State Tony Crosland announced the creation of thirty polytechnics to be managed under the control of the local education authorities, and the establishment of a binary line that divided the expansion forecast in the Robbins Report between the universities, on the one hand, and a new 'public sector of higher education' comprising the polytechnics and colleges, on the other.

1974 Publication of *Power and Authority in British Universities* by G. C. Moodie and R. B. Eustace (London: Allen and Unwin), the first major research-based study of university governance in the post-Robbins era.

1981 The imposition of a reduction of 8.3 per cent on university budgets, as an element in the Thatcher government's overall reduction in public expenditure. This, taken with the abolition of financial support for international students, amounted to a cut of 15 per cent in the funding of the university sector 1981–4. The cut was administered differentially among the universities by the University Grants Committee (UGC) and was accompanied by a 3 per cent cut in student numbers. This was the first real cut in university budgets since the Second World War. Following the outcry over the reductions Secretary of State Sir Keith Joseph announced that he would intend to exercise greater policy control over higher education than previous ministers had done.

1985 The UGC introduced a research selectivity exercise intended, through peer review, to evaluate institutional research performance, discipline by discipline, and to distribute Quality Research (QR) funding to institutions accordingly, within a fixed university sector budget. The exercise was repeated, under the title the Research Assessment Exercise (RAE) and later the Research Excellence Framework (REF) in 1989, 1992, 1996, 2001, 2008, 2014 and (planned) 2021.

1985 Publication of the Report of the Committee on Efficiency Studies in Universities (the Jarratt Report) (London: Committee of Vice Chancellors and Principals (CVCP)), which recommended that vice chancellors should be regarded as chief executives and that university councils (governing bodies) should 'assert themselves'.

1988 The Education Reform Act replaced the UGC with the Universities Funding Council (UFC) and removed the polytechnics and colleges from local education authority control and placed them under a new Polytechnics and Colleges Funding Council (PCFC). The legislation established a new governance structure for the polytechnics and colleges, which reduced the role of academic boards and empowered polytechnic and college directors (principals) to act explicitly as chief executives, answerable to unicameral governing bodies.

1992 The Further and Higher Education Act abolished the UFC and the PCFC and replaced them with Higher Education Funding Councils (HEFCs) for England, Wales and Scotland. At the same time it abolished the binary line and granted university status with full degree-awarding powers to the polytechnics and the Scottish Central Institutions (the Scottish equivalent of polytechnics), while retaining the internal governance structures created by the 1988 Act.

1993 Responsibility for the research councils was transferred from the Department of Education and Science (DES) to the Department of Trade and Industry (DTI).

1997 Publication of the Report of the National Committee of Inquiry into Higher Education (the Dearing Report) *Higher Education in the Learning Society* (London: HMSO), which recommended inter alia the introduction of a tuition fee of £1,000 payable by UK students supported by an income-contingent loan scheme. The recommendation was rejected by the Scottish government but implemented in England, Wales and Northern Ireland in 2000. It also argued for an increased strategic role for governing bodies and a reduction in the size of their membership to no more than twenty-four.

2003 Publication of the White Paper *The Future of Higher Education* (Cm 5735 London: HMSO), which recommended raising tuition fees for UK students to up to £3,000 per annum. Only two institutions chose to charge less than the maximum figure. The new fee levels came into force, except in Scotland, in the 2006–7 academic year.

2006 Responsibility for higher education was transferred from the Department for Education and Skills (which had been reinforced by a transfer of vocational training responsibilities) to a Department for Innovation, Universities and Skills (DIUS), which reunited the research councils and higher education. DIUS was later merged into the larger Department for Business, Innovation and Skills.

2012 Following the government's 2010 Comprehensive Spending Review, at which cuts of 25 per cent were imposed on public expenditure, tuition fees in England were raised to a maximum of £9,000 (and later to £9,250) with provision for loans to students from the Student Loans Company (SLC) repayable over thirty years providing their income reached a prescribed level. Under these arrangements tuition fees replaced recurrent grant to universities in England except for government subsidies to fees for courses in science, technology, engineering and mathematics (STEM) and courses in medicine and veterinary science. In Wales, lower-level fees were charged initially but have now been raised to £9,000; in Northern Ireland the suspension of the Northern Ireland Assembly and Executive has prevented any decision to raise fees above 2006 levels except with respect to inflation; in Scotland there has been no decision to charge tuition fees to Scottish students.

2016 The Higher Education Governance (Scotland) Act mandated Scottish universities to include two trade-union representatives on their courts (governing bodies) and to make the chairs of those bodies elected positions by the staff and students of the university with the aim of 'democratizing' the universities.

2017 The Higher Education and Research Act abolished the Higher Education Funding Council for England (HEFCE) and replaced it with the Office for Students (OfS), a body designed to be a market regulator rather than a funding body. Funding councils continued in Wales and Scotland. Research funding

including the research councils and the operation of the REF and the distribution
of QR funding was transferred to a new body, UK Research and Innovation
(UKRI), which was placed under the Department for Business, Energy and
Industrial Strategy (BEIS), while responsibility for teaching in higher education
was transferred back to the Department for Education (DfE). The Act also
relaxed regulations to encourage the expansion in the number of private higher
education institutions under the title of 'alternative providers'. New Regulations
introduced to accompany the creation of the OfS emphasized the extent to which
the government wished to see the higher education system in England operate
according to market principles.

2018 The OfS came into full operation in England with effect from April.

Chapter 1

Introduction

Forms of governance, at both national and institutional level, critically shape the culture, creativity and academic outcomes of higher education. Governance, as defined in this study, is not just a matter of constitutional structures, but encompasses how decisions are made and by whom, how different levels of governance interface with one another, what pressures are exerted on policy by internal and external forces, and how institutions and their members respond to them. Historically, British universities have been considered among the most, if not *the* most, autonomous in Europe, a conclusion fully supported by the European University Association (EUA) Autonomy Scorecards (Estermann, Nokkala and Steinel 2011; EUA 2017). In the classic study of British university governance, *Power and Authority in British Universities* (Moodie and Eustace 1974), a picture is drawn of a university system in which 'the supreme authority … must therefore continue to rest with the academics for no-one else seems sufficiently qualified to regulate the public affairs of scholars' (Moodie and Eustace 1974: 233). This assessment, which arguably remained true until the mid-1980s, must now be decisively revised, although the belief systems deriving from it remain buried deep in many universities' cultures. This study will show how what was a broadly uniform governance culture running through the university system has fragmented under state, societal, financial and market pressures, and how the state itself, with some important regional variations that did not exist forty or so years ago, has chosen to play a much more proactive role in the direction of higher education than could have been imagined in the mid-1970s. To emphasize this, the chapters in the book follow sequentially through changes in system governance to changes in institutional governance and, finally, to an assessment of the implications for the direction of higher education itself. The consequence of the fragmentation is a much more diverse and variegated governance context confronting an altogether wider assortment of risks and pressures in a more fluid economic and social climate.

Much current writing about university governance concentrates on governance at the level of the governing body to the exclusion of concerns about governance at other levels in the institution. We believe that this begs a large question as to whether the governing body, albeit it may be the de jure locus of critical decision-making, is in practice, as some feel it should be, the de facto heart of institutional policy formation and strategic decisions. For most academics, for example, governance is much more concerned with departmental or faculty/school/college structures or directions from their universities' executive boards. Implicit in this study is the concept of 'shared governance', that is, a partnership between academic and lay governance or, drawing on our evidence, a partnership between lay involvement, the academic interest and the student voice. The study, therefore, seeks to explore the different layers of governance in British higher education from the nation state through to the various levels of governance within university institutions. What this reveals is a set of interrelationships that go a long way towards determining the climate of academic life and the strategic direction of the institutions.

This study has been undertaken as part of a wider research programme on the governance of higher education in the UK and continental Europe conducted under the auspices of the Centre for Global Higher Education (CGHE) (director: Professor Simon Marginson), funded by the Economic and Social Research Council (ESRC) and the Higher Education Funding Council for England (HEFCE). This research is concerned with studying the interaction between global influences, national governance reform programmes in higher education and institutional governance, and to assess how, together with internal societal, financial and market pressures, they have exerted change in British and continental European higher education governance systems. It is intended that this British volume will be followed by further volumes and/or other publications covering these themes.

For the British study we undertook some ninety-five interviews, almost all of which were face-to-face, recorded and transcribed. We conducted nineteen interviews with people involved in central policy issues in higher education, in government, and in official and representative bodies, in England, Wales, Scotland and Northern Ireland. The remainder of the interviews were with people working in the institutions themselves. We selected six broadly representative institutions in England: a Russell Group university, a pre-1992 university, two post-1992 universities, one in London and one in a large provincial city outside London, a post-post-1992 university* and one private

---

* The term 'post-post-1992 university' is, in general usage, ascribed to institutions that have been given university status since the elevation of the polytechnics in 1992.

'alternative provider" institution. In Wales and Scotland we interviewed one pre-1992 and one post-1992 university in each system, and in Northern Ireland both of the two universities. In each institution we aimed to interview the chair of the governing body, the head of the institution, a senior administrator, normally the registrar/secretary, three academics (one senior, one middle ranking and one relatively junior) from different disciplinary fields and the president of the students' union or a senior student officer. In total this gave us twelve institutions where we took evidence in depth: three Russell Group, three pre-1992, five post- or post-post-1992 institutions, and one private alternative provider. In addition, we had access to interviews at an Oxbridge university conducted by Aniko Horvath for another CGHE project, which made for valuable comparisons with our own list of governance interviews. We believe this represents the most extensive empirical study for a project on the governance of higher education in the Britain since Moodie and Eustace's, and, in fact, exceeds theirs, in that they did not regard it as necessary to review national policymaking, because in practice in that period there was not much to review. They did not, for example, include the role of the University Grants Committee (UGC) in their study, although it provided the crucial framework for the internal balance of decision-making power within institutions. Nor did they interview in depth in particular institutions.

The interviews were conducted over 2016–17, when the British higher education scene was subject to far-reaching structural change: in England, the 2017 Higher Education and Research Act (HERA) reinforced the government's decision, embodied in the replacement of a grant-plus-tuition fee funding system by a totally fee-based system (subject to some additional grant to top-up science, technology and mathematical (STEM) disciplines), and the removal of an institutional cap on student numbers (except in medicine and dentistry), to create a fully blown market in higher education. In Scotland the Higher Education Governance Act 2016 imposed significant representational changes on Scottish institutional governance, and in Wales, in 2018, a White Paper introduced the concept of a tertiary education in place of a university-only-based system that was more adapted to Wales' economic environment. Only in Northern Ireland, where the political situation has frozen the prospect of development, has legislation not occurred, but here the retrenchment in funding and the consequential cutting

---

This is the form of words used by the Department for Education to describe those privately funded institutions whose students are eligible, as higher education students, for tuition fee loans from the Student Loans Company; some have been granted university status, others degree-awarding powers, while others have their qualifications validated by existing universities.

back of student numbers has produced change of a different character, with the prospect of further change if Brexit produces a reduction in the number of students from the Republic attending the two Northern Ireland universities.

If we take the findings of *Power and Authority in British Universities* as summarizing the governance of universities in the post-Robbins era, the 1991 White Paper *Higher Education: A New Framework* (DES 1991) and the 1992 legislation marked, in hindsight, a very clear break with the previous governance culture of the British university system. Moodie and Eustace were concerned to describe the internal pressures on a stable institutional governance system, inspired by the attack on professorial hierarchies by the 'non-professorial radicals' and by the even more disruptive incursion of the student voice in university affairs. They described both how senates expanded their powers at the expense of university councils (governing bodies) and the rise of a non-academic administrative class described by one vice chancellor as an 'academic civil service' (Sloman 1963: 87): in contrast to modern criticisms of professional staff as instruments of managerialism, the Registrar of Oxford claimed that a good administration was the best guarantor of the ability of a university 'to practice democratic control by academics of the policies which shape their environment' (University of Oxford 1964: para 556).

The 1992 legislation, however, introduced fundamental changes to the structural framework of the higher education system. First, it provided for the devolution of the previously unified British higher education system for Wales and Scotland, and abolished the Universities Funding Council (UFC), the brief successor body to the UGC, replacing it with Higher Education Funding Councils for England, Wales and Scotland (leaving Northern Ireland, always a constitutional anomaly, to the care of the Northern Ireland Office advised by the English Funding Council, HEFCE). The funding councils were to be *funding*, not planning, bodies, thus emphasizing a more marketized system, and were emphatically no longer to carry the label of being 'buffer' bodies between the universities and the government, although all three funding councils, to a greater or lesser extent, continued to exercise that role. Second, it gave the polytechnics and the Scottish Central Institutions full university status and legitimized a much more directive form of university governance for them, which, significantly, both reduced the policymaking powers of academic boards, as compared to pre-1992 university senates, and increased the powers of vice chancellors to act as chief executive officers who reported to smaller governing bodies, themselves intended to act much more like company boards (Shattock 2006). The clear evidence that the government was much more comfortable with the New

University governance model, and its official endorsement for the whole system in the Dearing Report (NCIHE 1997), gave considerable impetus to the previous recommendations of the Jarratt Report on governance and management in the pre-1992 universities, which called on university councils to 'assert themselves' and for vice chancellors to be required to act in a more CEO-like mode (CVCP 1985). Looking back, the 1992 legislation represented a watershed that separated the higher education world of Robbins, and of Moodie and Eustace, from the world of the Office for Students, of dominant chief executives (and dominant chairmen of governing bodies) and of a 'business model' of university governance. It also placed the pre- and post-1992 institutional governance structures side by side, which, over time, led to a diffusion of governance models, borrowing from both sides of the former binary line and, cumulatively, to a steady drift towards more top-down decision-making structures and to a reduced participation in strategic policymaking by academic staff. In addition, devolution gave space to cultural and educational differences between England, Wales and Scotland, which encouraged significant divergencies from a uniform national higher educational system.

These changes, in themselves, would certainly have affected the stability of the higher education system, but they were also accompanied by a series of further developments that imposed interconnected pressures on both government and institutions. These pressures, not listed below in any order of severity, represent a backdrop to any understanding of the reordering of the governance of the system and of institutions that has since taken place:

The importance of reputation Prior to 1992 the binary line offered a tidy division of reputation between the universities and the polytechnics, based primarily on research performance, which bore comparison with the segmentation between the University of California and the California State University system in the United States, or the division of universities from Fachhochschulen in Germany. In Britain, the Research Assessment Exercise (RAE)[*] had begun to differentiate institutions within the university sector but the existence of the dual funding system[†] ensured that the university system remained easily distinguishable from

---

[*] The first Research Selectivity Exercise, as it was then called, was held in 1985–6 and was designed to assess the quality of research in British universities and differentiate the level of their recurrent grant accordingly.

[†] Government funding for research is available to British universities via project funding from the research councils or, prior to 2012, through recurrent grant, or, thereafter, except in Scotland, through tuition fees. This approach is strongly defended by the academic community because it prevents project funding becoming too great a determinant of the directions that research should take.

what was then described as the 'public sector of higher education'. Although league tables based on the RAE began to appear in the British media from 1986, the *Good University Guide* (now *The Times and Sunday Times University Guide*) and other student recruitment-oriented guides began publication in 1992, to be followed by the Shanghai Jiao Tong University and the *Times Higher Education* (THE) world league tables in 2004. League tables have exercised a fundamental influence on both government and institutional strategies (Hazelkorn 2011) not only from the point of view of abstract prestige but in the hard managerial sense of promoting the recruitment of home and international students, thus influencing the size and shape of the institution and its financial security.

Funding structures The introduction in 2000 of tuition fees to be paid by home students as a supplement to recurrent grant from government was followed by their increase in 2006, and the subsequent substitution of tuition fees for recurrent grant in 2012. This created a fundamental change in the relationship between government and the institutions and their students in England, Wales and Northern Ireland. It also prompted the greatest policy divisions between the four individual governments, with Scotland refusing to introduce tuition fees altogether and preserving free access to higher education, with Wales pursuing an alternative fee option and with Northern Ireland unable to proceed beyond the English 2006 fee increase in the absence of a government able to make the necessary decisions. The remarkable effect of the Scottish decision is that Scottish universities now seek to recruit English and Welsh students as if they were international students because they bring their £9,250 tuition fee in England and their £9,000 fee in Wales with them and so do not count against the student number targets imposed by the Scottish Funding Council.

The creation of a market To some extent higher education has always offered market analogies: from 1981 the government's refusal to subsidize funding for international students created an international recruitment market to replace the income lost in the 1981 cuts;* the introduction of the RAE stimulated a market for RAE-able staff. But the substitution of tuition fees for recurrent grant, followed by the removal of the cap on home student numbers, created

---

* In the Thatcher government's first budget, reductions were imposed across all government departments including the universities' budgets. This represented the first reduction in recurrent grant to universities in the post-War period, and was imposed by the UGC using controversial quality and disciplinary criteria.

full-on market conditions in England and Wales. The result has been a greatly increased volatility in the recruitment field for home students, exacerbated by demographic factors and by some institutions grasping the opportunity to grow their student numbers, either for academic reasons or simply to enlarge their footprint. In Scotland and Northern Ireland such market conditions do not apply: in the former, a continued restriction on home numbers has led to higher rejection rates, while, in the latter, the contrary applies with home entry targets being cut back to match a reduction in state funding. Marketization in England has led, as in the independent school sector, to an 'arms race' in university building, financed by extensive spending – estimated by HEFCE to amount to some £40 billion over the fifteen years 2002–17, with another £14.6 billion due to be spent between 2017 and 2019, pushing borrowing up to £11.7 billion (*THE* 1 February 2018). The presence of a tranche of low-cost alternative providers represents a new element of competition, especially to universities that are ranked in the lower divisions of the league tables. The existence of a market implies enhanced competition: successive governments have believed that competition drives up quality but, within the higher education system, many believe that too great a concentration on competition can detract from a concern for good education, the exercise of scholarly values and a true commitment to research.

Academic and financial accountability Ever since the Parliament's Public Accounts Committee (PAC) obtained access to universities' accounts in order to comment on their financial management in 1967, and especially since the near bankruptcy of University College Cardiff in 1987,* accountability for government funds spent in universities has been an established feature of institutional management. The introduction of the Research Selectivity Exercise in 1985–6 was partly predicated on the accountability principle that the dual funding system rewarded universities whether or not they were appropriately research active, but the determination of the research ratings was achieved through academic peer review. In the 1992 Act, responsibility for the quality assessment of teaching was vested in a Quality Assurance Committee coming formally under the control of HEFCE, but the assessment was again to be made by a panel of academics, and the committee itself was representative of the

---

* In 1987 University College Cardiff came close to bankruptcy and was only rescued by a merger with a neighbouring institution. The UGC was heavily criticized by the PAC because of its lack of financial control, and this resulted in the replacement of the UGC by the Universities Funding Council and by the imposition of a new and strengthened audit regime.

sector and included the Committee of Vice Chancellors and Principals (CVCP). Accountability had been achieved, but the formalities of academic responsibility had been preserved.

In England two further steps have, however, been taken along the road of external scrutiny, both of which strongly encourage government or lay intervention. The first was the introduction of the Teaching Excellence Framework (TEF), which was designed to assess through a range of metrics whether institutions merited Gold, Silver or Bronze Star awards, or a Fail, for their teaching. Proposed as a counterpoint to the pressures on institutions imposed by the Research Excellence Framework (REF), which was itself, of course, machinery created by government, the TEF was formulated to complement the government's market philosophy. Its snappy, populist and easily quoted awards were more user-friendly than the wordy, jargon-ridden reports by the Quality Assurance Agency (QAA), which were largely unread by applicants for places in higher education. The simplicity of the awards fitted neatly into a league table format. The TEF may not be seen as any more useful than QAA reports, according to research commissioned by the DfE, which found that, in 2018, only 15 per cent of applicants used TEF results to help with their choice of institution (McKie 2019).

The second was the decision by HEFCE to require institutional governing bodies to take a de facto as well as a de jure responsibility for the maintenance of academic standards in their institutions, rather than regard it as a matter entirely for the senate or academic board. The decision was reinforced by the requirement that the chair of the governing body formally sign a form issued by HEFCE committing the governing body to give an assurance on the maintenance of academic quality. This requirement breached a notional red line that governing bodies concerned themselves with management, finance and strategy, and that academic policy and issues surrounding teaching were strictly matters for the academic community. In some universities, lay governors were sufficiently concerned at this accretion to their responsibilities that they insisted on physically attending meetings of senates and academic boards to see how these responsibilities were exercised there; in others academics and senior management teams found themselves presenting papers to their governing bodies justifying academic processes, which were widely followed across higher education, to sometimes sceptical and unsympathetic audiences. In either case it was clear that an academic Rubicon had been crossed and, while in academically successful universities that commanded strong fields of applicants, formal assurances from senates and academic boards and descriptions of the procedures involved were sufficient to satisfy governing bodies, in institutions of lower standing, where recruitment problems were apparent, the threat of lay intervention in what had previously been the academic heartland of decision-making became increasingly possible. The HEFCE requirement seriously threatened the traditional bicameral structure of university governance and put at potential risk the accepted norms of academic accountability.

Representation of higher education to government Before 1992 the established mode of representation of higher education interests to government had been through the CVCP (later retitled Universities UK (UUK)) and the Committee of Directors of Polytechnics (CDP). When the merger took place it did so on the CVCP's terms, but the position fragmented when, in 1994, a group of the most research-active pre-1992 universities broke away to form the Russell Group, quickly followed by most of the rest of the pre-1992 universities in a so-called '1994 Group'. In the meantime, divisions on the post-1992 side led to the creation of three separate groups, the University Alliance, Mission Plus and Guild HE. These organizations inevitably competed in their own interests for the government's ear and severely weakened the UUK's ability to marshal an argument on behalf of a unified system. The existence of Universities Wales and Universities Scotland, each created to represent the interests of their universities to their governments, completed a fragmentation of policy representation that dissipated the strength of the universities' voice in national policy.

Reorganization in system governance The 1992 legislation established Higher Education Funding Councils for England, Wales and Scotland. In Wales and Scotland, this was followed by a wider devolution of powers establishing a governing Welsh Assembly and a Scottish Parliament. In none of the three countries has the Funding Council structure survived unchanged. In England, where the changes have been the most radical, it immediately became clear after the new tuition fee structure was announced in 2010 that the position of HEFCE was at risk, because a large part of its remit, the allocation of funds to universities, had been rendered redundant by the transfer of funding for teaching from grant to fees. In thirteen years, 2003 to 2016, three White Papers (DES 2003; BIS 2011; BIS 2016), a government higher education strategy document (BIS 2009) and a government-appointed review (Browne 2010) offered different sets of organizational and funding structures. In Wales, higher education was transformed into tertiary education with the Funding Council taking over further education; and in Scotland the Funding Council, having narrowly survived abolition, found itself linked to an Enterprise Board, although it retained its responsibility to a minister. In research, the development of the government's Innovation agenda saw a growing separation between policy on funding for research and policy on funding for teaching and learning, culminating in the assignment of responsibility for them to two separate government departments, the Department for Business, Energy and Industrial Strategy (BEIS) and the Department for Education (DfE). In addition, the merging of the research councils under a common overlord agency, UK Research and Innovation (UKRI) in 2017, meant that there was a danger that research strategies could become wholly detached from general academic policy considerations.

Individually and in combination these changes have been severely disruptive to the unified world of higher education, something that seemed to be predicted by the ending of the binary line. Although, at the research level, a unified resource allocation system through the REF remains, both Wales and Scotland are concerned to establish regional research strategies and, at the system level, devolution is driving differentiation; the espousal of a radical marketization policy in England is not being adopted in Wales and Scotland. These differences in national policies are being reflected in the governance of institutions.

But diversification is being driven in England, Wales and Scotland by other factors, by financial pressures, by market conditions and by reputational ambition. In England, a 'business model' of university governance is increasingly gaining ascendancy, especially in the less research-active institutions or in institutions where student recruitment is an issue, but this is not found, or not found with anything like the same intensity, in Wales or Scotland. In Wales, new governance challenges are faced in multi-higher education/further education institutions that have arisen out of institutional rationalization. In Scotland, the requirements of the 2016 legislation, making chairs of governing bodies elective positions and requiring trade-union representation on university courts to be mandatory, mark a first instance of government intervention in institutional self-governance arrangements since the Second World War. This emphasizes the growing distance that is occurring between the systems in England, Wales and Scotland, while the stagnation of government in Northern Ireland illustrates how much easier it has become for individual systems to become adversely differentiated as a result of local political or economic factors.

One of the outcomes of our research is to demonstrate that the study of institutional (university) governance is difficult, if not impossible, to separate from the study of the governance of higher education at the national government level. This is exemplified in Chapter 2, which describes the changes in government policy in England, and it is given added force by the comparison in Chapter 3 with the policies adopted in Wales and Scotland and how these policies are reflected in the governance of Welsh and Scottish universities. (In Northern Ireland, the absence of representative government has had a profoundly negative impact on the governance of the province's higher education system.) This interface between governments and institutional governance provides a critical context to which institutional governance must react and adapt. National government policy may frame developments in institutional governance, as in England, or engage in direct intervention, as in Scotland, but, in all four of the separate systems of higher education in the UK, it represents a crucial influence on the way institutional governance is conducted. This was not always the case, as the Moodie and Eustace study demonstrates, but no study could, in our view, be conducted now without an acknowledgement of the extent to which governance at the state level impacts on the ways in which institutions govern themselves. We believe that this is probably true in continental European and in other Anglophone settings as well.

One of the key themes of any study of the governance of higher education must be the question of the degree of autonomy it enjoys. We distinguish autonomy as existing at three levels: the system level, the institutional level and the individual pedagogical and research level. We further distinguish as to whether it exists at a substantive or only at an operational level, the latter being defined as self-government, which is significantly circumscribed by a higher authority. When Moodie and Eustace were writing in 1974, for example, universities enjoyed autonomy at the system level as well as at the institutional level, but this was reduced to autonomy much more at the operational level under HEFCE and the Welsh and Scottish Funding Councils. We explore in Chapters 2 and 3 the extent to which any of the four systems can now be said to be even operationally autonomous and the effect this has had on institutional autonomy. In Chapter 5 we discuss inter alia the degree to which, in a very diverse set of institutions, substantive or even operational autonomy can still be found in the pedagogical and research world of the individual academic, and we ask what the implications might be for these findings on the intellectual, critical and creative contributions that higher education can make to society.

What our research tries to draw out is the extent to which governance structures at national and institutional levels have changed. Chapters 2 and 3 describe changes at the system level, with Chapter 3 showing how devolution to Wales, Scotland and Northern Ireland has diversified the previously unified UK system, and how government policies in Wales and Scotland contrast with those followed in England. Chapter 4 is concerned with the institutional picture and describes how national policies and financial and environmental change have affected institutional governance while Chapter 5 attempts to draw conclusions about how these changes are impacting on research and teaching. Chapter 6 explores the growth in global governance and regulation in higher education and contrasts this with the more 'commercial' approaches to globalization to be found in Britain. Chapter 7 describes some of the policy implications that the findings of the research suggest for the British higher education model. The chapters are briefly summarized below.

Chapter 2: The transformation from a self-governed
to a 'regulated' higher education system

This chapter describes how the state has extended its role, not just in policymaking in higher education but in the direction of the system, culminating, in England, in its management through an explicit market, which is controlled by a regulator, the Office for Students, and how the associated changes have impacted on institutional governance. It provides some historical background for system governance before 1992, and traces its evolution from higher education self-government, through the Higher and Further Education Act of 1992, to a system of control by regulation established by the Higher Education and Research Act of 2016. It suggests that state dominance in England has been accompanied by an increasing political or ideological underpinning, which can be seen in the creation of a private sector of higher education, the 'alternative providers', and in the regulations designed to encourage its increase and the number of its institutions.

Chapter 3: The impact of devolved government: Wales,
Scotland, Northern Ireland and England

Devolution has provided the opportunity for a greater differentiation of higher education, and for the development of four increasingly distinct systems, with England's being by far the largest. A comparison of the four systems illustrates the extent to which the English system has been driven in a different direction from the rest, and makes it possible to assess the effects of policies based on the principles of 'competition and choice', as against those pursued in the other systems. It also shows how the political stalemate in Northern Ireland has disadvantaged the Northern Irish universities. It concludes that the impact of devolution has been broadly positive, in that the political, social and economic characteristics of the different nations have become more closely reflected in their higher education systems, but that issues of coordination, especially with England adopting such a different style of governance, have proved difficult to reconcile.

Chapter 4: The changing pattern of institutional governance

University governance has been significantly destabilized by changes imposed externally, then translated internally, and the balance is moving decisively in many universities towards a fully top-down organizational culture. The impact of increasing government intervention, particularly in England, the 'laicization' of university governance, the uncertainty of relationships between governing bodies and academic governance, the decline in the participation in governance by the academic community, the rise in the power of the executive and the increasing shift towards a 'business model' are described, to offer a backdrop against which institutional changes have occurred. In spite of this, however, our research suggests that, although the space occupied by collegial discussion of academic issues below the levels introduced by the new forms of governance, is narrowing, it is still possible to see universities as to some, though to a varying extent, as bottom-heavy organizations.

Chapter 5: University governance and academic work: pressures on innovation and creativity

This chapter links governance, and governance changes, with threats to creativity and innovation in teaching and research. It shows how the system divides itself between those institutions that remain driven by academic priorities and those institutions where the stress of concern about student recruitment encourages the dominance of marketing considerations at the expense of teaching based on interest and intellectual curiosity. It describes the UK research funding system and shows how the changes to the governance of research could come to weaken the dual funding system. The organizational separation of REF funding from teaching funding implies that effectively the state has distanced itself from concerns about institutional funding, consigning institutions' futures entirely to the market. Moreover, the arbitrary removal of the cap on institutional numbers threatens the continuing development of research in less research-intensive universities by putting their financial viability in question as they lose student numbers to more advantageously placed institutions. Overall, this chapter argues that strengthened authority structures are endangering experimentation, creativity and innovation by reducing opportunities for internal debate, for open-ended discussion of policy issues and new thinking, the necessary adjuncts of good academic work. There is little or no space for what Stark et al. (2009) call the 'organization of dissonance'.

Chapter 6: Globalization and higher education governance

This chapter opens with an account of the evolving architecture of global regulation and coordination, the EU Modernization and research agendas, the influence of international agencies and the impact of rankings. It suggests that the role of global governance is likely to grow. By contrast, our research indicates that, at the senior levels of national and institutional policymaking, British higher education remains largely unaware or uninterested in this development, their focus being much more directed towards the recruitment of international students, primarily for financial reasons, on the prospects for winning funding for research from EU sources and on their position in international ranking tables. Britain is a major contributor to the globalization of higher education, but its institutions do not incorporate it into their governance and policymaking frameworks and treat their international activities as a separable 'add-on', rather than as an integral component of their mission. The reputation of British higher education remains high internationally, but its focus on globalization simply as a market for exploitation places it at risk as competitor higher education systems engage more closely with the details of global regulation and coordination. The reluctance of British universities to give consideration to models from other systems, except perhaps the United States, may be attributable to local funding issues, but may also be an unwillingness to recognize how globalization is affecting higher education.

Chapter 7: The strategic implications of the changing governance structures in British higher education

This chapter draws on the research findings of the previous chapters to suggest ways forward to address some of the shortcomings in British higher education's present system of governance. It is critical of the role of the state in creating financial instability in the system. It draws attention to what it sees as the imposition of a partisan politicization of policy in England, and contrasts the situations to be found in Scotland and Wales. The chapter goes on to argue that stronger unified representational machinery is required in England to maintain the independence of the university system. It suggests ways to bridge the separation of national responsibilities for research and teaching so that a more unified approach can be achieved for the management of the system. It is sceptical of the claims made for 'for-profit' higher education and suggests a pause in the authorization of any new institutions. In light of the changes described, the chapter asks whether university governance remains fit for purpose in current conditions, and reviews the opinions of those interviewed. It is critical of the 'business model' of university governance, and some conclusions are reached about lay governance, the place of the academic community and the provision for the involvement of the student voice in institutional governance. It considers the role of the state in the governance of English higher education and argues that the failure to exercise a duty of care could have long-term damaging effects on the quality and international reputation of the system. At the same time, it urges institutions and national policymakers to engage more with the global governance agenda lest Britain, a keen participant in international higher education, finds itself isolated and outflanked by its international competitors.

Chapter 2

The Transformation from a Self-Governed to a 'Regulated' Higher Education System

System governance pre-1992

Higher education was never at the forefront of British government thinking after 1963, either in regard to the structuring of the governance of higher education at the national level or about the mechanisms required to pursue policy once the immediate decisions arising out of the Robbins Report (Robbins 1963) had been taken. There were too many other, bigger issues around. Nevertheless the austerities of the Thatcher period opened up important issues of system management, which the reliance on the post-Robbins settlement had allowed to develop, if not unseen, certainly unaddressed. The 'Thatcher' cuts to university budgets in 1981 and the University Grants Committee's (UGC) reaction to them, administering them differentially according to its view of quality and national need, highlighted the extent to which government had followed a 'hands-off' policy towards the universities and left their management, with all the implicit policy issues, to be determined by the UGC, acting, as Carswell described, 'as a collective minister' (Carswell 1985). The position of the UGC was also subject to question from its failure to prevent University College, Cardiff, the premier university institution in Wales, to slip to near bankruptcy. In the meantime, on the other side of the binary line, the failure of the National Advisory Body (NAB) partnership of the Department of Education and Science (DES) with the local authorities to resolve the issues of growth among the polytechnics and colleges brought to a head the long-sustained ambition of the DES to bring them under direct national control. The result was the abolition of the UGC and the NAB and, after a brief interregnum under two new funding bodies, the Universities Funding Council (UFC) and the Polytechnics and Colleges Funding Council (PCFC), the two sides of the binary line were brought together under a new mechanism, a Higher Education Funding Council (HEFC). The 1992 legislation that created the funding council system also devolved responsibility for the management of higher education to Wales and Scotland thus creating a Higher Education Funding Council for England (HEFCE) and similar bodies for Wales and Scotland. Devolution was prompted not so much by recognition of deep-seated national differences, although it was certainly argued in Scotland that these existed, but because of the political impracticability of transferring the Scottish Central Institutions, the equivalent of the English and Welsh polytechnics, out of the control of the powerful Scottish Education Department, which had nurtured them, into a larger, UK-based higher education system.

The essence of the UGC system was that the committee, made up primarily of carefully selected senior academics and chaired by a leading academic, acted as an intermediary or, as described by contemporaries, as a 'buffer', between the demands of government and the needs of the university system, thus preserving a prized autonomy of the system as well as the autonomy of the institutions within it. This worked well while the UGC was located under the Treasury, which had no pretensions to be responsible for broader university policy issues, but less well after the publication of the Robbins Report, when the universities were transferred to the new DES. Nevertheless, until the implementation of the Thatcher cuts, the informal process where the senior civil servant conveyed the wishes of his or her minister to the chairman of the UGC on an informal, non-directive basis, served to maintain the belief that the autonomy of the system was not transgressed (Shattock 1994). At the same time the UGC maintained close relationships with the institutions themselves: the Committee made quinquennial visitations to each university and its range of subject committees also made visits to their disciplinary colleagues on a university-by-university basis. These visits combined an inspectoral role with the task of keeping the main Committee informed about academic development in the universities as well as keeping the institutions informed on UGC thinking. In the 1950s it had been the UGC, not officials in the ministry, who initiated policy discussion about the forecast rate of student number expansion and its financial implications, and it was the UGC, not a minister, that proposed founding the 1960s 'New Universities'. It was natural for a vice chancellor whose university had a problem or was wanting to launch a new initiative to discuss it personally with the UGC chairman: universities fully exercised their autonomy, but within a controlled environment. This was a self-governing system: the UGC and the universities shared a culture based on an established form of institutional governance, the core of which lay in the relationship between the vice chancellor and the senate, with the council, the governing body, occupying the governance role of last resort rather than that of a front-line, decision-making body. The UGC had issued a model charter and statutes for the new 1960s universities to draw on, which emphasized the decision-making powers of the academic community and it was the first body to be consulted by the Privy Council when universities sought amendments to their statutes. At the national level, the UGC operated in close consort with the Committee of Vice Chancellors and Principals (CVCP), itself a body very conscious of the need, in issuing policy statements, to stay aligned with senate opinion across the country.

The UGC's decision in 1981, however, to be selective in where the cuts imposed by the Thatcher government were to fall, followed by the research selectivity exercise in 1985–6, shattered the implicit sense of an identity of interest between the institutions and the UGC. Cardiff's maverick financial behaviour also showed that the old informal relationships could not be relied upon in situations of institutional stress and poor institutional governance. Seeking to retain sector autonomy, the UGC responded to an invitation from the secretary of state (Sir Keith Joseph), as did the NAB, to provide public advice on a future strategy for higher education and engaged in an extended consultation with the universities themselves. In its report to the secretary of state, the committee defined its historic intermediary role as follows:

> The UGC stands between the Government and the universities as it has done for 65 years. Recent difficulties have led to its being criticised more than before; but they have also shown that an intermediary body is essential. We are not the servants either of Government or of the universities. As one half of our task we shall continue to assert to Government the needs of the universities for resources which will enable them to provide teaching and research of the highest quality as they must always aim to do. As the other half of our task we shall guide and encourage universities towards the changes we are convinced they must make in order to serve the national interest into the 1990s and beyond. (UGC 1984)

This would have been an accurate statement of the UGC's position at any time back to 1946. The secretary of state chose to ignore the UGC's main recommendations in a subsequent Green Paper (DES 1985).

The UGC no longer commanded the full confidence of government. In the 1980s the UGC had found itself in a position where it believed itself forced to take 'dirigiste' decisions for the good of the university system. This damaged the trust in which it was held in the universities and, at the same time, gave it a political salience that brought it into conflict with the government and its political priorities. Secretaries of State for Education, like Keith Joseph, Kenneth

Baker and Ken Clarke, chose, themselves, to exercise policy-determining roles over the university sector in directions inconceivable in the 1970s, setting the stage for a reformulation of national policy machinery and a redefinition of the relations between universities and the state.

The Further and Higher Education Act 1992

The 1980s were a period of some turbulence for higher education on both sides of the binary line. As Richard Bird, the senior civil servant in charge of higher and further education, wrote, summarizing the period, policymaking was 'disorderly' and 'the creation of an embracing strategy was always beyond reach'. However, he added, if there was 'a guiding philosophy' at all it was the 'promotion of some sort of market whose functioning compels greater attention to the customer' (Bird 1994). This reflected the underlying instincts of the Tory ministers who served as secretaries of state through this period. At the end of the decade, marketization appeared firmly on the policy agenda with both the PCFC and the UFC encouraging a bidding war for additional student numbers by inviting institutional applications for expansion at a reduced unit of resource. The polytechnics and colleges accepted the invitation but the university sector did not, bidding by agreement for extra numbers at a common guide price. University resistance to marketization in this form was palpable: accused of acting as a cartel, they nevertheless won their point, thus preserving a common unit of resource for teaching across the university sector.

The great importance of the 1992 Act was the abolition of the binary line and the translation of thirty polytechnics into universities. In replacing the PCFC and the UFC, however, the creation of a Funding Council model swept away the managerial and planning philosophy of the UGC. In the 1991 White Paper, *Higher Education: A New Framework*, the government nailed its colours firmly to the mast of a more marketized future:

> The Government believes that the real key to achieving cost effective expansion lies in greater competition for funds and students. (DES 1991: para 17)

This represented a decisive philosophical switch from the UGC's approach, which was based on a close and interactive relationship with the sector. The removal of the binary line and the realignment of the teaching budget made this easier to implement (Shattock 2012). A second important change was to abandon the central direction of policy to separate funding bodies in Wales and

Scotland. The new Higher Education Funding Council system represented a step towards implementing a new philosophy: the councils were explicitly funding, not planning bodies, established to transmit government funding to institutions rather than to manage a sector. The UGC's paraphernalia of subject committees and visitations was abolished; the chairman or chief executive was no longer a person a vice chancellor would consult over an individual institutional issue, but became a distant, bureaucratic figure operating at a strictly system level; communications were more formal and technical than with the UGC, and much less adapted to scrutiny at senate, or indeed governing body, level than in the past. The relationship between the institutions and the funding councils was contractual, institutions receiving funds against stated levels of performance, with great emphasis placed on accountability, both financial and academic. The climate of exchange was impersonal, and officer-to-officer, and the Funding Council board members were kept remote from decisions about individual institutions, and their discussions were restricted to system-wide issues. In England, the sense of an impersonal bureaucracy was enhanced by the decision to locate the Funding Council out of London on the campus of the former polytechnic, the University of the West of England, on the outskirts of Bristol. Gone were the days when a vice chancellor or registrar might drop in for an informal chat with a UGC conveniently located in central London; relationships were accordingly at arm's length, and bureaucratic, rather than intimate and personal, very much mirroring those that had existed between the polytechnics and colleges and the NAB.

Although the 1992 legislation devolved responsibility for higher education to funding councils in Wales and Scotland, their impact was initially relatively modest. The Research Assessment Exercise (RAE), which had operated effectively in 1985 and 1989, was kept firmly in the hands of the English Funding Council (HEFCE) in 1992 and thereafter. It was agreed that the remit of the Quality Assurance Agency (QAA), again the responsibility of HEFCE, should extend across the whole of UK higher education. This made good sense because, in terms of student numbers, England constituted by far the largest component of the UK system with 79 per cent of the student numbers (against 13 per cent in Scotland, 5 per cent in Wales and 3 per cent in Northern Ireland) (DES 1991). Moreover, devolved responsibility was not intended to imply any differentiation of funding levels, with the White Paper committing itself to the policy that 'funding allocations by each territorial secretary of state to the relevant body will be informed by the Government's general policy in higher education' (DES 1991: para 48).

For the pre-1992 universities, the contrast between the UGC and HEFCE models required a considerable adjustment; the post-1992 universities and colleges, on the other hand, were used to a bureaucratic relationship with their funding body. Post-1992 institutions, however, found themselves eligible to enter the RAE. This proved to be a mixed blessing because, although some institutions managed to win additional funding from the exercise, reputationally the post-1992 sector as a whole suffered in league table terms in comparison with the performance of the pre-1992s. This was to exercise an unspoken influence on policy, especially in England, both at the national and at the institutional ends of the market.

Over the period of its life HEFCE played an important stabilizing role in a sector that eventually covered some 136 institutions, 109 of them universities. It justified the claim to be an intermediary body and engaged, robustly at times and with expertise, with the officials of whichever ministry it found itself under. Its two most important functions were the allocations of targets for funded home student numbers and the management of the Research Assessment Exercise, later the Research Excellence Framework (REF). The first gave it a controlling influence over the expansion of the higher education system (a power it shared with the funding councils for Wales and Scotland). Because funding was itself so restricted, institutional targets were vigorously policed and cutbacks in allocations of numbers could be imposed where targets were exceeded. (The funding councils' remit did not, of course, extend to the recruitment of international students so that institutions became increasingly schizophrenic, exercising fierce controls internally on home student recruitment but acting sometimes like nineteenth-century merchant adventurers in seeking to attract international students paying high-value tuition fees.) In its second function, the strength of HEFCE's position reflected the increasing importance that the government attached to the economic benefits of university-based research. While the original rationale of the first Research Assessment Exercise in 1985–6 was primarily to redistribute funding from the least to the most research-active areas in universities, the growing recognition of the importance of research concentration both scientifically and for reputational advantage meant that HEFCE occupied a unique cross-departmental role in linking research performance in the universities with considerations relating to national economic development. It is probably no coincidence that it was over questions of the degree of research concentration that HEFCE recorded its most public disagreements with its political masters (Shattock 2012: 100–1). HEFCE was never just a conduit pipe for state funding, as it was probably intended to be, and

Taggart overstates the position when he describes the shift in relationship with government from the UGC days as:

> it was once the role of the state to provide for the purposes of the universities; it is now the role of universities to provide for the purposes of the state. (Taggart 2004: 113)

However, it grew into a large-scale mechanism for controlling higher education institutions through financial and academic accountability procedures, through its control over home student numbers and through its role in assessing research excellence.

Where HEFCE could be said to have failed was in its role of representing the financial needs of higher education to government. The 1992 White Paper envisaged a doubling of higher education numbers by 2000. The solution proposed was greater competition, but by 1997, when the Dearing Committee reported, the unit of resource had fallen by 36 per cent since 1989 and the universities were in revolt, threatening to charge tuition fees themselves to bridge the financial gap (DES 2003: para 1.31). Reversing this trend, and finding a solution to paying for the continued expansion of higher education at a time when there were enormous pressures on the national finances elsewhere, became the key policy issue for the governance of higher education over the next two decades. The position of HEFCE was predicated on its role as the distributor of government funding to institutions and the decision in 2010 to fund teaching via student tuition fees removed from it its prime raison d'être. But its replacement represented a further policy shift in the governance of English higher education.

The departmental superstructure

It was apparent in 1963, at the time of the Robbins Report, that higher education did not fit well into the structure of government departments. While it was clear to almost everybody that the universities could not continue to be the direct responsibility of the Treasury, an alternative location was hard to find. Robbins offered the compromise of a new department that would also have responsibility for the research councils but this was rejected in favour of an upgraded Ministry of Education to become the Department of Education and Science, with a second permanent secretary to deliver the post-Robbins developments. (The second permanent secretary post was discontinued a year later when the Labour Party took power from the Conservatives.)

Civil servants, discussing redistribution of responsibilities within Whitehall, warn that the influence of political and personal factors in the construction of Cabinet membership may carry more weight than apparent reflections of changes in policy. Nevertheless any account of the changes of government departmental responsibility for higher education suggests a lack of clarity in defining policy and an uncertainty in the governance of the sector, which is reflected in the lack of stability in the way it has been run. As in other respects, 1992 represents the point at which significant change began. In 1963 the research councils had been transferred to the DES, along with responsibility for higher education (although local authority-funded higher education remained funded through the Department of the Environment), but industrial innovation was located in the Ministry of Technology. The two sides of research were coordinated by a Cabinet-level Central Advisory Council for Science and Technology. By the end of the 1980s, the recognition of the contribution of research to economic growth had hardened considerably and the White Paper, *Civil Research and Development* (Cabinet Office 1987), recommended that selectivity and exploitability should be central criteria for the allocation of resources. Lacking an obvious departmental base, the Office of the Chief Scientific Adviser to the Government in the Cabinet Office was chosen to coordinate policy across Whitehall and, in 1992, the research councils were transferred from the DES, thought to be insufficiently committed to the research agenda, to that Office. In 1995 they were transferred again, this time to the Department for Trade and Industry, leaving HEFCE, the RAE and responsibility for the distribution of the resources deriving from the RAE (entitled QR, or quality research funding, in the RAE formula) with the renamed Department for Education (DfE).

This structure was to survive the Blair premiership, although the 2003 White Paper promised a sharpening in the RAE concentration of resources, but in 2007, Gordon Brown, Blair's successor, restructured the governance of higher education by removing HEFCE altogether from the DfE and creating a new department, the Department for Innovation, Universities and Skills (DIUS) with John Denman as secretary of state, thus bringing the research councils and the Technology Strategy Board back under the same roof as higher education. Two years later, allegedly to provide a larger brief for Lord Mandelson, who was to become First Secretary, DIUS was merged with the Department for Business, Enterprise and Regulatory Reform to become the Department for Business, Innovation and Skills (BIS). Mandelson's reign lasted for a year to be succeeded by Vince Cable as Secretary of State in the Coalition Government, underpinned by David Willetts as Minister of State, who had been a long-time shadow Minister for Higher Education in opposition. Cable was succeeded in the brief Cameron government by Sayid Javid who, in 2016, was reshuffled to provide a place for Greg Clarke, in charge of a yet further departmental merger of BIS, this time with the Department of Energy and Climate Change to form the Department for Business, Energy and Industrial Strategy (BEIS). Most significantly, the new department relinquished HEFCE and its successor body the Office for Students (OfS), back to the DfE, allegedly to give Justine Greening a bigger department and thus more weight in Cabinet, but retained the organization of the REF and the distribution of QR funding. At the same time, the 2017 Higher Education and Research Act merged the seven research councils under a new body, UK Research and Innovation (UKRI) within BEIS, with a further new body, Research England, answerable to it, to which HEFCE REF staff were transferred. Willetts, and his successors Jo Johnson, Sam Gyimah and Chris Skidmore, were each appointed jointly to BEIS and the DfE as Ministers of State for Science and Higher Education to seek to keep the two key functions of higher education, research and teaching, operating in tandem.

The main conclusion to be drawn from this account of the changing structures and personnel in the governance of higher education is that they are driven much less, if at all, by issues in higher education itself and much more by extrinsic factors, political decisions about ministerial appointments, the disposition of government and departments and the way the prime minister at the time wished to conduct the nation's business. Such decisions were also taken on the basis of immediate, short-term considerations without much, if any, thought for the implications for the governance of the higher education sector and for the institutions that comprised it. The decision, in particular, to separate the machinery for funding student numbers and the machinery for funding research via the REF and QR between two different government departments struck at the institutional interrelatedness of teaching and research and any system-based assessment of the coherence of institutional strategies. The presence of a single second-rank minister to coordinate policies is unlikely to mitigate the polarizing effect of separate policymaking in two independent and distinct departments.

Funding and its impact on system governance

By 2000 the 1991 White Paper forecast of UK student numbers had been exceeded by almost a third, the distribution between the component systems being England 83.3 per cent, Scotland 8.9 per cent, Wales 5.4 per cent and Northern Ireland 2.3 per cent. Since 1997, when the CVCP committed itself to charge tuition fees to home students, prompting the establishment of the

Dearing Committee, the question of how to pay for a continuing expansion of numbers represented the most important policy issue in higher education. As one senior policymaker told us, 'public spending pressures really trump most considerations in public policy most of the time' and the 'financing [issue] has been the dominant thing over the last 10 to 15 years' (1). The Dearing recommendation for the introduction of tuition fees of £1,000 per annum, although it broke the policy log jam over charging fees to students, did little to alleviate higher education's funding problems, because the additional income was lost in the government's decision to continue its predecessor Conservative government's policy of imposing reductions on the higher education budget for the first two years of the life of the new government. (The decision by the Scottish government not to charge the Dearing fee marked the first substantial break with a unified national higher educational policy.)

The funding issue did not, however, go away. Blair writes in his autobiography that, by 1999, he realized that reform was necessary, but his interest lay not in the whole system but in a restricted group of leading universities: it was clear that it was 'a myth that all universities were of the same academic standing' (Blair 2010: 482). Policy on funding moved from the DfE to the Cabinet Office, where work was led by Andrew Adonis, Blair's Head of Policy Unit. Dinner with a subset of the Russell Group led to the establishment of a working party chaired by Charles Clarke, the Secretary of State for Education, but operating out of the Cabinet Office. This resulted in a White Paper entitled, somewhat immodestly, *The Future of Higher Education* (DfS 2003), which recommended the creation of a Graduate Contribution Scheme under which universities would be given 'the freedom to set their own tuition fee between £0 and £3,000' (DfS 2003: 76). The White Paper assumed that research-intensive universities were 'the best universities' (para 2.17) and, tacitly, that universities would charge variable levels of fees depending in part on their appreciation of their individual 'mission' (a shorthand for recognizing the level of their research intensity). 'We need to move to a funding regime', the White Paper stated, 'which enables each institution to choose its mission and the funding streams necessary to support it, and to make sure that our system recognises and celebrates different missions properly' (DfS 2003: para 1.39). It was, therefore, a surprise to the government when only two universities chose not to charge the full £3,000. There was no subsequent appetite to clarify divergent missions or to try to link mission with tuition fee charging levels: the Blair government had shot its bolt on controversial policy issues in higher education.

The Blair initiative sought to address the issue of the reduction in the unit of resource but did not provide a solution to how the continued growth in higher education numbers could be tackled. The White Paper allocated increased resources for research and for research infrastructures, but did not provide state funding for the anticipated improvement in the age participation rate for 18- to 30-year-olds from 43 per cent to 50 per cent. By 2006, when the new fee levels were introduced, the Cabinet Office was already back at the drawing board, devising alternative funding approaches. David Willetts, as shadow minister, travelled the world to discover what funding structures other countries used to match continuous increased demand. The triggers for a further scheme were the Browne Review (2009) and the 2010 Government Comprehensive Spending Review (CSR). The former represented a commitment given to Parliament to review the effects of the 2003 tuition fee decisions and was described by Willetts as 'crucial in shaping the debate' (Willetts 2017: 66). The Spending Review placed a requirement for savings of 25 per cent on BIS over the next financial period with the reductions to be front-loaded. Once again, the Cabinet Office went into action involving Willetts, Oliver Letwin, the Cabinet Office Minister, the Conservative Party Central Office, in the person of Jo Johnson, and civil servants from the BIS and the Treasury. The goal, as Willetts, the key architect of the scheme, described it, was 'to save public money without depriving universities of cash' (2):

> We have at last [he wrote later] ended up with a model which properly delivers and funds what the great reformers of the early sixties envisaged. Unlike many other systems it has student choice at its heart. It leaves with universities the responsibility of who they should admit and allocates funding according to the choices of students. And as it is a graduate repayment scheme it does not count as public spending – this is not some strange device but reflects the reality that money provided by the Exchequer should be repaid later. As it took most funding of higher education teaching out of public spending it made it possible to boost funding per student. (Willetts 2017: 68)

The result was a saving in public expenditure of £36 billion and an increase in funding to the system of £1.5 billion (Willetts 2017: 67).

The funding scheme was technically ingenious: students borrowed the money upfront through the Student Loans Company (SLC) and repaid it after graduation from earnings, unless those earnings fell below £21,000 per annum. The loans ran for thirty years and were repayable at a retail price index plus 3 per cent interest rate. Because the scheme assumed repayment of the student loan, government borrowing to enable the loan to take place did not, under Treasury rules, count against the government's borrowing account. The scheme looked good on paper but has proved much less sustainable in practice: since the recurrent grant to universities to pay for teaching was replaced by tuition fees (except for a supplementary figure for science, technology, engineering and mathematics (STEM) courses), BIS could record a 40 per cent saving on its budget in the CSR. However, because the Treasury believed that price competition would force tuition fee levels to average out at £7,500 per student, while all universities, following the 2006 precedent, chose to charge £9,000, the maximum permitted in 2012, the level of borrowing by the government to pay for the student loans greatly increased. The initial expectation was that after thirty years 70 per cent of the loans would be recovered, but forecast repayment levels have proved to be progressively more pessimistic and the best estimates now envisage a recovery rate of well below 50 per cent (McGettigan suggests no more than 20 per cent (McGettigan 2015)). The evidence of students graduating with debts of £50,000, at a time when the housing market is at its least favourable to young people, was sufficient to turn a technical issue into a political one, with political commentators arguing that the switch in the student vote to the Labour Party in the 2017 General Election was directly attributable to the tuition fee policy. In an emergency debate in the House of Commons in July 2017, Johnson argued: that the scheme had increased university funding by 25 per cent, making it better now than at any time in the last thirty years; that to attempt to write off the student debt would add £3,500 per person to the National Debt; and that abolishing fees and writing off the student debt would cost £12 billion a year for five years or a one-off cash cost of £89.3 billion (Johnson, Emergency Debate 19 July 2017). Nevertheless the Labour Party's threat to act on fee levels, or even abolish them, certainly lies behind two government announcements: the first, at the Conservative Party Conference in October 2017, to raise the earning level for loan repayments from £21,000 to £25,000; and the second, to establish a new government enquiry, the Augar Review of post-18 education and funding. This was in effect a full re-examination of tuition fee levels, their rates of repayment and the extent to which they reflected the cost of teaching different subjects.

The panel reported in May 2019. It recommended revising the decision, taken less than 21 months previously, that the earning level for student loan repayments should be reduced to £23,000, abolishing the 3 per cent interest on repayment of the debt, extending the repayment period to 40 years and reintroducing means-tested maintenance grants of up to £3,000 a year. At the same time it sought to upend Willetts' model (see page 27) by capping maximum tuition fee levels at £7,500 per year and making up the difference from the existing maximum of £9,250 through the provision of a teaching grant from the state. It went further, however, by recommending that the grant should 'reflect more accurately the subjects;

reasonable costs' (recommendation 3.5 page 96) (shorthand for adjusting the grant to the assumed actual costs of teaching the degree and implying a significant reduction in grants for all but STEM and medical and veterinary subjects) and that funding for students should take account of the 'social and economic value [of higher education] to students and taxpayers' (shorthand for excluding applicants with weak qualifications on the argument that there were 'too many students who will not benefit from a degree' (page 99)). To squeeze the sector further, because the panel concluded that the previous scheme had been too generous to higher education, it suggested that the tuition fee level should be frozen until 2022–3.

These recommendations (and at the time of writing they are only recommendations) represent a sharp break in terms of policy between the governments of David Cameron and of Theresa May. The report makes it clear that it is much less enthusiastic about handing over policy to market forces, though one can dispute how far practice actually followed rhetoric in the way the previous regime managed higher education. Nevertheless, a return to a situation where the state provides even partial funding through a teaching grant puts it very obviously back into a funding driving seat, where it was before, though without a HEFCE to act as an intermediary between the state and the institutions. The sector was assured by the responsible minister, Jo Johnson, that the reforms agreed in 2010 and implemented in 2012 were the long-term solution to higher education's funding issues, but within seven years it is proposed they be extensively revised and the new recommendations offer the prospect of ministerial or Treasury cherry-picking even if the overall thrust of the report is not accepted. Institutions cannot be blamed for strategic uncertainty when policy development at the national level is pursued in such a short-term, stop-go manner. In 2012 universities and colleges found themselves funded through what one former civil servant who had been closely involved in the process called 'the least worst way to fund higher education' (3), only to find that within five years the government had set up another committee to revise it.

The development of the market as an instrument of policy

An interest in a greater reliance on market forces in making policy has been of long standing. Bird, in his reflections on policymaking in the 1980s quoted above, suggested that the promotion of some sort of market lay in the background of decision-taking. But the first real attempt to harness market forces was the Labour government's proposed introduction of variable tuition fee levels in its

2003 White Paper. It is perhaps not surprising that the government adopted the conventional mind-set that universities and colleges could be ranked, effectively, according to their success in research, because this was the reputational message deployed in the media league tables and by the presentation by HEFCE of the RAE results. From a top-down perspective the market implications were clear, but from an institutional perspective it was immediately obvious that the correct market response to variable fees was to position an institution at the upper end of the tuition fee range since to charge a lower fee was to admit shortcomings, which would be bound to affect recruitment. As the National Audit Office was to conclude three years later:

> Providers are incentivised to charge the maximum, even for courses that cost less, because not to do so could suggest poor quality and reduce demand instead of increase it. (NAO 2017b: para 3.5)

It is astonishing that the precedent of 2006 was not taken into account when the borrowing costs were calculated by the Treasury in 2010. But it is clear that, in addition to the pragmatic arguments for a new solution to the higher education funding problem outlined above, there were ideological and political considerations with regard to the employment of a market philosophy, and which were brought into play as the scheme was developed. The Browne Review argued that the enhancement of student choice and increased institutional competition would drive up quality:

> Students will control a much larger proportion of the investment in higher education. They will decide where the funding should go and institutions will compete to get it. (Browne 2010: para 4.1)

This, in the review's view, was 'a surer way to drive up quality than any attempt at central planning' (Browne 2010: para 4.1). These arguments were echoed in the 2011 White Paper, *Students at the Heart of the System*:

> Our reforms to higher education funding will promote a more diverse, dynamic and responsive higher education sector where funding follows the student and the forces of competition replace the burden of bureaucracy in driving up the quality of the academic experience. (BIS 2011: para 1.45)

The belief was stated most boldly in the 2016 White Paper:

> Competition between providers in any market incentivises them to raise their game offering consumers a greater choice of more innovative and better quality products and services at lower cost. Higher education is no exception. (BIS 2016: para 7)

A key adjunct to this statement was to remove HEFCE's controls over institutional student number targets (condemned in the White Paper as 'micro-management', though in fact they were the product of Treasury pressure in a previous era), thus enabling those institutions with strong fields of applicants that wished to expand to do so at the expense of other institutions less strongly placed in the market. It may be too early to assess the long-term effects of this new freedom on the size and shape of the higher education system in England, but a National Audit Office analysis of the effect over the first three years suggests that, in a stable period for enrolments, applications increased by more than 10 per cent among higher-ranked universities and showed a substantial fall in lower-ranked institutions (NAO 2017b: Figure 6). The likelihood is that the market will continue to strengthen the 'best' universities and weaken the less strong. Rather than competition driving up quality, the danger, according to the NAO, is the creation of a two-tier system, where some institutions exist on a borderline of economically viable recruitment and teaching quality.

A glance at the statistics of applicants and acceptances issued by the Universities and Colleges Admissions Service (UCAS) might suggest the existence of a pure market dominated by competition between institutions trying to attract the best-qualified candidates. However, this ignores the attractions, for and against, of institutions sited in particular regions (London, the south east or the north), or that many students from less-advantaged backgrounds, irrespective of their academic qualifications, prefer to attend their local institution ignoring issues of reputation (a fifth of students continue to live at their family home while in higher education). In addition, student choice may concentrate entirely on the particularities of a given subject or degree course and disregard institutional reputation. Research evidence points to the fact that students from disadvantaged backgrounds are less mobile in their choice of institution and are more likely to live in their family home while studying (Gibbons and Vignoles 2013). Moreover, research has shown not only that economic and social disadvantages are reflected in admissions to higher-ranking institutions but that they continue to be reflected in subsequent graduate earnings even when compared with peers who studied at comparable institutions (Britton et al. 2016). The NAO has found that 'the lowest ranked universities saw an 18% increase in the share of students from low participation areas between 2011 and 2016 compared with 9% in the highest ranked' (NAO 2017b: Figure 6), flagging up the danger that the new higher education market rather than providing a more level playing field, will in practice increase the social class differentiation between students at higher- and lower-ranked institutions.

The Browne Review argued that one of the keys to the operation of a higher education market was that applicants were able to make an informed choice about the institution they wished to study in. HEFCE was accordingly asked to ensure that institutions produced Key Information Sets (KIS), which showed basic data on a comparable course-by-course basis to assist student choice. The issue of consumer protection, however, was referred to the Office of Fair Trading, itself in the process of a merger with the Competition Commission to form the new Competition and Markets Authority (CMA), which was brought into being by the Enterprise and Regulatory Reform Act 2013. The CMA's report, *Advice to UK higher education providers on Consumer Protection Law* (CMA 2015), had the effect of transferring the regulation of a fundamental aspect of higher education's autonomy outside the control of higher education authorities, even to the extent of the CMA issuing posters for institutions to exhibit on the presentation of course information, course changes and unfair treatment. Taken together with a promise to monitor practice in the sector and the threat of undisclosed penalties for failure to observe the CMA's recommendations, this reflected a clear indication of the government's intention to seek advice from outside the sector to reform the machinery for controlling higher education. How effective these particular steps to improve market information were might be judged by the NAO's finding that only 20 per cent of prospective students appeared to utilize the Unistats collection of comparative data published by HEFCE in making their university choice (NAO 2017b: para 2.12).

Unsurprisingly, one immediate effect of the removal of the cap on student numbers has been the introduction of a new volatility into the admissions process. Another has been the 'arms race' that has developed across the system for improved physical facilities, so that university borrowing has shot up to pay for new buildings intended to enhance institutional attractiveness (HEFCE estimated that over the period 2015 to 2019 the sector was planning to spend an average of £4.5 billion, 51 per cent more than in the previous four years (HEFCE 2016: para 6f)).

The creation of new governance machinery: the Office for Students

The decisions to finance higher education via tuition fees rather than recurrent grant and the removal of controls over student numbers spelt the end of the line for HEFCE. Although its continued existence was confirmed by the 2011 White Paper, by the time of the circulation of the first draft of the Higher Education and

Research Bill, it had been replaced by a new body, the Office for Students (OfS). Arguing that the demands of consumers and taxpayers required a heavyweight market regulator to intervene in the market in the same way as the Water Services Regulation Authority (Ofwat) or the Office of Communications (Ofcom) did in the water industry or telecoms, Johnson described the OfS remit in the following terms:

> It is a fundamentally different way of looking at how the sector is regulated. It's a classic market regulator rather than a funding council whose principal job up until now has been to ensure that the sector was suitably funded and the financial sustainability was assured. This is a regulator that is going to be driving value for money in the provision of higher education. That's a core concern right now for students who are bearing the cost or a significant part of the cost of their higher education. (Adams 2018)

The OfS had a bad start, with revelations as to the political nature of the appointment of some of its board members, notably a prominent member of the 'free schools' movement, whose appointment had been promoted by the minister himself. Following a petition signed by more than 220,000 people concerning the views he expressed on other matters, the member withdrew from the board. Perhaps more damaging, bearing in mind the government's stated intention that a key element of the OfS's role was to represent the interest of students (the consumers), was the refusal to give the National Union of Students (NUS) a seat on the board, even though it had had observer status on the HEFCE board. This was followed by the arbitrary rejection of three of the student candidates nominated by a panel appointed to make a preliminary selection for OfS board membership, apparently on the grounds that they expressed views at variance with the government's. The OfS must expect more than usual public scrutiny over its selection of the student panel, which is to be created to parallel the consumer advisory panels under the Office of Gas and Electricity Markets (Ofgem), the Civil Aviation Authority and the Office of the Rail Regulator to underpin the role of the student member of the board. A further weakness in the membership was that the board contained not a single experimental scientist.

The government drew exclusively on non-higher education sources for advice on its reforms. It could have asked HEFCE or even UCAS for a report on good practice in regard to admission procedures but it chose to go outside the sector to the CMA for advice, which was explicitly drawn from consumer law. A civil servant involved in drafting regulations for the OfS admitted that 'the language is very much akin to the language of the utilities industries', but excused this by arguing that the new funding system could be seen as comparable to 'other regulated industries' and compared student consumer rights to those of 'an energy bill payer' (4). The draft Regulations themselves quote the Prudential Regulations Authority of the Bank of England as the model for its risk-based approach to regulation (DfS 2017: 94). It also consulted the National Audit Office but, significantly, received a critical response, which it seems to have ignored.

The functions of the OfS were defined in the Regulatory Framework. It is worth asking why such regulations were needed, because there was no precedent for this procedure when HEFCE was established? The answer, one must conclude, was two-fold: first, the new approach represented such a radical break with past procedures that the OfS needed some formal protection from post hoc criticism as to the way it conducted its business; and, second, the urgent political and ideological objective of easing the further opening up of the system to the expansion of private higher education required legitimization. Without the latter issue the material could probably have been condensed into a letter of guidance from the secretary of state to the chair of OfS. As it is, the Regulations offer a mixture of prescription on process and aspiration as to the role of the organization. Underlying them there is an undercurrent of defensiveness and suspicion of the sector: fourteen paragraphs are devoted to defining occasions where the OfS might need to intervene into an institution including using powers of entry and search, and twenty-three paragraphs and subparagraphs are devoted to institutional deregistration; fines can be levied for institutional breaches of the Regulations (the Minister suggested in a speech to the Jewish Society that an example might be for a failure to observe the provisions on Freedom of Speech). These paragraphs seem to reflect a recognition that the sector is less than supportive of the new provisions and that they are a great deal more minatory than the sector is used to.

The basic provisions of the Regulations require institutions to apply for registration in one of two categories with or without capped tuition fees at the higher level. In the former they become eligible for receipt of government grant (for STEM subjects, etc.), for QR monies, for Tier 4 licences for visas for international students, and their English students become eligible for government loans for tuition fees through the Student Loans Company. In the second category, intended for private institutions, institutions are not eligible for government grants or QR payments and their students' eligibility for loans is restricted to a lower level of fees. These provisions are not new and were fully in operation before legislation; what was new was the requirement that existing public universities should be required to apply for registration to obtain access to rights that they had formerly possessed and pay a substantial registration fee, to be fixed by the secretary of state, for the privilege.

Registration involved an assessment of risk for which the OfS required data on student numbers, admissions data, continuation and completion rates, Teaching Excellence Framework (TEF) performance, degree outcomes 'including differential outcomes for students with different characteristics' (OfS Regulatory Framework 2018: para 136), details on student complaints, graduate employment and financial sustainability, and the OfS could also seek information from students and student bodies. The Register will 'provide a single authoritative reference for students, businesses, providers, other regulators and members of the public about a provider's status' (OfS Regulatory Framework 2018: para 71). The registration process for established institutions, while bureaucratically onerous, is otherwise relatively straightforward. However, where concerns were expressed, but disregarded, was in the arrangements for new entrants, where pressure from the first generation of new alternative providers has led to the abandonment of previous Quality Assurance Agency (QAA) conditions. Under a section headed 'New and faster options for market entry' the regulations declare that 'the conditions of entry are designed so that providers do not need to have a track record of delivery of higher education to meet them' (OfS Regulatory Framework 2018: para 41), and the financial sustainability requirements are loosened as far as to accept a legally binding guarantee from a third party rather than a record of institutional financial performance. Applications for degree-awarding powers do not need a track record of even three years (as compared to the previous six) but probationary powers can be granted from the day of a course's launch providing 'a clear commitment to the assurance of standards supported by effective (in prospect) quality systems' can be identified (OfS Regulatory Framework 2018: para 216). It is hard to square these provisions with the stringent concerns about risk set out elsewhere in the document.

The OfS is not, however, simply a regulator. The drafting of the Regulations gives it latitude to extend its influence into institutions beyond the formal regulatory role, and a test of its effectiveness may be how capable it will be in resisting ministerial efforts to make it more interventionist than its initial indications claim it will be. One sign that it may seek a wider policy role (and perhaps raise conflicts with its regulatory functions) lies in the following paragraph:

The OfS is well placed to champion particular issues, themes and approaches. Although OfS will not, in general, dictate how autonomous providers should act or what methods they should use the OfS will be able to shape sector wide debate and focus. Through its influencing power, the OfS may promote innovation in particular areas or encourage the dissemination of information about what works best to enhance particular outcomes. (OfS Regulatory Framework 2018: para 45)

Critics might seize on the words 'in general', but leaving them on one side, the most striking conclusion to be drawn is that the market alone is not deemed to be sufficient to bring forward innovation. This paragraph could easily become a vehicle for interventions of a qualitative nature; if so, the spread of expertise on the membership of the OfS board needs to be addressed urgently.

The creation of a private sector within higher education: the rise of the 'alternative providers'

One important, but little remarked, reason for removing the cap on English student numbers was to allow new alternative providers to acquire student numbers for tuition fee/student loan arrangements without existing public institutions being required to reduce their targets to accommodate them. Politically this would have proved to be a battle that the coalition government would have been unlikely to have won. At the last count in 2017, HEFCE recorded 115 alternative providers where degree-awarding powers had been granted and home students had become eligible for state-paid student loans, but analysis highlights considerable diversity, with a third of the providers having fewer than 100 students and only eleven having more than 1,000; 48 per cent of the students were studying business and management courses; 56 per cent of the UK students were from ethnic minorities; 75 per cent of the students were over the age of 21; 39 per cent were over the age of 30. The range of institutions covered by HEFCE's list defies easy categorization but includes for-profit institutions, mostly owned by private equity companies (e.g. BPP University and the University of Law), private institutions that operate under charity law (e.g. Regent's University and Richmond University College, both of which started life as private colleges providing US study abroad programmes), small specialist institutions (e.g. MA programmes run at Christie's Auction House) and institutions established consciously to challenge the educational culture of the public institutions, of which only two have been founded: the University of Buckingham as far back as 1974, and the New College of the Humanities (NCH), as recently as 2011, which offers a liberal arts-based education with 1:1 tutorials.

This diversity certainly meets the expectation in the 2017 Act that opening higher education to alternative providers would increase the variety of institutions and programmes in the sector, but doubts remain as to whether such institutions will ever achieve a level playing field with the public institutions or will represent anything other than a new, lowest tier in a hierarchically structured higher education system. Buckingham, for instance, offers a cautionary history: founded in protest against what a group of academics and others regarded as the encroachment of the UGC on the freedom of universities, and taking its first students in 1976, it committed itself to generous staff-student ratios, which it has maintained, and to a two-year degree structure. But although the quality of its teaching is clearly recognized in the annual national Student Satisfaction Survey, after more than forty years it has only 2,600 students, most of them international students, and only a modest record in research.

In the new generation of for-profit private institutions the influence of their private equity company owners can clearly be seen. The companies invest in the institutions but expect to sell them on after four or five years at a significant profit. Thus BPP was bought by the Apollo Group in 2009, which in 2017 was taken over by a consortium of private equity investors called Apollo Education; the College of Law was bought by Montagu Private Equity in 2012, and sold on as the University of Law to Global University Systems in 2015. In each case the change of ownership led to extensive changes in the institution's leadership team. The student market of all these institutions is primarily international and the range of disciplines taught is essentially determined by recruitment considerations. Thus Regent's University, located partly on the former premises of Bedford College, University of London, in Regent's Park and partly on premises in the adjoining Marylebone Road, now has 3,600 students, 85 per cent of whom are international, and teaches a broad humanities/social science programme but no science. Decisions by OfS on private institutions have an enormously important influence on their future: the effect of BPP acquiring degree-awarding powers is said to have increased its market value by £50m; the Greenwich School of Management and the British and Irish Music Institute, both for-profit institutions owned by a private equity company, Sovereign Capital, drew £19.9m and £24.4m respectively from the state in student loan payments in respect to tuition fees; without such support for their students it is unlikely that either institution could survive.

The role of the OfS is thus critical to the future of the current alternative providers and for the entry to the market by new institutions; the regulations have been drafted to encourage more. The 2017 Act even suggests that new applicants should pay heavily subsidized registration fees. One is forced to ask whether this represents a political/ideological policy intrusion into the higher education sector. Most of these institutions are, unsurprisingly, sited in London and the south, the most attractive locations for international students, and the only ones sited outside this area are the branch campuses of vocational institutions like BPP and the University of Law. Without low interest rates and the boom in private equity investment, the world of the alternative providers would also look very different. Home students make up a small minority of their student body and contribute less than 1 per cent of the total UK student population. No private providers have appeared in Wales, Scotland or Northern Ireland. Monitoring these institutions' financial sustainability and their maintenance of academic standards will prove costly, in comparison with the public institutions, especially in the case of the specialist single discipline colleges, which are likely to be vulnerable to changes in the environment or in market fashion. Questions of internal governance have been ignored: most academic staff are employed on short-term or easily terminated contracts, and have little say in academic governance let alone in institutional strategy; governing bodies are dominated by owner interests – the Greenwich School of Management's governing body, for example, consists of only five members, two of whom are shareholders, and financial decisions have to be endorsed by a higher body within the company. Apart from Buckingham, alternative providers have no research capacity; they are not the Harvards or the Yales of the future, but are more likely to be, for the most part, low-fee institutions, overly dependent on recruitment targets and essentially aimed at international students, teaching inexpensive, easily marketable subjects, with science and technology teaching concentrated in the larger public universities. Their contribution to UK higher education is likely to be negligible; they will never be more than fringe institutions.

The sector's representative bodies

Before 1992, the university sector had a long tradition of representation by a single body, the CVCP, which was funded by membership subscriptions paid by institutions and which employed its own staff who conducted research on policy questions. The CVCP had close relations with the UGC both at chairman and at officer level and most policy issues that involved the sector were discussed informally before they entered the public domain. The CVCP was respected by government largely because it was a coherent body representing a relatively homogenous group of institutions. Until 1992 the polytechnics were represented by the Committee of Directors of Polytechnics (CDP). This body was less well financed, operated with a minimal secretariat, the funding for which, until 1988, was controlled by the local authorities as the polytechnics' owners. The CDP may have been a less professional body than the CVCP, but arguably it was politically more effective, particularly in the period up to the 1992 legislation, which gave the polytechnics university status. In 1992 the two bodies merged, but very much on the CVCP's terms retaining the CVCP's name and its premises in Bloomsbury. The rapprochement did not last, however, and, in 1994, seventeen of the leading research universities, while retaining their membership of the CVCP, broke away to form the Russell Group (now comprising twenty-four universities), ostensibly to give more effective representation to their research interests. This began a slow process of fragmentation of university interests, where 'mission groups' assumed representative roles while continuing in membership of the CVCP, which rebranded itself as Universities UK (UUK).

The first to follow the Russell Group exodus was most of the rest of the pre-1992 universities, which, anxious to press the interests of smaller research universities, created the 1994 Group. At its largest, the 1994 Group comprised nineteen universities, but questions about its role and distinctiveness reduced it to eleven and, when a subset of its members were invited to join the Russell Group, the 1994 Group folded altogether. Meantime, on the other side of a now non-existent binary line, the Coalition of Modern Universities was formed. This, however, was later to split into the Alliance Universities – some eighteen self-styled 'business-engaged' universities, who stressed their commitment to vocational, technical and professional education and to research in these fields – and the MillionPlus, nineteen universities (mostly less research-active) whose name derived from the claim that together they enrolled over a million students; this group was heavily committed to increasing access and to widening participation. They have been joined by a fourth 'mission group', GuildHE, formerly the Standing Conference of Principals (SCOP), comprising thirty-two colleges and universities, mostly former higher education or art colleges, some of which have since achieved university status.

The establishment of the mission groups very clearly weakened the representative status of UUK, because each wished to argue its special interests with government and, in so doing, were competitive with each other. The differing locations of their headquarters say a great deal about their character: the Russell Group, housed in prestigious offices in close proximity to the Houses of Parliament, the Cabinet Office and the relevant government departments;

the Alliance, located further away at the unfashionable end of Whitehall; MillionPlus even further away at the Elephant and Castle; and Guild HE, tenants in Woburn House, the headquarters of UUK. In their own way they reflect the diversity of institutional priorities: thus, the Russell Group wins 68 per cent of QR funding, while the bottom fifty universities receive 0.5 per cent. Whatever the value of drawing attention to the varying strengths of the higher education system, the creation of different mission groups has proved to be divisive and has given the government the opportunity to consult separately and to play one off against the other. Relationships between the groups are not close and the Russell Group's public stance as representing universities at the apex of the system, to the exclusion of the rest, does not encourage collaboration. The sense that the Russell Group believes that it represents the 'real' universities, and that this may also be the view of the government, permeates the system. Before 1992, the CVCP was *the* channel for university communication with government, but now it is only one of many. The representative position of UUK has been further weakened by the necessary creation of Universities Scotland and Universities Wales to undertake discussions with their respective governments post-devolution. UUK has, therefore, increasingly been reduced to acting on behalf of English issues whereas its original remit was always national. Moreover, before 1992, it was the channel recognized by university staff for the settlement of sector-wide issues, but the academic staff support for the Universities and Colleges Union (UCU) strike over amendments to the Universities Superannuation Scheme in 2018, and the fact that a number of vice chancellors openly expressed sympathy with their aims, suggests that trust between universities and UUK is at a low ebb. The result is that UUK has lost standing in Whitehall and the higher education sector has lost coherence in responding to government proposals for reform and change.

The National Union of Students (NUS) offers a contrasting profile to the official bodies that represent higher education institutions but, on occasion, it can pack a more powerful punch. Thus, it persuaded the then shadow secretary of state, David Blunkett, not to raise top-up fees immediately after the 1997 General Election, delaying the introduction of fees by two years (Shattock 2012: 134); the adverse student vote in response to the Liberal Democrats' decision in 2010 to renege on their promise not to raise fees was a significant factor in the latter's loss of seats in the 2015 General Election. The student vote in constituencies containing universities has now become a recognizable political factor for all political parties. However, at the more mundane level of negotiation over student-related issues with government, the NUS, with its highly politically focused staff, could often get further and faster than the official representative bodies, although it would always expect to be more influential with Labour than Tory administrations. The fact that HEFCE invited NUS representation on some of its committees, and that the OfS excluded it, tells us a great deal about the political attitudes of the two bodies.

System governance and institutional governance

According to the OfS's Regulations, its first duty is 'to protect the institutional autonomy of English higher education providers' (OfS Regulatory Framework, para 10) but the question that arises is whether the very existence of the OfS (and its Regulatory Framework) itself limits institutional autonomy. A civil servant's explanation of the reform was that 'the framework … sets the rules of the game but not how you play the game'. The 2017 Act, he argued, protected institutional autonomy by limiting the government's and the OfS's role to 'top down strategic prioritization' – 'the things we want to buy for the UK economy, UK tax payer, UK voter' – leaving universities within these limits freedom as to 'how they set their mission, how they select their students, how they teach their courses, how they conduct their research' (5). However, the Regulations bear on all these activities. Thus, universities not only no longer have substantive autonomy but are now limited to a level of operational autonomy, which is circumscribed by the new Framework Regulations. Governance at the system level, which was formerly mediated by HEFCE as a designated intermediary body, has passed into the hands of the minister because the OfS, at least as designated, is no more than a regulator unless the minister chooses to use it in some other way. Autonomy at the system level in England has now been largely supplanted by government.

   Over the quarter-of-a-century of HEFCE's life, it had preserved the perception of sector autonomy by acting, in some respects, like the previous UGC although, in its own self-description, like a 'broker' rather than a 'buffer', between the sector and the state. But the new governance structure has replaced it with an organization based on a philosophy and a funding system at considerable variance with what has gone before. Consultation with the sector has been minimal, except on technical details: universities with histories stretching back to the nineteenth century, and much further, have been required to apply to register as institutions providing higher education, subject to conditions laid down by government that reduce their legal independence; a new piece of reputational machinery, the TEF, first formally mentioned in a Conservative Party Manifesto, has been introduced solely on the initiative of the minister without reference to the institutions themselves; and a market has been created with explicit guarantees in the regulations that neither the OfS nor the government will step in to support an institution that suffers market failure. The fact that all institutions must provide a student protection plan in the event of failure or closure does not suggest great confidence in the market's success.

The consequence is that the academic community is widely convinced that university autonomy has been greatly weakened. The following comment by a lecturer at a Russell Group university sets this usefully into context:

> I think there's definitely a sense of decisions being taken at a level above the university which are often linked to what are believed are ... market forces or ... broad socio-economic trends which we, as academics, have no control over. And that is they are very much determining the shape of higher education in the 21st century and I suppose that manifests itself most obviously in things like the TEF, higher tuition fees reshaping the relationship between students and academics and altering the way that we need to behave in the workplace and the pressures on us as teachers ... I think there's a sense in which these things that we feel that we now have to be doing [as a service provider] and have to be implementing, and have to be delivering to students, because of this new context. This increasingly consumer-style context in which students are accessing higher education, isn't really something that as academics we decided to do or we decided would be a good thing for universities ... There is a sense that there are people higher up in the university who are making strategic decisions that are being driven by these broader forces ... So I think there is a sense of disempowerment. (6)

Willetts' book *A University Education* opens with the words: 'I love universities' (2017: 1). Whether or not this represents more than a literary flourish, there is no evidence that his successors have the same feelings towards higher education institutions, indeed rather the contrary. However much the relationship between the institutions and the government changed in the replacement of the UGC by HEFCE, there remained a belief that HEFCE represented a force of advocacy towards sensible and institutionally manageable decisions on policy. The growth in importance of the 'mission groups' as channels of communication to government, and the effect on the status of UUK as the voice of the sector, further reduced the effectiveness of any central body that might act as a break on poorly thought through government initiatives. HEFCE may have seemed to be a producer-led organization, although it had a good record of relations with the NUS, but its successor, as the regulator of a market, makes the claim to be very much on the side of the consumer, apparently leaving institutional rights and legitimate interests vulnerable. The whole process of the creation of the OfS, from the sources of external advice that were drawn, to the analogies quoted with utilities industries, to the controversy over some of the first appointments to the OfS board, suggest an underpinning of political ideology that regards the role of universities and colleges as service providers there-to-be criticized, rather than institutions whose students are part of a common enterprise. The change of nomenclature from 'higher education institution' to' higher education provider' is symbolic of a radical change in how the institutional components of the higher education system are to be valued.

This sense of institutional disempowerment is compounded by the way, over the last decade, responsibility for higher education has been shuffled between government departments to the position where the REF and QR funding are to be hosted by a different government department from that concerned with the bread-and-butter issue of teaching students. The appointment of a minister to have joint responsibility for these two critical components of the management of a research-active university is no guarantee that policy in Research England will not be absorbed by UKRI or research council thinking, over time, restricting the powers of institutions to direct QR funding as they see fit. For the most research-intensive universities, this could involve up to 50 per cent of their recurrent income. Institutions that, apart from the 1960s New Universities, served long periods of apprenticeships as university colleges or as polytechnics, might reasonably feel belittled by the dismantling of the QAA safeguards for the granting of degree-awarding powers, especially when such a step is based on the argument that the new providers will bring innovation into the system; they will look for evidence that this is indeed the case, rather than the product of political ideology. The new market in higher education could, on the other hand, become an iron cage reducing innovation and universities' powers to act.

Universities benefit from financial stability to do good academic work, but in the last thirteen years they have had two radically different funding schemes to cope with, plus the Browne Review; and in 2019 the report of the Augar Review was published which, if the recommendations were accepted, would demand significant operational changes to the governance and management of higher education and severe university belt-tightening in some parts of the sector. Moreover, the report leaves undecided a series of issues: the Treasury's agreement to a return to the teaching grant, the extent to which the grant is to be modified to recognize subject costs, and the controversial question of restricting entry to higher education for less well-qualified students. The resolution of any one of these issues could have a further destabilizing impact on English universities and colleges. Instability of this order makes institutional financial planning and the financing of building programmes to cater for prospective growth in student numbers frustrating and forces institutions to concentrate on short-term decision-making. For universities without substantial reserves or high creditworthiness, risks increase and strategies lurch from one scenario to another. Institutional thinking becomes reactive and short-term. A key driver of the latest review is the Treasury's concern that universities are charging a common tuition fee at the limit of the figure permitted, thus reducing the proportion of the student loan likely to be repayable, yet this was a natural market response that a government, anxious to launch a market, should have been able to anticipate. Its encouragement of cheaper alternative providers, partly to compensate, risks creating a sector that will suck in bureaucratic time and resources and, on present showing, is offering little support for the view that market competition automatically raises quality and standards. Thus higher education institutions in England exist in an uncertain climate where the national governance structure should have provided stability. Institutional governance reflects this. As we explore, in Chapter 4, how governance has developed at the institutional level, we must keep in mind the uncertainty of national policy on higher education and the extent to which it has fluctuated over the period. There is little sign that this will change.

Chapter 3

The Impact of Devolved Government: Wales, Scotland, Northern Ireland and England

Until 1992, all British universities were funded centrally and such guidance as they were given came from a single source, the University Grants Committee (UGC) or, after 1988, the Universities Funding Council (UFC). Polytechnics and colleges in England and Wales were the responsibility of their local authorities, coordinated by the National Advisory Body (NAB) and, after 1988 by the Polytechnic and Colleges Funding Council (PCFC), while in Scotland the Scottish Central Institutions came directly under the Scottish Education Department. As far as the universities in Wales and Scotland were concerned, Aberystwyth, Bangor, Cardiff, Lampeter, Swansea and UWIST (all formally colleges of the University of Wales), and Aberdeen, Edinburgh, Glasgow, Herriot Watt, St Andrews, Stirling and Strathclyde Universities, were all funded on the same basis as the English and the two Northern Ireland universities, with student number targets set by the UGC/UFC. The decision to establish separate funding councils for Wales and Scotland (the Northern Ireland universities, because of Northern Ireland's constitutional status, continued to be the responsibility of the secretary of state for Northern Ireland, advised by a committee of the UGC/UFC) did not, in practice, have much visible impact on the two higher education systems: the three funding councils worked closely together, with representatives attending one another's meetings; and funding formulae used by the Higher Education Funding Council for England (HEFCE) were applied in the other three systems. The absorption of the polytechnics, the Scottish Central Institutions, and the colleges of higher education into the university systems, and the rationalization of funding levels that this involved, tended to obscure the fact that devolution was not the radical step it was initially thought to be.

This was to change after referendums in Wales and Scotland in 1997 and the 1998 Good Friday Agreement in Northern Ireland. This led to a formal devolution of government functions, defined in three Devolution Acts in 1998, which transferred substantial areas of public administration, including higher education, from Whitehall to the devolved governments, the National Assembly in Wales, the Scottish Parliament in Scotland and the Northern Ireland Assembly. In Wales, further legislation in 2006 clarified the relationship between the Assembly and the Executive and gave the Assembly legislative powers including in education. In Northern Ireland the Executive was a five-party power-sharing body, which took decisions only on the basis of formal rules governing a quorum. All three governments were to be funded under a common (Barnett) formula, which provided a primarily population-based share of comparable spending in England, and was to be apportioned, normally every three years, in the UK government's Comprehensive Spending Review (CSR). The funding was not earmarked for particular administrative areas, leaving the three governments free to determine their own spending priorities. These arrangements have continued in force including through the years of financial austerity. The Scottish government was thus able to exercise its new powers in 2000 by deciding that it was not going to follow England in introducing the post-Dearing £1,000 tuition fee. This decision remains in force.

Because England's university and student populations are so much larger than those of the other three administrations (England: 136 public universities, Wales: 8, Scotland: 19, N. Ireland: 2; England: 83 per cent of the UK student population, Wales: 5.4 per cent, Scotland: 8.9 per cent, N. Ireland: 2.3 per cent, in 2018–19) and because the UK government itself is responsible for English higher education, developments in England can easily be regarded as representative of the UK as a whole. However, it is not just that in size that Wales, Scotland and Northern Ireland are comparable to other small European nations (Finland, Ireland, Norway, the Baltic states) but, post-devolution, the three higher education systems have developed their own characters and have not only diverged significantly from the pre-1992 UK system but also diverged, very markedly, from the otherwise dominant English model that has been established over the last two decades. The existence of these different governance structures and approaches provides a valuable perspective on the financial pressures and political ideologies that have driven changes in England. Devolution has turned out to be not simply an administrative device or a response, particularly in Scotland, to strong political pressures, but has come to reflect significant cultural and historical differences from the higher education system in England.

Devolution did not extend to research, however: the research councils remained the main source of research project funding and, by agreement, HEFCE, while it existed, remained responsible for the organization of the Research Assessment Exercise (RAE)/Research Excellence Framework (REF) and for the allocation of quality research (QR) funding, although the other two funding councils (and their governments) and the Northern Ireland Office were left to distribute their shares of the QR funds as they thought fit. The UK's Innovation agenda, therefore, remained a matter for national decision-making and was committed to the pursuit of national priorities. This has met with some resistance in Scotland, where there is a wish to establish Scottish priorities, and some concern in Wales that its more limited priorities, in terms of expenditure, will be lost sight of in the UKRI's strategic vision.

Towards a tertiary education system in Wales

Structurally, Welsh higher education is more integrated with English higher education than those of the other devolved nations: 27 per cent of Welsh students undertake their studies outside Wales, predominantly in English universities, and 56 per cent of the students actually studying in the Welsh system are from outside Wales, again predominantly from England. It has one Russell Group university, Cardiff, which is by far the largest university in Wales, its income constituting half of the annual income received by the whole Welsh system. However, Welsh higher education is distinctive in other ways at the system level: its political culture gives priority to consensual decision-making rather than the much more directive approach adopted in England. This is a characteristic that is enhanced by the intimacy of the system. As one senior official explained:

> You can get the whole of Welsh higher education round a table ... which means that there are conversations that you can have and ... a closeness of working relationships which you really couldn't operate in a sector the size of England for example, and I think that provides opportunities and certain dis-benefits as well. ... HE providers are able to get much closer to government than would be the case for most universities in England. (1)

This assessment is confirmed by a vice chancellor who said:

> It does make a difference in terms of there is a closeness [with ministers] and accountability and the way that it is discharged is that there is an intimacy in that relationship because everybody knows everybody and there are only nine

universities if you count the Open University.* So for a minister they've only got that number to think about whereas the equivalent minister in England has got ten times that number, if not more. (2)

Another interviewee commented on his preference for the familiarity that this proximity gave as compared to the pre-devolution situation where secretaries of state responsible for higher education normally had English parliamentary constituencies and rarely visited the province.

Relations with the Assembly are similarly close. Such closeness may be of even more importance in discussion between ministers and Universities Wales and the NUS for Wales. On the other hand, a downside of devolution is that Welsh universities are more exposed to political influence: universities can use their proximity to ministers to their advantage but can also suffer because ministers are now much better informed than they were in the past. Many members of the Assembly, which must approve all major government policy initiatives, also have close personal links to higher education in Wales, either through their own careers or through family members. A senior civil servant felt that 'the state has gained a great deal from devolution and the role of higher education because it feels a much stronger sense of connection with these organizations and of ownership towards them' (3), while recognizing that this view might command less support in Cardiff, Wales' only Russell Group university, because of its national and international connections, than in some of the more regionally engaged universities.

A further distinctive feature as compared to England, is the universal support for education and its economic regenerative role; the pre-1992 universities themselves were in part created in the nineteenth century from the financial contributions of working men and women and, historically, university education was seen as an active force for the alleviation of poverty and for social justice: the Heads of the Valleys Institute in South Wales for example offers an example of the engagement of a university with the economic decline of the former mining areas of mid-Wales. In discussions about the reconfiguration of an institutionally over-provisioned higher education system, the government accepts that some campuses, however uneconomic, must be preserved because of the essential contribution they make to their local economy. Wales, along with Northern Ireland, has the lowest gross domestic product (GDP) per capita among the UK's regional economic groupings and is below 75 per cent of the EU GDP average.

---

* The Open University in Wales is funded by the Welsh government but remains constitutionally part of the Open University based in Milton Keynes.

Devolution in 1998 dealt the Welsh government a poor hand as far as higher education was concerned, both because it found itself with too many institutions for its population base, even though the pre-1992 institutions continued to sustain themselves by attracting English applicants, and because it inherited a system not well adapted to the country's economic circumstances. As a result the government, which since then has been either Labour or Labour-dominated, has sought to encourage a reduction in the number of institutions through mergers. Of course, achieving mergers does not of itself produce reductions in expenditure but it does have the effect of pushing decisions about the need to close campuses onto the institutions themselves, making planning an orderly rationalization easier than if it was attempted by administrative fiat, or simply by the operation of the market. The principle of operating through consensus, albeit sometimes concealed in a velvet glove, has generally been effective in bringing the number of institutions down from twelve to eight plus the Open University; and the government was willing to accept the legal challenge of Cardiff Metropolitan University not to join a merger with other institutions to form the new University of South Wales.

It also sought to reorient the system. Having commissioned a report on the governance of the sector (Hazelkorn 2016), the recommendations of which included substituting 'Tertiary' for 'Higher' in its name, and having obtained approval from the Assembly, the government proceeded to issue a consultative White Paper, *Public Good and a Prosperous Wales – Building a Reformed PCET Sector* (2018), prior to legislation. This approach has made it possible to perform a transformation in the character of Welsh higher education with the Royal Welsh College of Music joining the University of Glamorgan, which itself then merged with University College, Newport, and Merthyr Tydfil College (a key contributor to the Heads of the Valley scheme) to form the University of South Wales and the Swansea Metropolitan University, together with Lampeter and Trinity St David, and the remnants of the University of Wales, combining to form the Trinity St David University with two further education colleges, Coleg Sir Gar and Ceredigion, joining the Trinity St David University group. The approach contrasts sharply with the 'hands-off' logic-of-the-market approach adopted by the Office for Students (OfS) in England. One other success is that the government has introduced a greater sense of common purpose in the institutions, offering a counterweight to the rivalry and parochialism that had flourished beneath the bonhomie encouraged by the intimacy of the system.

Nevertheless, Welsh higher education policies cannot avoid being influenced by England. While HEFCE was in existence the Higher Education Funding

Council for Wales (HEFCW) stayed closely in touch with its decisions and attended its meetings as an observer, and Welsh government policy on tuition fees was closely aligned with the policy adopted in England, although the approach followed in Wales was significantly different: fees were charged at £9,000 as in England, although not all institutions initially charged the maximum figure, but every Welsh student received a fee grant of £4,954 because the minister believed that the full £9,000, even with student loan support, would discourage Welsh students from entering higher education, so that the actual cost to the student was around £4,050. However, how the minister squared the circle was to deduct the fee grant from the recurrent funding made available to HEFCW thus significantly reducing the funding available to institutions. This resulted in an absence of capital spending, inadequate expenditure on maintenance and infrastructure costs and, according to one well-placed interviewee, a deterioration in the appearance of Welsh universities in comparison with their English neighbours. The Welsh government's decision to accept the main recommendations of the Diamond Report on higher education funding and student finance arrangements in Wales (2016) means that from 2018–19 Wales has opted for a £9,000 tuition fee (but not £9,250) supported by loan arrangements, and by grants and loans for student maintenance, which brings it more into line with the English model while offering a better deal for students from disadvantaged backgrounds. This will leave HEFCW with only QR monies to distribute. Unlike HEFCE, however, HEFCW continues, like the former UGC, to see itself as carrying out a 'buffer' rather than a brokerage role, and undertakes visitations of institutions on a three-year cycle rather like the old UGC. It sees itself as 'not to be captured by the sector but … [to be in a position for government to take its advice] because we do know what's possible and not possible and what's reasonable and what's not reasonable which helps to avoid government getting in a silly place as well' (4). Again, like the UGC: 'we transmit government aspirations to the sector but we also inform the government about what might or might not be the limits of sensible aspirations' (5). With further mergers potentially in prospect, and with the additional responsibilities for further education consequent on the decision to adopt a tertiary education approach, it promises to continue to play an important intermediary role in the Welsh system under the proposed title of the Tertiary Education and Research Commission.

Although HEFCW has 'to recognise that for Welsh higher education to do what it has to do, what it needs to do for Wales, it has to be a player on a UK-wide system' (6), in other words it has to align itself in some procedures to benefit from the UK's standing and reputation. It has, therefore, gone along, though in a watered down form, with HEFCE's requirement that governing bodies should provide a guarantee about their institution's quality of education (see Chapter 5) but has stated that this must be supported by an external quality assurance view, normally from the Quality Assurance Agency (QAA) itself, because it believes 'that governing bodies are not typically well equipped to form judgements about academic quality' (7). This was a position warmly supported by the chairs of governing bodies that were interviewed. Again, unlike England, the HEFCW continues to support active and routine institutional reviews by the QAA, both to provide a guarantee of academic standards and for the use of its reports to assist students applying for university entry. Welsh universities have not entered the Teaching Excellence Framework (TEF): as a senior official expressed it, 'The Welsh Government is not into markets. It's not part of its political philosophy' (8). On the contrary, Wales is committed to consensual decision-making with relatively long chains of consultation, but, bearing in mind the distribution of small institutions of higher education over its unfavourable geography, it has probably made as much progress in adapting to a more appropriate structure than a more robust approach could have achieved and it has accomplished a philosophical transformation of its vision of higher to tertiary education, which provides much more flexibility for future structural change without political bloodshed. Moreover, it has not swept away key pieces of national governance machinery but has retained, and in some ways reinforced, its intermediary body, which has retained its own trusted arrangements for maintaining close working relationships with the institutions. The Welsh tradition is for public education: Wales has only a tiny number of private schools and no alternative providers at the higher education level. The government has indicated it would accept proposals for private higher education that would operate under charity laws but would not entertain propositions for for-profit institutions. In effect it rejects one of the key ideological bases of the developments in England.

This rejection of the concept of higher education as a market and of the 'business model' of institutional governance has consequences for the way institutions are run: the role of governing bodies is much less emphasized and the academic community in most universities has a higher profile in decision-making. The concept of the dominant governing body or of the quasi-'executive' chair (see Chapter 4) to be found in some English universities is entirely foreign to Wales. This does not mean, of course, that in institutions that have been subject to mergers and reductions in staffing there are not accusations of a lack of consultation and of the heavy-handed exercise of institutional authority but the commitment to the importance of university education and its role in society seems to be unaffected. Nor do there seem to be any even mildly xenophobic reactions to the high number of English staff teaching in Welsh universities: one senior executive, when asked what proportion of the staff were people who identified themselves as Welsh, replied: 'that's something I never think about, I've no idea' (9). From an English perspective, governance at national and institutional levels in Wales could seem reprehensibly unreformed but, on the other hand, even though the higher education system has suffered significant restructuring and severe cuts in income, the value systems of the academic community remain remarkably robust and collegiality undiminished. Similarly, among the students there seems little evidence of consumerist attitudes: as one students' union president explained: 'we've always had open partnership and discussions with the University; I don't think the change in fees has impacted or changed that' (10).

The assertion of a Scottish higher education identity

Scottish higher education is much less integrated with English than the Welsh system. As one senior official explained: 'It's not because we want to be different, it [Scotland] just is different and it's [England has] got decreasing relevance to how we see things up here' (11). Scottish higher education is increasingly drawing away operationally from its English counterparts: Scottish Funding Council (SFC) representatives ceased to attend HEFCE meetings before it was replaced by the OfS; neither the NUS (England) nor the Universities and Colleges Union (UCU) maintain close links with their Scottish opposite numbers; Universities Scotland exercises all the functions and more of Universities UK (UUK) in England; in Scotland, only 6 per cent of Scottish resident students, as compared to 27 per cent of Welsh, choose to cross the border for their higher education. There are two main reasons for this: the history and the politics of the devolved government in Scotland. Education and university education in Scotland have a longer and more distinguished history than in Wales or Northern Ireland: education was excluded, along with the church, from the provisions of the 1707 Act of Union. The 'ancient' Scottish universities played a critical part in the Scottish Enlightenment and were beacons of scholarship in the nineteenth century when the English civic universities were in the process of finding their feet. By the beginning of the First World War, Scottish schools were already awarding their own school-leaving examinations, differing from the School Certificate in England, and a complementary four-year degree system was fully established in the universities, instead of the three-year period in England. One further difference is that over 20 per cent of Scottish higher education is carried out in further education colleges.

In the post-1992 period, the new Scottish Higher Education Funding Council (SHEFC) set its face against the English idea of 'teaching-only' universities. The government's argument is that

> being a university is the teaching and the research, and the two are combined: the research informs the teaching and so on, and ... [we would] just logically expect all our universities to be research active, it makes them universities. (12)

An academic in a post-1992 university, and thus a beneficiary of the argument, confirmed it:

> Research is often what excites certain people, or research is something you can involve students in ... the fact is that research fuels and feeds policy ... and to have institutions divorced from that, that are divorced from access to policy-makers, makes them really instrumental to the point of delivering an agenda that is being created elsewhere, so they become service providers as opposed to being able to contribute. (13)

Even though the post-1992 universities performed poorly in the 1992 RAE, they were not categorized as second or third division institutions by the funding council.

The second reason for Scotland's distinctiveness from the other three nations is the political nature of its government. The parliamentary elections in 1999 resulted in a Labour–Liberal Democrat government, but this was succeeded in 2007 by a Scottish National Party (SNP) government, which has been in power ever since. One senior university interviewee commented, in discussing government–university relations, that the SNP is 'a profoundly socialist government' (14), though this would be regarded as an overstatement by most political commentators. Most university leaders and senior academics argue that the SNP, when it came to power, did not fully understand the position of universities and their tradition of autonomy in Scotland, as elsewhere in the UK, but saw them simply as part of the public sector. Unlike in Wales, there was no instinctive respect for the idea of a university; one senior university figure suggested that the government and half the civil servants in Holyrood thought the universities were 'big secondary schools' (15). It could probably be added that very few people in the universities were particularly sympathetic to the SNP or fully understood what the SNP's political and social drivers were likely to be.

The government's immediate priorities were widening access to universities, particularly from the 20 per cent least advantaged population (identified by the Scottish Index of Multiple Deprivation) and ensuring that universities contributed to Scottish economic development. These priorities parallel those in Wales but were pursued much more aggressively. The appointment of a Commissioner for Fair Access focused attention on the first with a direct reporting relationship to the minister, but the chief bureaucratic instrument of control, with the potential to considerably restrict institutional autonomy, was the requirement that institutions complete Outcome Agreements with the Funding Council. Implicitly, the process was intended to monitor progress in implementing the letter of guidance issued by the minister. The agreements, which are renewed every three years, are very detailed, reaching down into the statistics of the admission of students from predetermined areas of deprivation or the progress of research projects that have an economic or regenerative impact, and include targets that are monitored on an annual basis. The agreements have to be negotiated with the Funding Council and signed off by the university court (the governing body), thus potentially drawing the Funding Council into a close involvement in the determination of institutional priorities and imposing on university courts an institutional monitoring role at a significant level of academic detail. In one university at least, the court was involved in seeing every draft of the university's outcome agreement – three occasions in all – and agreeing to every single target (16). To date, while the process of monitoring Outcome Agreements has been immensely burdensome administratively, it has not been accompanied by direct intervention from the funding council or the ministry. The potential, however, remains for the Outcome Agreement process to be employed to enforce government priorities on institutions at an extremely detailed level, including individual degree programme targets and admission arrangements.

That this has not happened is probably down to the continued existence of the Funding Council. The original, 1992, SHEFC was merged with its further education analogue in 2006 (they already had a joint secretariat) to become the Scottish Funding Council, but in 2017 the government proposed abolishing the Funding Council and incorporating its role within a Scottish National Enterprise Board, which was to have statutory decision-making powers. This could have had the effect of subordinating universities to an entirely economic development role. But the SNP government did not have a majority in the Scottish Parliament and the proposals were opposed. The structure eventually approved retained the Funding Council reporting directly to the minister but also linking it with a non-statutory Enterprise and Skills Strategy Board, on which it was itself represented; it retained responsibility for the distribution of QR funding, which gives it primacy within Scotland for the support of research. The SFC has never been as powerful as a 'buffer' body as the Welsh funding council, the role of defending university interests to government having been largely taken by Universities Scotland, but its role in negotiating outcome agreements with universities has shown it to be an effective intermediary body. From the point of view of institutional governance and the protection of institutional autonomy, it has enabled universities to sustain their own strategic priorities while responding positively to the demands of the state.

The prime mark of Scottish distinctiveness rests, however, with the decision not to charge tuition fees to Scottish students. From the moment Alex Salmond made the statement that 'the rocks will melt with the sun before I will allow tuition fees to be imposed on Scotland's students' (quoted in Riddell, Weston and Minty 2016), a political roadblock was created to discourage any retreat from a policy based on a fundamental Scottish principle. The White Paper on Scottish independence made it clear that it regarded the rejection of fees as 'a core part of Scotland's educational tradition and the values that underpin our education system' (Scottish Government 2013). The principle that 'access to education should be based on the ability to learn not the ability to pay' (Scottish Government 2007) represented a critical divide in Scottish thinking from the market orientation current in England.

The application of the policy had important implications for Scottish universities: undergraduate student numbers were capped so that institutional expansion could only be achieved at the postgraduate level or by the recruitment of English or international students; funding became tighter by comparison with England because the government's funding allocations did not keep pace with the additional income generated in England by the increases in tuition fees in 2006 and 2012. The control of student numbers, at a time of rising home applications, made admission levels more competitive, rejection rates higher and conflicted with the government's policies on access and widening participation: critics argued that meeting widening participation targets had the effect of displacing middle-class applicants; Riddell et al. argue that the true beneficiaries were students from more affluent families who could afford to pay tuition fees but were not required to do so. Paradoxically the policy made universities considerably more market-orientated because, in order to make up shortfalls in SFC funding generally calculated at between 6 per cent and 10 per cent less than the average unit of resource in England, universities chose to recruit international students or enter into international partnerships for students very much more actively. And, after 2012, a new market appeared made up of English students bringing with them tuition fees of £9,000 and became, therefore, subject to active recruitment. The result was that the budgets of high prestige universities, or universities in locations near Edinburgh or Glasgow, made them much less dependent on the Scottish government than might otherwise have been expected (the proportion of dependence on state funding varies from 20 per cent, in Edinburgh, to 80 per cent in the Highlands and Islands); the number of English students rose by 14 per cent, and universities became affected internally by many of the same 'commercial' forces as their opposite numbers in England. A further result was to polarize relations between the universities and government over issues of funding, with university pressure, conducted by Universities Scotland, for the government to retain parity with funding levels in England in the face of government backsliding, extensively reported in the media. (A perverse consequence was the reductions in further education college budgets, where a high proportion of higher education students and a significant proportion of access and widening participation students were being taught.)

The fees issue in 2000 established the separate identity of Scottish higher education and was given a good deal of support within universities. The second major exercise in imposing a Scottish dimension on higher education policy, a reform of university governance in the Higher Education Governance (Scotland) Act of 2016, was met with almost universal opposition from the universities. The purpose of the legislation was to 'democratize' the governance of the universities and to give stakeholders, the students and staff, a greater say in how universities were run. The Act entrenched trade-union and student representation on the university court, provided for two members to be elected by and from the body of the staff in addition to any elected from the senate, and made the position of chair of the court (in Scotland called 'the senior lay member') subject to election by staff and students instead of being elected by the court itself. The Act was also drafted to permit the remuneration of the chair of court, as it is thought to encourage the electoral process to draw on a wider social range of candidates. In addition, the legislation prescribed constitutions for senates/academic boards that again seemed to be aimed at protecting the interests of staff and students as against the heads of schools and university principals. The momentum of these reforms moved in an entirely opposite direction to those taking place in England, which, from the Dearing Report onwards, have tended to emphasize the need for greater external lay involvement and a more managerial role for the vice chancellor.

It is too early to assess the impact of these changes but they deserve comment, if only because it is the only example since the 1992 UK Act where any government within the UK has sought to legislate in respect to the detail of institutional governance. More importantly, it was imposed on a university system over an extensive barrage of protest. It is not surprising that a senior university figure described as a very significant challenge the task of retaining 'the autonomy and the diversity of higher education institutions in Scotland as against an increasingly – although interventionist might be too strong – certainly top-down, controlling government' (17). A good example of the way government interest can be exerted can be seen in discussions to revise the Scottish Code of Good Higher Education Governance, where the draft circulated for consultation in 2017 was heavily criticized for its directive style, drawing the comment from one lay member that some of its provisions display 'a sense in which various bodies feel that they must dance increasingly to the tune of the Scottish Government' (18). As with the Outcomes Agreement process, described above, the enforced changes to institutional governance structures may, in practice, have only a modest effect but the opening of the chairs of courts' position to election primarily by students (since they heavily outnumber staff) ignores the evidence of elections in students unions, and rectoral elections in the ancient Scottish universities, where only tiny proportions of the student body take part and are liable to be over-influenced by special interests. Good governance may be severely tested if university funding is subjected to further cuts.

Like Wales, one of the great differences from England is the size of the university system, nineteen universities, and the intimacy between senior university figures, principals and chairs of court with ministers. As one senior figure said:

> And that obviously has two sides, the closeness of government has a good side. The good side is that we have immediate access to government, we don't have to go through junior ministers or civil servants, we speak directly to the First Minister or Deputy First Minister or they pick up the phone and speak to us. Now that has positives and negatives. (19)

The speaker went on to say that the negative side was that the government's political agenda was very much for the need for universities to contribute to the government's targets in the economy, health and well-being, and that conversations could turn on outcome targets. The relationship is not as congenial as it appears to be in Wales. Another commentator said:

> One of my concerns is that intimate is not quite the word to describe a sometimes uncomfortably close relationship between the Scottish Government and higher education institutions in Scotland. Not that it's become claustrophobic or

controlling but it certainly is one of the challenges ... to keep that relationship at an appropriate distance. (20)

One of the strengths of the Scottish university system, however, is its cohesiveness. There has been no question of setting up separate mission groups, as in England, and the isolation of, for example, the Russell Group from the rest of the system does not exist in the same way between the four ancient universities or the pre-1992 universities and the rest of the system. As one principal said, the first reaction that English visitors attending a meeting of Universities Scotland have is 'they are struck by how well we stick together and how coherent we are and consistent and how well we work together as opposed to England' (21). This cohesiveness among the institutions gives Universities Scotland its strength, as compared to UUK, and is responsible for the way the university system has for the most part been able to withstand the interventions of a government, which, if it had its way, might try to subordinate the higher education system much more closely to its political and social objectives.

This is not to say that the SNP-led government is not proud of the international ranking of its most high-profile universities and of their research achievements, but its view of research is essentially instrumental to the needs of Scotland: 'they want universities to be skills factories' grumbled one senior university figure (22). But the universities have resisted this, compete vigorously in the REF and are as concerned about their research for reputational reasons as are universities in England. Indeed, the fact that all universities are expected to be research active, even though a research hierarchy exists, with Edinburgh winning one-third of the research funding of the whole system, contributes to Scottish universities seeming to be happier and better-balanced institutions than are often found in England. Without a neo-liberal government in sight, university courts do not assume the all-powerful role that is presumed in some parts of the English system. They take an active role in the determination of institutional strategy and in the detail of the Outcome Strategy, which they are required to sign off, but strategic plans are in general well-trawled within the academic community, certainly at senates/academic boards, and are then considered at court strategy day meetings. One chair of court described the role of the court in a way that would not have been out of place in the UK in general well before 1992:

> The governing body's view, and I mean we, we had a big say in the development of our strategic plan ... The governing body's role is two-fold, it's first of all to be a critical friend to the university, and to ensure that the right questions are being asked but there's an advisory role so that we are bringing our individual expertise

that we bring from the outside world ... so we might bring marketing expertise, we might bring finance expertise, we might bring building development expertise, whatever ... so we are bringing other expertise that we can offer to the university senior management, but the strategy of the university lives, to me quite firmly in the senior leadership of the university. (23)

Again, senates/academic boards continue to play a role in policy, and not just academic policy, and, in the view of academics expressed with various levels of positivity, continue to represent the views of the academic community. Course approvals and course reviews are carried out in a spirit of quality enhancement rather than quality assurance (Scotland rejected the standard QAA approach in favour of Enhancement-Led Institutional Review (ELIR) many years ago); one academic interviewee described the contrast he found as an external examiner to an English university where he was expected to give assurance, to say that the programme ticked the boxes, but did not offer suggestions for improvement (24). A student president in a post-1992 university, discussing relations with the university, said: 'I never feel really like there's a hierarchy' (25). Academic creativity is limited, however, by the tight control of student numbers. In a situation where there is considerable pressure from applicants on target places, it is difficult, if not impossible, to start new programmes without closing popular courses except at the postgraduate level, where number controls do not apply. Although academic life could be described as less regimented than sometimes can be found in England, academic performance suffers the same stifling burden of bureaucracy that is apparent in England. One academic interviewee quoted his principal as saying that the university was subject to 526 lines of accountability. Another complained of the need to rewrite his research plan each year to ensure that it continued to meet government economic priorities for inclusion in the Outcome Agreement.

In 2008 the government and the universities reached agreement through a tripartite advisory group, set up after the universities had complained about a lower than anticipated budget allocation, that there should be a new relationship between the two parties: the government would maintain parity of funding with England, SFC regulations would adopt a lighter touch and the universities would commit themselves to a closer alignment with the government's priorities and strategic objectives. The result was a significant increase in funding (Raffe 2016). It is not surprising that a decade or so later, after continued economic turbulence, the government is accused of not keeping its side of the bargain and the universities are irked by the level of accountability required of them. Scottish per capita GDP is roughly the same as in England, although with pockets of serious economic deprivation, so that it is not unreasonable for Scottish universities to benchmark themselves against funding for English higher education. A senior official admitted that 'a private fee-based approach might provide the English universities' system with more resource to invest in facilities' and it could lead to a situation when in the future 'we say "what happened to that world-beating university system?"' (26). This alone might explain the more edgy and abrasive relationship with government than exists in Wales, but in Scotland's case the reasons are also political: the changes in the universities' governance structure embodied in the 2016 Act represent a serious attempt to weaken the universities' powers of self-government, albeit one can be fairly confident that universities will find ways to reduce their impact. Organizationally, however, what distinguishes the governance of Scottish higher education from England's is not its uncertain relationship with government but its cultural cohesion and resilience. This is based on a tradition of collective action and of institutional autonomy derived from its older universities, and on the fact that all the institutions are regarded as research active, which reinforces more participative, more collegial relationships in internal governance.

Stalemate in Northern Ireland

Northern Ireland constitutes the smallest of the devolved higher education systems but is in many ways the most politically, though not academically, distinctive. The system comprises four institutions: two universities, Queen's University Belfast and Ulster University, and two university colleges, St Mary's and Stranmillis, both located in Belfast. The colleges are small, at around 1,000 and 1,500 students respectively, while the universities are comparatively large by UK standards, at 23,000 and 26,000 students respectively. There are also six further education colleges, which teach some higher education, foundation degrees and higher national certificates. Of the two universities, Queen's is strongly traditional: it was founded in 1849 as Queen's College, Belfast, and was once part of the National University of Ireland; like its civic university counterparts in England it is a member of the Russell Group. Ulster is multi-campus in Belfast, Coleraine, Londonderry (Magee) and Jordanstown, formed as a result of a merger in 1984 between the university in Coleraine, a 1960s foundation, and the polytechnic in Belfast. Although Ulster's distributed campus imposes different organizational structures to Queen's, the two universities share a pre-1992 governance constitution, differentiated only by Queen's calling its governing body the senate and its senate the academic council.

A further dimension to the Northern Ireland scene is its close connection with its neighbour, the Republic of Ireland: students from the Republic make up a significant proportion of Northern Ireland's international student population (1,400 out of 2,000 at Ulster University; and the Magee campus of the university in Londonderry has a large local student catchment from just across the border). Relations between the two university systems are strongly collegial and the two governments have reciprocal arrangements over tuition fees and maintenance grants in Northern Ireland and registration fees and maintenance grants in the Republic of Ireland. Interchanges between the two systems are as painless as, for example, between Scotland and England. At the same time 26 per cent of Northern Irish students choose to study in the rest of the UK, while only 5 per cent of Northern Irish places are taken by students from the rest of the UK, and 90 per cent of the system's international students are EU students from the Republic.

In such a small system one would expect an intensification of the intimacy between institutional and political leaders, but in Northern Ireland the relationships are of a different order, although, of course, in a relatively small community there is a high level of social familiarity between the worlds of higher education and government. The Northern Ireland system has never had an intermediary body like the UGC or HEFCE for the distribution of funding but civil servants in the Northern Ireland Office took advice from these bodies and the two universities have always participated in the RAE and the REF and benefitted from QR funding like the rest of British higher education. With the creation of a Northern Ireland Assembly and the Executive, devolved ministerial responsibility for higher education and further education was introduced, but through the Northern Ireland Department of Employment and Learning and, later, the Department for the Economy. While government funding was provided as in Wales and Scotland via the Barnett formula, on policy issues ministers tended to follow HEFCE closely. Political interest in education in the Executive focused on the school system and not on higher education. The policy vacuum only increased when the Executive collapsed and the Assembly was suspended. As a result the universities have had a much more arm's-length relationship with government than is the case in either Wales or Scotland. As one senior university figure explained: 'Generally government policy doesn't influence us too much … we are very much an autonomous institution rather than something that government is all over' (27). On the other hand, both universities' academic policies are driven closely by their UK league table positions, with Queen's benchmarking itself against eight fellow Russell Group universities and Ulster endeavouring to raise its league table position.

The two universities have, however, suffered severely through the suspension of the government because of the absence of any process to determine whether a transfer to funding via income-contingent loans would be politically acceptable. In effect, policy is frozen in a hybrid higher education funding system where tuition fees are held at the 2006 English figure, uprated by inflation to £4,030, combined with a supplementary grant from the government of around £3,500, leaving a gap of some £2,500 in comparison with the tuition fee income received by English universities. The supplementary grant must, however, compete in a situation where GDP per capita is, with Wales, the lowest in the UK. The government's spending priorities are for health and primary education and the supplementary grant has, therefore, seen reductions of 2 per cent per annum in recent years. These shortfalls in funding, and the absence of any political process to reverse them, have determined the course of governance change in the two universities. However, it is not at all clear, even if the Executive and the Assembly were restored, that the funding situation would necessarily be improved, since neither the Democratic Unionist Party nor Sinn Fein are sympathetic to moving to an English tuition fee solution, and Sinn Fein's policy in the Republic is to oppose tuition fees altogether. In any case, there is no inclination in government or in the previous Assembly to copy the English market-based approach. In a situation where government is unable to take decisions, officials concede that it is natural for the universities to want to enhance their autonomy.

One way the universities have exercised their autonomy has been to negotiate with the government an agreement that their intakes should be reduced in line with the budgetary reductions in order to preserve the unit of resource. This led Ulster to reduce its numbers by over 1,200 in 2015 and shed 210 posts, and resulted in its vice chancellor foreseeing a reduction of 25 per cent in student numbers over four years (Doyle 2017); Queen's cut 10 per cent of its budget and similarly reduced its numbers and posts. One result is that UCAS has calculated that the chances of a Northern Irish student gaining a university place in the UK system has fallen to a ratio of 75 per cent of applicants as compared to 85 per cent for English students. In both universities this accommodation to changed circumstances was only achieved with considerable pain and by putting a great strain on decision-making and governance processes. At Ulster it also led to a much publicized industrial tribunal.

These conditions, which are directly or indirectly the result of the Northern Ireland government's handling of higher education, have led both universities to make significant changes to their governance structures: both have reduced the membership of their governing bodies, from thirty-five to twenty in the case of Queen's, and from forty to seventeen in the case of Ulster, and both have merged and reduced the number of their faculties from five to three at Queen's and from six to four at Ulster. Both have also tightened, or reinforced, their central decision-making structures. Queen's retitled its central University Management Group to be the University Executive Board and devolved more power to the deans who became pro-vice chancellors, and Ulster strengthened its Senior Executive Team and created executive deans. When difficult decisions over cutbacks were involved the Queen's Executive Board recommended direct to the governing body; at Ulster decisions were arrived at painfully at a joint meeting of their governing body and the senate. In both universities decision-making power seems to have become more concentrated. At one, described by a senior university figure as 'a very top-down institution' (28), he estimated that only about forty people might be involved in discussion or consultation but that the level of discussion was never that great. The bases for key decisions were reached at faculty level, but the central executive committee took the final decision, which was confirmed by the governing body. In neither was the senate a powerful decision-making body: in one it was apparently bypassed by the central executive committee; in the other it was described by a former member as a body that rubber-stamped decisions by the central executive committee (29).

A further reinforcement of central direction within the universities has been the issue of reputation and their positioning in UK and world league tables. This is not simply a question of institutional ego but a reflection of the influence of league tables on the recruitment of international students and the income they generate, which in part has served to compensate for the shortfalls in government funding and fuels the universities' independence from government: Queen's, for example, aims to increase its proportion of international students from 8 per cent to 20 per cent. Reputational positioning thus becomes a key element in the maintenance of autonomy. However, it carries with it a reinforcement of central authority. At Queen's, the consequence of benchmarking itself with other Russell Group universities has been to bring in more postgraduates and international students where there is no government control over tuition fee levels, and to set targets for research income and publications. These targets have been devolved down to faculty, school and individual staff levels. Although there was consultation, as one academic said:

> A lot of academic staff felt that the big decisions had already been made by the time the consultation happened ... it was almost like a performance management system gone mad ... and it was much too pressured without recognising the realities of academic performance. (30)

At Ulster, the governing body, it is said, deliberately looked for a vice chancellor to raise the University's ranking in the league tables, and a new strategy was adopted boosting research and international student recruitment. In both universities it can be said that the effort to raise the universities' international profiles has reinforced a centralization of authority and increased the pressure on individual members of staff. But although it may have affected the autonomy of individual members of staff over research, there was clear evidence that, at the ground level, the essential principles of academic autonomy have been maintained. Thus one senior academic said:

> One still has considerable latitude in the construction of a syllabus and a curriculum in an individual module ... we have subject benchmarks, we have peer pressure from colleagues within and without about the curriculum but ... colleagues have enough freedom to manoeuvre. (31)

In the other university an interviewee described a straightforward process for an individual to propose a new academic initiative, discuss it and win support from colleagues, put it to a faculty and, if they supported it, leave it to the dean to carry it forward to the senate. Both universities are under acute strain from austerity and from pressure to raise their academic profiles and, while both sets of pressures seem to be targeted down to individual members of staff and although autonomy in research may at times be compromised, autonomy in teaching and collegiality in respect to curriculum development seems to have been preserved. Austerity may have reduced academic participation in governance at the strategic decision-making level, but it has not pre-empted the norms of academic initiative, consultation and debate at the academic level.

The four systems compared

It is clear that although the Welsh and the Scottish systems are in a process of diverging from the English model, England and the English approach to markets and competition are the elephant in the policy room that cannot be ignored. (The Northern Ireland system, operating in a policy limbo as it is, is more concerned with survival.) Exchanges of funding council papers and monthly four-way telephone calls between civil servants have kept the four systems in touch, when bureaucratic processes like the TEF or the involvement of governing bodies in the guarantees of academic standards, both processes emanating from England, could be discussed. But the relations between the higher education systems and the different sets of political processes have ensured that the systems have continued to move further apart (a process that will be encouraged by the abolition of an intermediary body in England to parallel the proposed Welsh Tertiary Education Commission and the Scottish Funding Council). In the twenty years since government devolution took effect, this has had a marked impact on the governance of the different systems and on their character. In spite of the need to undertake institutional rationalization, the Welsh consensual approach to policymaking has enabled useful reform to be undertaken without great damage to the institutions involved. In Scotland, the more aggressive SNP government has met its match in Universities Scotland, where the unity of the Scottish university system has been fostered by the absence of divisions between research-intensive and teaching-only universities; although the universities lost the battle over the reform of their governance, they have survived the absence of tuition fees much better than is sometimes believed south of the border. Moreover, they have retained a sense of internal collegiality and academic participation in governance that contrasts with what is to be found in many English settings. There seems to be more space for the individual academic. One academic, who had moved to a Scottish university from an English civic university, said that 'the thing is that you can actually do things here and get things done by showing initiative. The downside is that there are lots of initiatives going on which you are supposed to be doing' (32).

The SNP may have imposed a potentially unworkable institutional governance structure and Outcome Agreements, but this interventionism pales almost into insignificance in comparison to the changes arising out of the English Higher Education and Research Act, which require legally independent universities to apply for registration to be recognized as higher education providers controlled by 63 pages of conditions, which make them subject to a regulator whose Regulatory Framework extends over 158 pages, and which requires them to pay expensive subscription charges for the privilege which are to be fixed arbitrarily by the secretary of state. Whatever the value of exploiting market forces and competition to guide the development of higher education, this represents the most far-reaching assertion of the state's power of governance control in the modern history of British higher education. Unlike the efforts of Universities Scotland, there was no comparable reaction by representative bodies in England: Universities UK, which was later, it claimed, unable to object to the appointment of an inappropriate member to the OfS board because it had already been publicly announced, was quiescent, perhaps because the most powerful mission group, the Russell Group, was not threatened by the proposals. As a consequence there was almost no public discussion of them. None of Wales, Scotland and Northern Ireland is inclined to follow England's policy lead: of the four systems, England's is the outsider.

Thus we have reached a situation that would not have been predicted in 1992 or even in 1999: that we would have four distinct systems of higher education in one country. Of course this must be qualified by the fact that the four systems are bound together at the research level and in terms of the REF, and that all of them have Russell Group universities, which collectively defend the interests of research-intensive universities. But there is no doubt that devolution of higher education to Wales and Scotland has been beneficial in increasing the diversity of British higher education, and in strengthening the political and cultural bonds between the two systems and their environment. There is, however, an important downside. In both Scotland and Northern Ireland entry to higher education is restricted: in Scotland's case, on a point of principle in respect to the payment of tuition fees; and, in Northern Ireland, to protect a declining unit of resource. In both there is evidence of funding shortfalls, as there have also been in Wales until the promised increase in fees to the level in England. The political argument justifying this situation is that it represents choices made by responsible governments (or in Northern Ireland's case, a not-so-responsible government) as to how to allocate resources. But from an educational point of view, the situation is inequitable. Wales and Northern Ireland have, jointly, the lowest GDP per capita of all the regions in the UK and need heavy investment, social as well as educational, to remedy historic economic disadvantage; Scottish 18-year-olds should not have their life chances restricted by the application of abstract principles. The UK government ought also to be concerned about the loss of talent to the country as a whole that is involved.

In 1992 one of the dangers that critics of the original devolution decision foresaw was a descent into parochialism. That this has not seemed to have affected the universities may be attributable to the continued centralization of decision-making on research and to the reputational and the 'commercial' value of national and international league tables. Conversely, one of the benefits was thought to be the injection of greater diversity into the national higher education picture. This has been partially realized in the sense that two of the four governments involved have introduced radical new political visions, one of the left, the other of the right, but three out of the four have created different models of system governance that have been the product of their own political, social and economic cultures. The most direct impact of these changes can be seen, negatively in Northern Ireland, and considerably more positively in Wales and Scotland. In Scotland, the single most important factor has been the cohesiveness of the university system, something which seems to have been lost in England leaving the universities weakened when radical change was put on the agenda. In Wales and in Scotland the evidence suggests that the quality of academic life for staff and students has been sustained through the pressures of governance change at the system level, but one cannot state this so confidently for all the institutions in England; in Northern Ireland it is urgent that system-level governance is restored.

Chapter 4

The Changing Pattern of Institutional Governance

In 1992 university governance seemed to have set itself into a new pattern: the pre-1992 institutions, Oxbridge excepted, had a lay governing body – the council (with academic representation, normally up to a third of the membership, nominated by the senate) – an academic senate, faculties and faculty boards headed by elected deans, and academic departments; the post-1992 universities had lay governing bodies of no more than twenty-four members (normally only two of whom were academics elected by the academic staff as a whole), an academic board, advisory to the vice chancellor only, faculties headed by appointed executive deans answerable to the vice chancellor, and academic units (sometimes schools, sometimes departments, sometimes academic programme teams). The post-1992 constitution, which was set out in the 1992 legislation, was very clearly more hierarchical than the pre-1992 and gave unicameral authority to the governing body with the vice chancellor operating explicitly as a chief executive. The academic boards' functions were limited, more or less, to course approvals, academic regulations and examinations. This was not a constitution imposed by government but one that had been sought by polytechnic directors in 1988 primarily to give them the ability to manage and direct the strategy of institutions that had often been run chaotically under local authority control (Shattock 2012). The pre-1992 institutions were much more bottom-up and participative in their governance style but already the effects of the imposition of the 1981 cuts and three rounds of the Research Assessment Exercise (RAE) (in 1985, 1989 and 1992) had encouraged the creation of what Clark was to call, later in the decade, 'a central steering core' (Clark 1998). The process was accelerated, as universities expanded, by the devolution of budgetary authority and resource allocation powers to intermediary bodies such as deans' offices or faculty management committees standing between departments and the centre.

Senates, however, even though their powers were being eaten away by vice chancellors' Monday morning management groups or by invigorated senate executive committees, remained the beating heart of university governance, with governing bodies largely exercising a 'long stop', 'critical friend' role, in spite of the Jarratt Report's injunction that university councils should 'assert' themselves (CVCP 1985).

A snapshot across the unified university sector in 1992 would, therefore, have revealed a relatively tidy pattern of two individual systems sitting side by side reflecting a historical division of function (Shattock 2006). Twenty-five years later this pattern has been almost completely overturned, without national legislation (except in Scotland), but as a result of incremental change by institutions and by pressure from government, particularly in respect to the role of governing bodies for greater apparent accountability or for a closer approximation to a business model of decision-making. What has emerged is an extraordinary diversification of institutional models that have brought with them quite highly differentiated models of governance. This institutional diversity has been driven by reputational ambition – the effect of league tables, the signal they give to international students, the impact they make on the employment prospects of graduates – changes in funding structures, the creation of a market and the imposition of measures like the Research Excellence Framework (REF) and the Teaching Excellence Framework (TEF), which combine accountability with raising the stakes in institutional competition. In addition, one cannot discount the impact of institutional growth: in 1994, excluding the Open University, only two unitary universities exceeded 20,000 students whereas in 2017 the number had risen to forty. More recently, the pressures of demography, aggravated by the creation of the post-post-1992 universities and the government's encouragement of a new category, the alternative providers, has further diversified the picture.

It is commonplace to refer to the diversity of the British higher education system, but it is often not realized how diverse the sector has become and how far the idea of a university has been extended. Thus the case study institutions that we have drawn on include wide differences in institutional mission, from one university that says:

> Our focus on competition and collaboration has always been global, so when we think about competition we worry about students going to Stanford, or Hong Kong or ... other places around the world (1)

to another university that draws its students, 56 per cent of whom are from ethnic minorities, from a twenty-mile radius and 94 per cent of its income from tuition fees, and that regards its stakeholders as being

> from the city council for instance, to the chamber of commerce, to the local enterprise partnership, to community and social groups, communities like X across the road there. (2)

One of our case study universities, whose activities were closely linked to its local community, described itself as an 'anchor institution'; another claimed the role as its city's key partner, alleging that the Russell Group university in the city had abandoned its historic civic role in favour of a research and international profile.

Huge diversity is also to be found in commitment to research and in dependence on attracting students so that one university sees its research reputation almost as its raison d'être, where a senior academic says that they mobilize resources

> by being very, very attractive to students who are coming here from all over the world and bringing resources with them to pay for their fees, by being very, very attractive to faculty who can bring funding and critically by doing things which matter, so that people who want to invest from industry ... see us as the preferred place for investment and partnering. (3)

Another describes itself as being

> in the part of the market where we always have to be thinking about recruitment, applications, conversions, student numbers; that's what drives our income. We do research but it's on a very selective basis but financially it's not that significant for us; the financial driver is student numbers. (4)

For that university the most significant change was not the rise in fees but the removal of the cap on student numbers; neither disturbed the first university at all.

Wide differences exist between inner-city universities, which have much higher proportions of ethnic minority students and are able to attract ethnic minority members to their governing bodies, and universities in out-of-town locations where the ethnic mix is quite different and where the commitment to regional communities and to industry may be no less strong but is much less marked. All the alternative providers, except Buckingham, are located in inner-city locations, both with regard to their headquarter sites and any satellite addresses, because that gives them greater proximity to their customer base. There is also great variety in the level of entry requirements with one university setting a grade D and an E at A level (but in practice accepting two Es) and another taking pride in raising the standard entry target to a B and a C (an initiative by the governing body, not the academic community) whereas many Russell Group universities are looking for three A's. The former see their mission to be widening access, the latter to select the best academically qualified from a competitive field. Diversity also derives from the increasingly different academic and governance cultures that exist between Wales, Scotland, Northern Ireland and England, which spring from the different approaches to system governance adopted, as described in Chapter 3.

It is not surprising that this diversity is reflected in institutional governance arrangements. At one extreme we find an entirely bottom-up approach to governance where:

> By engaging all of the academics and spending our time going from department to department, from college to college, understanding what people want, getting the university centrally to agree to that means that then when it goes back to the faculty it's what they want. (5)

At another extreme a top-down culture exists, where a lay-dominated governing body takes the lead in deciding to raise entry standards and improve institutional REF scores (6). In between there are a variety of positions: where the executive proposes but the senate must approve before the governing body considers the matter, to the executive proposing direct to the governing body (with or without wider consultation with the academic community), to the governing body and the senate holding joint strategy meetings, to the governing body, having agreed and taken ownership of a plan, taking charge of monitoring the executive's implementation of it. Below this high-level governance, academic internal governance structures relating to faculties, schools, deans and departments may constrain or facilitate academic work and may encourage or discourage academic innovation and provide a participative framework within which academic staff and students can express their views.

This diversity and its manifestations in governance practice significantly cross the clear division between pre- and post-1992 universities that was apparent in 1992. It is true that no post-1992 university approaches entering the research-elite group, but three of their College of Advanced Technology (CAT) forebears, given university titles in 1963, are now, in some league tables, ahead of some members of the Russell Group; and several pre-1992 universities have slipped down below several of the post-1992s in national rankings. In governance practice it is hard to distinguish between some of the pre-1992 civic universities and some of the post-1992s, when the size of the governing bodies, the make-up of their executive teams and the way that some pre-1992s have tacitly restricted the function of their senates, are examined. In describing and commenting on the governance of UK universities at the end of the second decade of the twenty-first century, we are addressing a diversity of governance practice that has been shaped, not by a new legal framework but by the extent to which institutions have reacted to the changing demands of the state, to financial conditions and to the pressures inherent in increasing competition and the application of market philosophies.

Uncertainty in the relationship between the governing body and the academic community

In the traditional pre-1992 university governance model, policy, meaning academic policy in its broadest sense, was decided by the senate, while the governing body acted as a sounding board, commenting and critiquing recommendations and providing authority for expenditure and for the issue of the institution's accounts. In 1970, Lord Annan, then Provost of University College, London (UCL), wrote a paper on university governance for the Committee of Vice Chancellors and Principals (CVCP) in which he asked:

> Is there a university in the country where [the governing body] is not a dignified rubber stamp? The true governing body is the senate. … Even Council's Finance Committee does little more than set the stage for cutting the cake. … We cannot and should not want to return to the days when Council really governed. We prefer self government by the academic staff. (Quoted in Shattock 2012: 215)

Annan was probably exaggerating the position somewhat, but the process of managing the cuts in 1981, the recommendations of the Jarratt Report in 1985 and of the Dearing Report in 1997, and the weight of the Committee of University Chairmen's *Guides on Governance* issued from 2002, all served to revive the role of governing bodies, a position reinforced by the evidence of the more robust lay governing bodies to be found in the post-1992 universities. From 1992 onwards the funding councils formally recognized the role of governing bodies as the single, senior decision-making authority in universities, as if all universities were unicameral, rather than bicameral bodies, by laying on them accountability and other responsibilities in the Financial Memorandum, which set out the conditions on which universities received their annual recurrent grant. The position of the governing body was thus transformed and the role of the senate was, in effect, written out of the script. No one in the pre-1992 universities was in any doubt at any time that their governing bodies had final responsibility for the finance and management of their institutions and could, in the last resort, override decisions by the senate or any other body or person in the university, but most pre-1992 universities' statutes defined the role of the senate as 'the supreme academic authority' in the university, thus emphasizing the historic division of responsibility for the 'business' side of the university as resting with the governing body and for the academic side with the senate, leaving the vice chancellor to broker any conflict that might arise.

Since 2012 the introduction of full-cost tuition fees in place of a recurrent grant opened up a new significant risk factor on the 'business' side of the university, which was reinforced by the decision to remove the cap on student numbers, projecting many universities into a much less stable environment. Governing bodies, many for the first time, had to become concerned about the relationship between financial viability and student numbers. The burden of fiduciary responsibility was noticeably increased and their dependence on the executive for sound management and good data correspondingly grew.

In 2016 the Higher Education Funding Council for England (HEFCE) introduced a new requirement for an Annual Sustainability Assurance Report to be signed off by the chair on behalf of the governing body (and not by the vice chancellor, as the 'accountable officer'). The details of the scheme, described in a Memorandum of Assurance and Accountability, which replaced the Financial Memorandum, originated from HEFCE's Financial Sustainability Strategy Group (FSSG) and its Sustainability Metrics Steering Group, and comprised an interlocking set of financial returns, all of which required approval by the governing body: an annual assurance return, audited financial statements, financial results tables with a commentary, the audit committee's annual report, a value for money report (described as optional but strongly encouraged as a 'non-burdensome opportunity to demonstrate the value for money which institutions provide to students and the public' (HEFCE 2015/16: para 5)), an annual sustainability assessment (this too was optional), a Transparent Approach to Costing (TRAC) return and a five-year financial forecast. Additional returns were required from the vice chancellor as 'accountable officer'. This constituted a heavy burden for lay governors who, since the responsibility for the data was pinned on them by HEFCE, had perforce to take such steps as they thought necessary both to understand the data and to assure themselves that it had been professionally and accurately prepared. In return HEFCE stated it would publish a sector summary, and that the chair of the governing body and the vice chancellor would receive HEFCE's risk assessment of the institution on which the governing bodies, if they had been conscientious in assessing the material, would have reached conclusions themselves some six to eight months earlier.

These burdens were, however, further enhanced, and the responsibilities they implied were greatly extended in 2016 by a requirement that the governing body provided assurance on the quality and standards of the university's academic programme. The process was refined in 2017–18 when the accountable officer, 'as a governor on behalf of all the governors' replaced the chair as the signatory of the Annual Quality Assessment Assurance Statement. This required the governing body to give assurance that:

- The governing body has received and discussed a report and accompanying action plan relating to the continuous improvement of the student academic experience and student outcomes. This includes evidence from the provider's own periodic review processes which fully involve students and include embedded external peer or professional review;
- The methodologies used as a basis to improve the student academic experience and student outcomes are, to the best of our knowledge, robust and appropriate;
- That standards of awards for which we are responsible have been appropriately set and maintained. (HEFCE Circular letter 37/2017, 20 October).

In a covering letter the chief executive of HEFCE referred governing bodies to a report on the 2016–17 exercise by the Leadership Foundation that she thought governors might find helpful. This report concluded: 'The requirement is straightforward and does not add to the substantive role of governing bodies' (Leadership Foundation 2017). Both assertions are open to question.

On the contrary, although all governing bodies, in approving institutional strategic plans would have had the opportunity to comment on academic planning, no governing bodies would have sought the involvement in the academic affairs of the institution that is implied in the Quality Assessment Assurance Statement: in the pre-1992 universities, there is a clear division in their statutes between the 'business' and the academic responsibilities of the governing body and the senate; in the post-1992 universities, while governance was unicameral in form, in practice responsibility for academic affairs was vested in the chief executive. The effect of the new requirement has been to pull already heavily loaded governing bodies into areas where they have limited competence, so that they must, in practice, rely entirely on the advice of academic bodies and the vice chancellor. This makes senates and academic boards vulnerable to interventions by lay governing bodies that lack professional expertise in the field but also lack confidence or need reassurance in the processes operated by senates and academic boards. As one vice chancellor told us:

> Our board ... was very uncomfortable. It wasn't uncomfortable because of what we were doing but it was uncomfortable that that responsibility had been parachuted into it and it's one of the things it's least well-equipped to be able to have a firm view on. (7)

Perhaps equally important, the introduction of this requirement has added to mounting concern, as much in the minds of chairs of governing bodies as in those of vice chancellors, as to where the divisions of responsibilities and the lines of separation of governance and management should be drawn. Our evidence suggests that this is now a very large issue in university corporate governance. Thus one chair, when asked what the greatest challenge to good institutional governance was, replied:

> Sorting out exactly what it is a governing body needs to concentrate on and what the executive and senate needs to concentrate on, having really clear lines of accountability and knowing what the appropriate level of detail is in the information coming to the governing body, and the appropriate level of challenge. (8)

A vice chancellor, asked the same question, replied:

> Ensuring that the non-executive element of governance is coupled in to the right degree, that it is able to make decisions at the strategic high level on the basis of good understanding without having to consume too much time of what are very busy people and not drawing them in too closely to the management of the organisation. (9)

Picking up the question of the narrow dividing line between governance and management, a chair echoed the point:

> The first challenge to ... any governing body, and we find it here with our lay members, is to make sure they stick with governance and don't stray into management. And some of the people we appoint because of their professional roles, and the normal roles they play on a daily basis dig into management all the time. (10)

Perhaps almost an opposite point, voiced by a vice chancellor, was that the greatest challenge to good governance was

> that the non-executive is not strong enough or skilful enough to hold the executive properly to account. (11)

Another chair, with a business background, said:

> I suspect that higher education is still waking up to the challenge which will come from independent non-executives to executive decision-making and getting comfortable with that process of challenge. So I think we are on a journey … and I think it will be given more edge and more teeth by the by the sort of transformation we are seeing in government policy. (12)

A senior academic governor from the same institution confirmed the point:

> I'm seeing board members increasingly wanting to find out more, and challenge more on the academic side, about quality for instance, [and] some of the metrics we use on a day-to-day basis as an executive to measure our performance; they want to understand that a lot more, and … that's going to make it more difficult to have a separation between executive and non-executive in my opinion. (13)

One result of the pressure on governing bodies is to look for new business-type solutions. One chair said:

> I'm not convinced that having unpaid non-execs is still the way forward … I think the way I have met the challenge, the regulatory challenge, is by getting a very high quality board, probably one of the better quality boards I see. A lot of people focus on local worthies who are perhaps not coming from the commercial sector and understanding the role of a non-exec or understanding the complex challenges which the sector has. What I've managed to find by getting … senior people who've made their way in the commercial world, has been the way to meet it. (14)

A vice chancellor offered a similar view but found the results not welcome to her senior academic colleagues. Faced with

> going in to a difficult period I wanted people I could go to who'd had experience in different worlds … so my view's been very much I need a strong council, and sometimes they are difficult, and I would say my executive group doesn't like it. (15)

What these eight statements demonstrate is the inherent uncertainty at the top level of institutional governance as to how, under the pressures of a new funding regime and the imposition of new regulatory requirements, good governance should best be carried out and what should be the most appropriate balance of powers between a lay governing body and the academic and managerial authority within the institution. Promises from the Office for Students (OfS) that these regulatory requirements will be implemented with a 'light touch' where institutions are operating successfully do not alleviate governors' concerns that, having taken a personal responsibility for returns that have been signed off in their name, they may be subject to post hoc scrutiny by external authorities as to the depth of their understanding of the material submitted. Moreover, system-wide summaries of returns may be used, in an increasingly compliant era, to influence changes in practice that weaken the notion of individual institutional autonomy. These dangers are most apparent in respect to the Annual Quality Assessment Assurance Statement, which opens the door to direct lay intervention and control over the conduct of teaching and research, the core responsibility of the academic community.

Senates and academic boards

Julie Rowlands, in her book *Academic Governance in the Contemporary University*, concludes that 'within many contemporary Anglophone universities academic governance has been redefined and is being practised in a way that limits the extent to which academics can participate and academic voices can be heard' (Rowlands 2017: 237). Our findings support this in respect of the role of senates and academic boards at British universities, but we would nuance the picture to take account of the institutional differentiation that exists within the British university environment. The idea of the senate acting as the de facto governing body and performing as the chief actor in strategic decision-making, as described by Lord Annan (p. 73), has been left behind, except at Oxbridge, and even in the pre-1992 universities it is clear that the senate has lost influence. However, in all but one of the pre-1992 universities interviewed, the senate remained a force in university governance, although academics who were members of senate were noticeably more positive about their senate's role than academics who were not. (Their statements may have been coloured by an element of self-justification or simply have reflected that, as members, they were more knowledgeable about the business senates conducted.)

There remains a considerable gap between the status of a senate in the power structure of a pre-1992 university to that occupied by the academic board in a post-1992 institution. As described by the vice chancellor of one post-1992 university:

> [The] academic board are advisory to me as the chief executive; they have no decision-making powers in effect but they do have considerable responsibility for the discharge of what we do, whether that be research or whether that be curriculum ... the balance [of relationship] is actually between the executive, with academic board advising the executive, and the governing body. (16)

The academic board thus has no direct relationship with the governing body, although, as the vice chancellor continued, issues at the academic board are reported to the governing body 'because it is part of the fabric which the governing body need to see' so that it has a better appreciation of how the executive reaches its decisions or recommendations (16). It is appropriate to add that two out of three academics interviewed in the university did not think that the academic board represented academic opinion and one of the two argued that

> It's mainly a rubber stamping exercise; there's very little debate; there are staff members represented on it but it's extremely difficult for them to put forward views which do not accord with what management [the executive] want to do. (17)

Indeed there were few academics in post-1992 universities interviewed who would not agree with the view that their academic board was a rubber-stamping operation: 'Our senate [academic board] is neither large, nor is it powerful. I would say the dominant power within our university is our governors' (18). 'It wasn't a decision-making thing' claimed another (19); and an elected of member an academic board said:

> We only feel we can raise the most important issues ... overall there's a sense that there's the academic community and there is a committee structure and those two have very little contact between each other. (20)

The conclusion to be reached is that in the great majority of universities with post-1992 constitutions, where the academic boards' powers do not extend beyond purely formal academic business, the academic boards' participation in wider governance issues is very limited, if it exists at all; their role is restricted almost entirely to curriculum, examination matters and quality control.

Pre-1992 university constitutions accord senates much greater decision-making importance, from extending the range of business covered by the words 'academic authority' to having the right to discuss any matters affecting the university. Historically, as we see from Lord Annan's statement, although once the dominant organ of university governance they still remain an important component, even if exercising nothing like the power that they once did. Thus in one pre-1992 university, where academics agreed that the senate provided an academic voice in its governance, the vice chancellor described it as merely 'there to hold the executive to account for things academic ... [and] help to shape policy but ... it is not an initiating body' (21); and two out of three academics described it as a rubber stamp. At another pre-1992 university, which described itself as intensely collegial, the senate could, it was reported, become engaged in passionate argument but a senior academic described it as 'a relatively managed affair' and 'largely on board' (22); the structure did not, however, he claimed, look different from five or even ten years ago. In a third pre-1992 university, a middle-ranking member of the senate, in answer to the question as to whether senate represented academic opinion strongly and well enough to the executive, responded: 'I think we do have a good representative body of people on the senate and that they speak up in meetings and I think that works quite well' (23). But another academic, from the same university, regretted the fact that 'there's an acceptance that the major decisions are made not by the academic community at large but by the management team and by the vice-chancellor in particular' (24).

The evidence suggests that senates in the pre-1992 universities have maintained a level of participation in governance that has never been achieved by the post-1992s, but that it is a great deal less than was previously enjoyed: they can query decisions by their governing bodies or their executive, and perhaps force reconsideration, but they are unlikely to be able to initiate them; they are important vehicles for the expression of academic opinion on a wide range of issues but they are not decision-making bodies except in relatively narrow academic areas, and even these are now being challenged by the Annual Quality Assessment Assurance Statement, which transfers final authority on these issues to a lay governing body.

Why has this decline in power and influence taken place? Two immediate clues emerge from our interviews. The first is drawn, by implication, from Wales and Scotland where the prevailing mood of governments has not led to pressure for governing bodies to take control of their university in the way that they have in England. Thus, in a pre-1992 university in Wales, we were told that, while it was fully accepted that the ultimate authority rested with the governing body, there was 'almost an unwritten constitution which says that council does not require accountability from the senate on clearly academic matters' (25). In Scotland, a pre-1992 chair spelt out a much more traditional vision of the role of a governing body than would be found in England (see p. 58). This is paralleled at the academic council (senate) level by a more robust tradition of an extensive process of consultation over any issues likely to be controversial or to generate outright revolt. Tradition in the four ancient universities also inclines to powerful academic bodies rather than the more constrained senates to be found in England. Even at a post-1992 university an active academic board was encouraged by the vice chancellor and there was general agreement among its academics that it not only represented academic opinion well but was willing to question propositions from the executive. (One academic, however, criticized it for spending too much time on discussion and not sufficiently holding the executive to account. He also described it as being essentially 'toothless', although valuable in communicating issues around the campus (27).) These examples suggest that it is the lack of dominant governing bodies in Wales and Scotland that is a significant factor in permitting senates and academic boards to continue to play a relatively important role in their universities' governance.

The second clue was the size of the university. In large universities with highly devolved systems of academic governance the relationship between individual academics and central policymaking is inevitably distant, unless they are actually members of the senate or academic board, but in small institutions the situation is very different. Thus one academic at a post-1992 university of around 7,500 students told us:

> It seems to me that everyone knows everything because it's small and systems have been structured in such a way that voices are heard and that decisions seem to be made collaboratively in the round, as it were. (28)

At another small university a lecturer emphasized that, with a fairly flat decision-making structure, everyone who wanted it got a say. In large universities institutions become impersonal and communication from the centre inevitably becomes restricted to electronic newsletters. Even when vice chancellors undertake tours of departments to consult on revisions of a university's strategic plan, as many do, particularly in pre-1992 universities, it is questionable whether the intimacy and sense of colleagueship to be found in the smaller institutions can ever be replicated. One reason why institutional governance has changed is that, since 1994, the average size of universities in student numbers (excluding the Open University) has grown from around 13,000 to over 16,700 in 2016–17, the latter figure being spread over some twenty more university institutions; many institutions have doubled in size.

There are, however, more generic reasons for the loss of influence of the most senior academic bodies. The first is quite simply the complexity of university business and the speed with which it must be transacted. Senates and academic boards normally meet once every term, which gives no time for responding to fast-moving issues where internal consultation is required. Senates, too, are often large, if not over-large, bodies. In one of the pre-1992 universities in our survey, where the executive, and particularly the vice chancellor, was blamed by one academic interviewee for being over-dominant, the senate membership was ninety-two. In two others, vice chancellors had initiated reform of senate membership but had only reduced it to sixty-two and fifty-five members respectively – in neither case, one suspects, as large a reduction as they were looking for. In a third, the senate had been more or less replaced, except for statutory business, by a meeting of heads of academic departments, which was used by the vice chancellor for discussion of strategic issues. As governments have become more demanding in their requirements for accountability, as the collection and interpretation of data for strategic purposes has become more important, and as funding mechanisms have become more dependent on tuition fees, there has been a greater need for close scrutiny and discussion as to the most effective responses. In such situations governance and management become elided. Smaller bodies, made up of experienced people and meeting frequently and regularly, become the preferred vehicles for decision-making rather than larger academic bodies.

Academic boards in post-1992 institutions have never been allowed to expand in size the way that senates in the pre-1992s have done. Partly this is because they have not had a provision in their constitutions that all professors should be members – the main reason why senates in pre-1992s have grown – and partly because there was little pressure within institutions to change the provisions originally agreed. However, a second reason that both senates and academic boards are often referred to as rubber stamps is structural. As universities have grown and as institutions have devolved aspects of central management to faculties or, more fashionably, colleges, significant areas of academic business have moved downwards to be decided, effectively, at faculty, college or even school level, leaving senates or academic boards with only formal responsibility for approving recommendations that proceed from these bodies. Even where senates and academic boards retain the function of close scrutiny of syllabus or examination changes, the role is generally delegated to a specialist committee. Senates and academic boards have, therefore, very much become for substantial elements of their business rubber stamps for recommendations from lower bodies.

But there is a wider reason why in England senates (particularly senates) and academic boards have lost influence. This is encapsulated in the statement by one pre-1992 chair: 'I think it is absolutely critical that the governing body owns the strategy and that that is never lost sight of' (29). Since the Dearing Report (NCIHE 1997), the 'unambiguous' authority of the governing bodies over the operations of their universities has been stressed in government communications. It has been considerably enhanced by the requirements issued by HEFCE in 2016 that governing bodies accept responsibility for the maintenance of academic standards, quality control and the continuous improvement of the student experience. There is no reference to the concept of 'shared governance', that is, the belief that responsibility for institutional governance is shared between the governing body and the organs of the academic community; the Committee of University Chairmen's (CUC) *The Higher Education Code of Governance* (CUC 2014; Revised 2018) makes only a single reference to the existence of senates or academic boards (para 4.2). It is perhaps, therefore, hardly surprising that in many universities the senates do not feel the sense of ownership of the university that they certainly felt in the 1980s and 1990s. Over time this will be further weakened as governing bodies are tempted to exercise their powers under the new HEFCE requirements.

Some pre-1992 universities have sought to preserve their senate's role vis-à-vis both their governing bodies and their executives by holding joint governing body–senate strategy meetings, which have clearly been valuable in providing joint ownership of strategic plans. But, under present circumstances, it is unlikely that many senates will accept responsibility for a substantial restructuring and redundancy programme, as they did when managing the cuts in 1981, preferring to leave the final decisions to the executive or the governing body itself. This is not to say that they would not be capable of taking tough decisions to reshape their university if circumstances demanded it and perhaps tougher than a governing body would take – the Ulster University senate, for example, voted through just such a package of measures – but there would be less incentive to do so when the ownership of strategy is so firmly located in the governing body. Perhaps the chief virtue of its survival as a key element in a university governance structure is, as described by a senior academic in a Russell Group university, as 'an academic place where academics at different levels could voice their views' (30). This transfer of responsibility represents a major shift in the balance of university governance and remains to be tested in the event of future sharp reductions in income or violent swings in the student recruitment market. It could well turn out that a senate–governing body axis would prove more institutionally effective than an executive–governing body axis, with the senate left out of the decision-making equation, because the senate would more clearly be seen as acting on behalf of academic interests than a narrowly based executive operating in conjunction with a lay-dominated governing body.

The rise of the executive

The first use of the term chief executive in relation to universities was in the Jarratt Report and it quickly found its way into the 1988 constitutions of the polytechnics, and thence into the post-1992 universities. It was used initially more cautiously by the pre-1992 universities and, because it tends to be associated with the commercial or business world, can be misleading as a description of the role of a vice chancellor, both because it does not seem to encompass the role of academic leadership and because in business parlance it could be interpreted as a synonym for managing director. But it was adopted with enthusiasm by polytechnic directors and written into the constitutions of the post-1992 universities. As the pre- and post-1992 universities have moved closer together, these distinctions have lessened. The two most quoted pieces of research on leadership in the British university context both stress, on the contrary, the importance of academic leadership. Bryman writes of 'the need for a leader to create an environment or context for academics and others to fulfil their potential and to ensure the work interests of staff are supported' and about the 'significance of fostering a collegial climate of mutual supportiveness' (Bryman 2007: 27). Bolden et al. describe academic leadership

> as a process through which academic values and identities are constructed, promoted and maintained. This can be contrasted with a whole host of activities conducted within institutions ... to organise and allocate academic tasks and processes, which could be described more accurately as academic management. Together these processes shape and inform a sense of purpose and objectives for individual academics which are operationalized through the process of self-leadership which is characteristic of academic work (within the UK at least). (Bolden et al. 2012: 42)

These writings, though valuable in emphasizing academic over managerial leadership do not, however, capture the realities of the role of a vice chancellor, for example in reaching a decision to borrow a large sum to put up a new academic building, in establishing priorities and deciding where redundancies might fall in a cost-recovery exercise, or even in winning over a sceptical chair and governing body to a new academic development. The truth is that the vice chancellor sits at the focal point of an institution's top governance process. No one should deny the importance of leadership in the role of a vice chancellor or the fact that the job has significantly changed over the period since 1992: universities have grown much larger, their finances have become more complex and involve greater risk, the world of higher education has become more competitive and the vice chancellor has become the 'accountable officer' to government, as well as being accountable to the governing body for the running of the institution. It is not surprising that vice chancellors have developed machinery to assist them in these tasks. Such machinery tended to have its origin either in a traditional 'Monday morning meeting' of a vice chancellor and his/her senior officers or in the executive committee that senates often set up to assist in the processing of senate business. One exception, at Warwick, was where a steering committee was established, as far back as 1970, essentially to control the vice chancellor's tendency to act like a chief executive. In time, however, it came to act like a university executive board and was the inspiration for Clark's 'central steering core', which he saw as one of the essential characteristics of the contemporary entrepreneurial university (Clark 1998). Over a period of time, the Monday morning meetings and the senate executive committees were fused into what were variously called the university management group, the executive board, the vice chancellor's leadership team or the university development board.

In any survey of such bodies two questions arise that may affect their de facto or de jure legitimacy. The first is the extent to which their membership is entirely ex officio, or whether they contain members elected or appointed by the senate or some other body. The post-1992 universities, which inherited a management system that included the post of vice-principal, tended from the beginning to have senior management teams made up primarily of appointed professional officers, while the pre-1992s included in their equivalent bodies pro-vice chancellors drawn from the senior ranks of the academic community. As the system became formalized post- and pre-1992 systems grew together, especially as the practice developed in the latter of appointing pro-vice chancellors from outside the institution and of increasing their numbers and tying the posts to particular areas of business, such as international recruitment, academic quality or the student experience. The practice of external appointments, usually via headhunters, changed the character of executive boards. When pro-vice chancellors were appointed or elected from inside the institutions they were tacitly regarded as having one foot in the academic camp and owing rather more than a token loyalty to their former colleagues and their academic community as a whole. Appointments from outside, on the other hand, clearly owed their loyalty first and foremost to the vice chancellor who had appointed them. They had not grown up in the institution's organizational culture (indeed they were often brought in to change it), and had no academic departmental base to fall back on if things went wrong. Thus, the question needs to be asked as to what these external appointments brought in that was actually new and could not be provided by internal appointments, especially as they represented the seedbed for appointments at other universities as vice chancellors. As one senior academic with recent experience of sitting on the appointing committee for a senior managerial post stated, candidates were

> very homogeneous, [had] very similar careers, saying very similar things in their covering letters and very much committed to particular management and governance styles, which were within a very narrow range ... the system produces a certain kind of leadership which leaves very little space for doing things differently, very little space for innovation and very, very tailored to the current imperatives of funding and the institutional state-structured system that we have which is, I think, at some variance from what the rank and file of university staff are like, and what they are interested in and what they think a university should be like. (31)

Moreover, with the almost universal practice of employing headhunters to assist in identifying vice chancellors, the turnover of pro-vice chancellors seems to have increased, so that the membership of the executive board has become less stable and the pro-vice chancellor members less and less integrated into their academic communities.

A further important principle arising from membership of the executive board was representation from the academic community itself. In the past deans in the pre-1992 universities were normally elected by their faculties, while in the post-1992s they were normally appointed by the vice chancellor. As universities grew and some central decision-making functions, including resource allocation, were devolved to faculties, both pre- and post-1992 universities moved more to make external appointments to what became executive dean-ships. In addition, waves of internal restructuring led to faculty mergers (often leading to the creation of colleges), which controlled significant elements of the institutional budget. As these units became larger the title of dean was upgraded to pro-vice chancellor and the postholder became yet another ex officio member of the executive board. (Keeping the membership of the executive down to a manageable size of twelve to fifteen has often been the undeclared reason for reducing the number of colleges/faculties.) Thus any direct representation from the academic community became largely subsumed by figures of authority recruited from outside the university, who saw their role not as representing the academic community they had grown up in, but a set of strategic and management requirements determined at the centre. Their responsibilities, as one pre-1992 academic put it, were for 'downward management' (32). As a result there is a tendency in the academic community to regard them with suspicion, as 'central management', as people who, as ex officio members of the senate or the academic board, can be relied upon to speak in favour of policies that have been devised in the centre, however managerialist, rather than senior academic colleagues likely to engage with divergent views.

Theoretically, executive boards should report to senates and academic boards as much as to the governing body but, increasingly, their prime responsibility has been to the governing body with the senate or academic board cut out of the loop. They can easily become, in some governing body-dominated universities, the conduit pipe through which a governing body's views are transmitted to the university at large. The description of such bodies as 'the executive' suggests, too facilely, an analogy with business. Indeed many chairs see themselves and their lay colleagues as acting as 'non-execs' in a quasi-business relationship holding the executive to account. One suspects that a government that was responsible for the OfS regulations saw relationships very much in this light as well. But the executive does not need to fall into this role. On the contrary, it can form a bridge between the academic community and the lay majority on the governing body, both challenging the academic community to face up to the pressures of the times and emphasizing to the governing body the academic priorities of teaching and research, and the most appropriate way of protecting them. However, this rarely seems to be the case. Our evidence points more to the executive acting as a senior management team, a sort of collective vice chancellor, responsible for piloting managerial decisions down through the academic organs of governance and being answerable to a lay governing body for doing so.

The 'laicization' of university governance

In the nineteenth and early twentieth centuries the English provincial universities fought themselves free of excessive control by lay governing bodies. In the 1930s the University Grants Committee (UGC) refused a request from Nottingham to be included in the UGC's grant list because it was too subject to lay control (Shinn 1986). But government policy since the 1990s seems to have moved in a contrary direction towards reinforcing powers of control by lay governors. If the Dearing Report set the tone, the Lambert Report of 2003 seems to have set the direction. (Richard Lambert was initially commissioned by the Treasury to look at industry–university relationships, but his remit was extended to include university governance because it was thought that messages from the Dearing Report on governance were not being picked up.) Lambert drew a distinction between pre- and post-1992 institutions and made his preference on governance style clear:

> The older universities were, historically, run as communities of scholars. Their management and governance arrangements were participatory; senates and councils were large and conservative. ... The new universities have constitutions that plainly differentiate management from governance; the vice-chancellor has a chief executive officer mandate and governance is the responsibility of a small 12–24 person, lay-dominated, independent governing body. (Lambert 2003: para 7.3)

Implicit in this statement and in Lambert's chapter on governance is the idea that universities need to be run more like business corporations in order to fit them for 'modern times': post-1992 universities are commended for having a 'more executive style of management', pre-1992 universities are criticized for being committee-bound. It is clear that this business model represents the organizational structure that successive governments of all political hues have sought to reinforce in universities in order to provide decision-making machinery receptive to government requirements. And it has, for the most part, been achieved, without consultation with the sector but through the more discreet method of instituting changes through the funding contract or, latterly, making them conditional on the exercise of the government's power to permit universities to raise their tuition fees; in this way they could be presented as procedural changes based on accountability requirements. Thus the Financial Memorandum and its successor, the Memorandum of Assurance and Accountability, have become the key drivers in changing the bicameral basis of pre-1992 university governance to something approximating a de facto unicameral structure that was delivered to the post-1992 institutions in the 1992 Act. As a consequence, in many of the pre-1992 universities, the previous form of governance based on a partnership of the council (governing body) and the senate has had superimposed on it a new decision-making hierarchy, which is concentrated in the governing body, demoting the senate, already weakened by the emergence of an executive, to a subsidiary, almost formal, role.

This process is not evenly spread through the pre-1992 universities but is, of course, much more strongly represented in the post-1992 universities. There is evidence that in some, particularly those that are research-intensive, strong senates have resisted their demotion; but there is also evidence that in some post-1992 universities, governing bodies have begun to assume dominant positions, even to the extent of determining academic policies. Three examples from our sample of universities will perhaps illustrate the variety of practice. The first is a Russell Group university where the vice chancellor was explicit that the university's strategy

> really is very, very much conceived and drawn up and guided and shaped by the executive, and council then is a kind of sounding board really for strategic development. I just think you cannot expect ... lay members of council genuinely to be able to conceive of and direct strategy in a business or an area of activity which is not one they are deeply familiar with. (33)

In a second pre-1992 university the position was not so clear-cut. Here the vice chancellor was very clear that strategy was the responsibility of the executive in consultation with the senate, and that the governing body was not capable of setting strategy, but the chair, while admitting that the executive was where 'the actual preparatory work' needed to be done, believed that such work should be carried out 'within very high-level parameters set out by the governing body in discussion with the executive', and that the governing body should have ownership of the strategy and should be responsible for monitoring its development (34). A third and more extreme case was in a post-1992 university where the governing body was so dominant that it recommended raising the student admission requirements, instructed that greater priority should be attached to research (and found £5 million from the university budget to give to the vice chancellor as investment funding), and excluded the vice chancellor from the committee to nominate a new chair. Where universities are high in the league tables and their success is linked to a strong academically related organizational culture, it seems that a governing body's role is most likely to be that of a sounding board or of a critical friend, but when a university is less successful and suffers recruitment problems or financial difficulties, the governing body can become utterly dominant and the chair becomes, in effect, an executive chair. But governing body involvement on this scale, without academic commitment to the solutions proposed, is unlikely to succeed in rectifying the problems.

One consequence of the pressure being placed on governing bodies has been a reduction in the size of their membership and a search for members with national rather than purely local professional reputations. This has undoubtedly strengthened the membership but has greatly reduced the number of members who are familiar with the institution simply because they live in the locality. But by raising the professional profile of members, in a situation where the government is demanding more information, financial and academic, to be certified or assured by the governing body the temptation to an activist membership group, many of whom will have travelled some distance to the meeting, will be to increase the levels of intervention. For example, one result of the requirements to provide assurance on the academic side has been for lay governors to ask to attend academic boards and other academic meetings in order to assure themselves that the academic business of course approvals, examinations and programme reviews is conducted in a way that they can have confidence in. In two cases from our sample, where the governing body was most dominant, the institutions had attracted outstanding people to serve as chair and had brought in high calibre people to help them turn the institution around. Laudable and public-spirited though this is, it is questionable whether lay governing bodies have the time, the academic experience or the familiarity with the institution to do this effectively. Most governing bodies meet no more than five times a year – four normal meetings and one strategy meeting – but even with committee meetings sandwiched between, this offers little opportunity to gain in-depth knowledge of the institution or the sector. In one university, the chair held regular pre-meetings with the chairs of governing body committees, with no university officers (including the vice chancellor) present, the expressed aim being to steer the main meetings towards preordained conclusions and to coordinate the cross-examination of the vice chancellor and the executive. Increasingly, in many universities, the line of authority through the institution will be lay rather than academically directed.

One test of the effectiveness of lay governance has been the question of vice chancellors' salaries. All governing bodies are required to have remuneration committees and the chair has access to a database (compiled by the CUC) holding details of the vice chancellors' salary and other emoluments; remuneration committees are required to present their recommendations to the full governing body. One of the clearest justifications for lay governance is the representation of the public interest in the governance of universities, yet the public reaction to the *Times Higher Education*'s annual listing of vice chancellors' pay tells us that the public interest is not reflected in the figures, whether as expressed by ministers or by the general public at large, and the annual salary increases far exceed the increases accorded by the vice chancellors' own wages and salaries organization to their own academic staff. There may be complex reasons that have allowed this situation to develop, but it is abundantly clear that chairs and governing bodies have damaged the sector's reputation by awarding salaries thought to be excessive and out of line with what the public would expect. Moreover, they appear to lack the management grip to remedy the situation.

The capacity of governing bodies to carry out the role demanded of them has also been considerably overestimated by the government in respect to its assurance and accountability requirements. These requirements were already heavy, but have been substantially increased by the responsibility placed upon governing bodies in regard to academic quality, which makes demands that they are least qualified to respond to effectively. Already some institutions are finding it hard to attract members of what they regard as the right quality to join them; at least one post-1992 university in Wales has been forced to go well outside the borders of Wales to meet its required membership. One solution to the burden increasingly placed on lay members, and particularly the chair, is to pay honoraria for their services. In Scotland, the 2016 Higher Education Governance Act gave specific licence for universities to pay honoraria to their lay governors, but this was in line with the general direction of the legislation to bring a new kind of governor into membership by encouraging people who could not otherwise afford the time to join governing bodies without sacrificing salary to do so. Although the CUC has formally set its face against paying lay governors, a surprising number of chairs in our sample saw it as a likely development if the burdens on chairs and members continued to increase, and it is understood that the practice has already been taken up in both Scotland and England. Any more general movement in this direction would surely raise issues of conflict of interest and accountability, especially in the light of concern over vice chancellors' salaries, which, in a university setting, would be difficult to resolve. But the very fact that it has been raised serves to emphasize the transformation that has occurred from bodies seen as partners in the governance of universities (the 'shared governance' concept) to bodies seen as non-executive directors holding senior academic managers to account.

Students in university governance

Our evidence confirms that students are now very closely integrated with institutional governance processes at all levels. The following statements by the president of a students' union and by an academic may be taken as representative of the sector as a whole, allowing for some variations in the number of student representatives:

> So as elected officers we sit on probably the most important committees that the university runs, and we sit on council, academic board and a few others ... I think council is probably the most important committee that we sit on, and within that committee we are allowed to bring papers, and do presentations and show what students want, what they are asking for in terms of change and ... students' needs. (35)

> The students will usually have a year rep on every subject, every course, so the year rep, or one or two of them would feed into the programme leader ... and then every school will have one or two [student] reps who sit on the main school committee. Every faculty will have one or two student reps and again they are very powerful at that level. I sit on the learning and teaching excellence committee, ... again there are eight or nine [student] reps on that one ... at the academic board level there's a student union representative so the student reps all feed their comments up to the student union representative. And their comments are taken probably more seriously than something from me. (36)

Student presidents have regular meetings with vice chancellors and, separately, with relevant pro-vice chancellors and professional officers; in two universities in our sample, they write reports on students' union activities for every governing body meeting, paralleling the reports written by the vice chancellor. The picture that emerges is of good relations between senior figures in the universities and senior officers of the students' unions and also between the students' unions and the senior bodies on which they are represented. Whether this amounts to more than universities wanting to keep students on their side and seeking to engineer a better response in the National Student Survey (NSS) is more questionable. And there can be some scepticism among politically astute students as to whether student membership is simply a pro forma obligation that the university has entered into. As one student said:

> I feel that we as representatives sit on a lot of meetings and a lot of boards and sometimes it feels that's just to tick a box rather than directly feed into decisions that are made. (37)

In general, observers report that student members of senior university bodies seem to show much less interest in strategic issues and much more in immediate bread-and-butter matters that can be argued through face-to-face with university senior officers. As one president said:

> I feel the most effective way [to produce action] is our 'keep in touch' meetings with the university exec. We can bring up any issue raised and it doesn't have to be essentially academic – it can do with anything on the student experience … so if there are pressing issues or big, national issues going on, then we can have that discussion. (38)

Two disincentives to raising broader and more contentious issues are, first, the position of the students' union within the university and, second, the extent to which student officers can mobilize support from across the student body. Unions often feel themselves – almost certainly unnecessarily – vulnerable in regard to the annual university grant to the union, and other support that a university gives it: one president explained that she was inhibited by the fact that 'biting the hand that feeds you' might have implications for the next block grant to the union and 'you are scared of what the repercussions may be for your successor' (39). As to the latter, the answer is that most student bodies are remarkably apolitical in relation to the university, one president explaining: 'really you have a couple of groups of very, very engaged students and then the majority of your student population just doesn't engage' (40), while another summed up the attitude of the student body succinctly: 'I would say generally positive but with a strong sense of apathy' (41).

Our evidence suggests that, for the most part, the relationship between student representatives and their university authorities operates in a rather cosy world. Students' unions represent large bureaucracies – a students' union in a large university might employ more than 100 staff – that have to be protected, and student presidential elections rarely attract votes from more than 20 per cent of students in one case in our study, that figure was only 10 per cent. Student presidents almost always come to the post having served a sabbatical year previously in a more junior position, and so are comparatively comfortable with handling matters with senior university officers or with being members of senates, academic boards and governing bodies. The university authorities are themselves made receptive by the influence of the NSS on league tables and of the student experience on their TEF results. Indeed, vice chancellors and presidents of students' unions have a commonality of interest in respect to reputation and league table positioning, the one to satisfy hawkish lay members, the other to act as a proxy to obtaining a good job.

Perhaps, therefore, the strongest impact of students on their universities is not at the higher levels of institutional governance but at the course committee, departmental or school committee or at faculty level where their elected representatives are able to engage with the institutional academic issues of curriculum, feedback, teaching arrangements and examinations that are their most immediate concerns. This activity is of a different character and much more representative of the attitudes and concerns of the rank-and-file than standard union business. If we believed the rhetoric of the higher education market and of the OfS regulations we would expect to find such representation infused with consumerism, and with students behaving as customers critical of the academic goods that their tuition fees had purchased. On the contrary, however, our evidence suggests a much more nuanced set of attitudes varying somewhat depending on the positioning of the institution. One post-1992 students' union president told us:

> Students see themselves as consumers when something goes wrong, so if they fail a module, … if they don't get good feedback, if they are kicked off a course through a fitness to practice panel, then that's when they are coming to our advisers as consumers and behaving as if this is a legal case, now you need to do something about it. So it's interesting; if a student's doing OK they are partners, if the student's bad they are consumers. (42)

Another student president, at a pre-1992 university, said:

> If you are now wanting us to start treating ourselves as consumers, it's kind of a Catch-22 situation. I can either start rallying more and say treat us like consumers, give us the rights of consumers, but then I'm bowing down to the further marketization of universities, which is something that all students fundamentally disagree with … if you want to treat me like a consumer I'll ask for my rights. But I don't want that to be the reality we live in. I would prefer to say right we still want this to be a public good because that's what we morally believe in and that's what we think it should be. (43)

A third president, at a Russell Group university, broadened the argument:

> I would say we're moving towards … that consumerist rhetoric and ideology. It has benefits you know for the likes of CMA [Competition and Markets Authority] guidance but it definitely has its drawbacks and I think it's where we are moving away [from considering] what the value of higher education is – it's suddenly become a thing about competition, it's become a thing about league

tables, about moving up the ranks, about what our competitors are doing, how internationally renowned we are, what grants we are getting ... (44)

This is not to say that consumerism does not exist in the student body, and academics interviewed quote some ugly examples of remarks made by students, but the strong consensus among academics was that it had not taken root as any kind of critique of university teaching:

> I don't think there has been a huge change. I think there's lots of people talk about now that students pay fees they've become consumers and they expect to pass. ... My experience has been that they are not any more or less demanding than they have been before. (45)

On the other hand, there would be general agreement that students have become more demanding, more 'instrumentalist' about future employment, more 'transactional'. Even in Scotland where there are no tuition fees, a post-1992 senior administrator suggested that

> students have higher expectations from the university; ... I think they see it more as a contract where they give something and they get something back ... we see this mostly through academic appeals and complaints. (46)

A second senior Scottish administrator, in a pre-1992 university, argued that 'you are seeing a resurgence ... across the UK actually, in the onus [being placed] on universities in terms of social responsibility coupled with a sense of entitlement' (47). Although there was general agreement among those interviewed that the introduction of tuition fees had made a difference, it was significant that in Scotland, where no fees were charged, the attitudes of students towards their teaching arrangements were no different to those found in England or Wales. In Wales the position is best summed up by the students' union president in a post-1992 university quoted above (p. 94):

> I think regardless of the change in fees the sort of governance and the student voice ... has ... largely been the same: we've always had an open partnership and discussions with the university. I don't think the change in fees has impacted on or changes that. (48)

In one respect, however, there may be a difference between universities in England depending on their institutional positioning. Whereas one vice chancellor in a small post-post-1992 university, located in a comparatively prosperous area, told us that his students, who were primarily from the locality, showed few signs of consumerism because of the local high employment opportunities, the vice chancellor of a large urban post-1992 teaching-intensive university, also with a large local catchment, said that their students had always behaved as consumers 'and they know it' (49), while an arts-based professor from the same institution spoke critically of the fact that

> we have been ... active participants in treating [students] as if [we were providing] them with an economic service rather than a professional, cultural relationship as an institution ... our whole orientation has been around treating students as customers. (50)

At another urban post-1992 university, though this was one with recruitment problems but with a similar local catchment area, students appeared to behave as consumers because of the university's vulnerability (a vulnerability that also applied to staff if the university suffered repeated student number shortfalls). As an example of the power this can put in students' hands, one academic teaching programme was forced into being reorganized to take place only on the first three days of the week so that the students could undertake or continue with paid jobs for the rest of the week (technically turning a full-time into a part-time programme). As the president of the university's students' union said:

> Students are consumers because this university is run by students – if students are not here staff are not here, so obviously they are consumers. They [the university] must look after these consumers. If they don't look after them they are going to leave next year, they are going to change university, go to a different university, they [the university] are really going to lose students. In 2011–12 we had around 25,000 students, now we have 14,000. (51)

Here we have the higher education market at work: when universities become vulnerable power passes to the consumer with academically questionable results. This was, in fact, the only students' union officer interviewed who gave support to the customer model of behaviour. On the contrary, our findings suggest that while British students are becoming more demanding and more litigious about their examination results, and sometimes talk about buying their degree, their attitudes are not driven by consumerism per se but by more general trends in society. Working relations with universities are exceptionally good by comparison with some periods in the past and, in participating in the design and monitoring of academic processes, students see themselves, and act accordingly, as partners with their academic teachers and not as self-interested critics; and the student input is welcomed by the academic community as making a positive contribution to course development.

Governance and the individual academic

Questions about autonomy lie at the heart of discussions about governance in higher education. As we have seen, autonomy at the system level has been replaced by ministerial and agency control. At the institutional level substantive autonomy has been replaced by operational autonomy and, within that, the role of academic self-governance has been weakened by the decline in influence of the senate and the enhanced role assumed by lay-dominated governing bodies. One might have expected the role of the individual academic in academic governance to have been similarly weakened. While it is limited by the fact that governance is much more top-down than in the past, our evidence suggests that below the top layer of governance, collegiality, extensive dialogue and academic interchange remain the essential background to decision-making. One of the main reasons for this is that, as universities have grown larger, decision-making on academic matters has tended to become devolved to intermediary bodies such as faculty or college boards and, in their turn, to specialist coordinating committees. While the chairs of these bodies have the task of passing communications downwards rather than upwards, the actual academic business is conducted between the teachers and researchers below the level where managerialism tends to flourish. While one can trace some variation in the academic independence and freedom enjoyed by individual academics between the older and the newer institutions, the differences are surprisingly small bearing in mind the large differences to be found at the higher levels of governance. A measure of similarity can be found in the following statements, the first from a Russell Group academic and the second from an academic in a post-post-1992 university:

> I don't want to be consulted on absolutely every decision but I do want to be consulted on the ones that directly affect me and where I can actually have some meaningful input. (52)

> In the bigger university it can still be really enabling as long as the people who line-manage you, or have responsibility for you, are listening and responsive. So it's about having a voice really and feeling that, you know, you are listened to in your university. (53)

New academic ideas, that is, for new teaching programmes, tend to start at the bottom with academic discussion with colleagues and move up through departmental committees to faculty groupings. A senior academic in a post-1992 university told us:

> We have great autonomy within this institution to [launch a new academic initiative]. I would consider that the most important thing there would be our

own faculty executive and the decision of our own executive dean. ... If academic responsibility and control lies anywhere it lies there at faculty level. (54)

In other words, not with the academic board or the executive.

A young academic from the same faculty commented: 'I think universities are one of the rare kind of places where people at the bottom can suggest the ideas that trickle up rather than the other way' (55). Another comment from a post-post-1992 university academic points up some of the constraints:

> I haven't felt that we don't have autonomy. It feels reasonably autonomous in terms of vision. We are permitted to articulate our own business plans, obviously targets [are] negotiated. Staffing appointments are done within the school ... obviously we refer to other people. So it feels reasonably autonomous. (56)

And these are echoed, but in a rather different way, at a pre-1992 university:

> At departmental level I guess you could have something that the departmental [head] didn't want to happen and that would probably be because it didn't fit within the wider strategy of the department. But I think it would always be up for debate. I can't think of an instance while I've been here from experience, when anybody said you can't do that or not allowed me at least to argue my case even if they then said to me well, for these reasons that's not going to happen. (57)

A parallel comment from a head of division in a post-1992 university makes the point that heads of department are no longer autocratic in the way that they were in the past when headships were permanent appointments:

> My job as head of division is to mediate, that is to try and recognise a critique that one member has [of a critical text], whether that critique is a valid critique of the particular thing we are dealing with ... or whether the critique is a broader critique about the institution, or about universities in general, which is not specific to that thing. So there's a lot of negotiation, there's a lot of persuasion and there's a lot of compromise in this ... I spend huge amounts of time negotiating with people and persuading and kind of cajoling and trying to shift people forward in a particular direction. (58)

It seems, therefore, that in spite of a sometimes repressive climate from above, academics still retain powers of initiative to generate new proposals and get them debated and adopted, although not across the full span of a university's development and only within a predetermined framework. The concept of the traditional freedom of the academic to pursue academic ideas, has not been suppressed by governance changes at the top of the institution, but it has been made more difficult to realize them. Two contributions from academics in pre-1992 universities comment on the relative freedom that academics enjoy:

> One still has considerable latitude in the construction of a syllabus and a curriculum in an individual module. OK we have things like subject benchmarks, we have peer pressure from colleagues within and without about the curriculum but it's still largely my impression that colleagues have enough freedom to manoeuvre. (59)

> I think academics have massive control, still, over what they do. They have more freedom than almost any other worker who exists. ... They have a huge choice about their use of time-management, the time when they are in the building etc., etc. There was perhaps a time when there was absolutely no regulation of them. There is now some regulation. Some of them don't like it but I think it's probably a good thing. (60)

What appears to have happened is that some of the main characteristics of academic life, openness to discussion, the search for consensus, the respect for contrary views and a concern for academic integrity, survive beneath the restrictions imposed by higher levels of governance and authority. Such characteristics may seem alien, inefficient or corrupting of efficient process to the average lay member of a governing body or the newly hired member of the university's executive team, but actually represent the warp and woof of academic life on which successful academic work depends. Universities thus remain, to a not inconsiderable extent, bottom-heavy organizations, a characteristic that the world of 'non-executives' and executive teams and of top-down management ignores at great risk to the quality of the academic product, but the space that this occupies is narrowing as the policy framework imposed by lay control or market considerations increases its hold on institutions

The destabilizing of university governance

What this chapter describes is the breakdown of the equilibrium of university governance that was in place in 1992: the pre-1992 system offered a clearly demarcated, bicameral constitution, the post-1992, a contrasting unicameral approach. The latter could be compared to the historical constitutions of US public universities, but the phrase 'shared governance' reflected the extent to which the academic community in the United States had successfully argued that lay and academic governance needed to work together in partnership. It was a reasonable expectation that the post-1992 universities would move in the direction of the pre-1992s, and some have, but, in general, under the pressures outlined in this chapter, the movement has been in the opposite direction. What we have seen is the gradual disempowerment of the academic community from the task of running their institutions, albeit in partnership with a lay governing body itself containing significant academic membership. Step by step, the power of the lay governing body over the academic community has been increased. Out of many questions two stand out: the first is what impact this will have on the academic product, which is the subject of Chapter 5, and the second is whether the government, the main driver of the change, overestimated the capacity of the new structure to carry out the tasks it requires. Can a lay governing body, meeting four or five times a year, even with committees meeting in between, which do not themselves have experience of academic work, be accountable for complex and costly institutions involving upwards of 30,000 staff and students, without becoming entirely dependent for assurance on the staff themselves who are running the business, especially when in the only piece of executive management for which they are themselves directly responsible, executive salaries, it is clear they have comprehensively failed. This may seem a harsh judgement but it prompts the further question: what disqualified the previous structure unless it was a concern that independent and autonomous bodies, governed on that basis, might be less compliant than bodies governed by lay people from outside the institution?

The decision to run higher education, except in Scotland and to a lesser extent in Wales, on a strictly market basis and to establish a regulator to manage the system taking as its essential criteria the student interest assumed that students themselves supported the market approach. The idea of incorporating market concepts into policy are not new and can be useful disciplines in institutional management. But the combination of a switch of funding via recurrent grant to funding via tuition fees simultaneously with withdrawing any limits on institutional recruitment may have been steps too far. While it benefitted some institutions it exposed others to risk and vulnerability through no fault of their own, but because of location or mission; this could only have an adverse impact on their students' university life and on the academic work of the staff. This might have been more defensible if the students were enthusiastic about a market, but our evidence suggests they are very clearly not. Students, in fact, primarily want to be partners in the teaching enterprise and are no more or less instrumental and transactional in their approach to it than the public at large. They are well integrated with their institutions' governance, identify closely with their institutions' strategies and show no visible support for the application of market-led policies for their own sake over those of good judgement and academic common sense. But market-led destabilization comes at a time of institutional governance destabilization; this combination is setting severe demands, in some institutions, on institutional management.

In the United States, advocates of the role of lay governance in public universities used to argue that a board of regents served as the 'moat and the bridge' in respect to the wider community (Epstein 1974), that is, it defended the university from external attack and acted as a connecting link with the public. There is little sign of individual governing bodies acting in this way in the UK. Moreover, the US use of the term 'trustee' implies a more long-term concern for the interests of the institution than the British use of the word 'governor'. The chairs' national body, the CUC, is essentially a compliant organization, taking its tone from a largely quiescent Universities UK, and has essentially gone along with the Dearing/Lambert argument for the increasing role of governing bodies. The concept of a governing body acting as if they were non-executive directors of a company, which was implicit in many of our interviews, is clearly at variance with ideas of shared governance or of a partnership of lay and academic interests in governance, but it reflects the view that a business model is somehow superior to a model that puts academic participation in governance at a premium in what, after all, are institutions seeking academic success. The successful expansion of British higher education since the 1960s, with only minimal institutional breakdowns, might suggest that a model that strongly involves the academic community, although sui generis, might nevertheless hold many advantages over models imported from very different organizations that have very different purposes.

Chapter 5

University Governance and Academic Work: Pressures on Innovation and Creativity

A university's core business is teaching and research, and it is performance in these activities that make up success both in reputational terms and in ranking tables. Both are dependent not simply on good performance as measured by standard indicators but on innovation and creativity in the development of new academic programmes or in new research ideas. One of the tasks of governance is to provide open structures that enable and encourage the academic community to contribute innovation and creativity. Against this there is the danger that a too dominant structure inhibits it, imposes restrictions on new thinking or creates decision-making hierarchies that are defensive in outlook, unreceptive to change and unwilling to take what might appear to be academic (or related financial) risks. Effective university governance must, therefore, try to preserve flat structures that enable lateral as well as vertical communication and a heterarchical academic culture that encourages what Stark calls the 'organization of dissonance' (Stark et al. 2009), where 'there is no hierarchical ordering of ... competing evaluative principles' and where 'in contrast to the vertical authority of hierarchies ... crosscutting network structures [are] reflect[ing] the greater interdependencies of complex collaboration' (2009: 18). Such heterarchical governance stimulates an atmosphere of open discussion, the freedom to explore new academic ideas and intellectual vigour, while, ideally, balancing it with robust financial and other safeguards. Such characteristics stimulate teaching and engage students and provide the essential climate for successful research.

In modern times this might seem an idealized picture, a counsel of perfection, but in fact some elements of these characteristics were to be found in all our case study institutions, in some only in part, while in others they determined the culture of the institution. For example, in England, of four institutions from among those that could be described as primarily teaching institutions, only the alternative provider had no apparent capacity or interest in research: in one, the vice chancellor argued that what distinguished his institution from a further education college was its 'underpinning by our research credibility' (1), while in another, a senior academic told us that 'I would be very surprised to find an academic who didn't think that teaching didn't need to be research-informed, research-fuelled, research-driven' (2). What was apparent, however, was how far institutions actually fell short in providing the appropriate conditions for good academic work and how far changes in governance structures were in danger of inhibiting innovation and creativity in teaching and research. There was severe criticism by one senior academic:

> I think academics have lost an extraordinary amount of autonomy. I think the marketization of higher education has been a complete disaster. I think there is a lack of respect for academia and academics generally, and I think that there is managerialism within academia and about academia which has been increasing radically over the last few years. (3)

This may not be true across the whole of British higher education, but elements of it could be identified in many of our interviews within the academic community. The sense that the conditions for the pursuit of high-quality academic work have worsened and are continuing to worsen is widespread, even in institutions that are most obviously successful. Criticisms that universities have become too top-down in their governance, and are insufficiently bottom-up, that good academic work is stifled by over-regulation and bureaucracy, and that too much academic business is now handled by non-academic professionals, are commonplace.

The research system

Historically, the UK has had a well-ordered national approach to funding research with, at its heart, a dual funding system from government: recurrent grant funding for research through the University Grants Committee (UGC)/ funding councils and project funding awarded on the basis of peer review through the research councils. The importance to the research system was that the two funding streams addressed different but complementary needs and were awarded by organizationally separate bodies using different methodologies. In addition, project funding has been available from charitable bodies, direct from government departments and, of course, from industry and commerce, thus offering a highly diverse, and sometimes a competing, set of funding sources.

Although there have been many attempts, for good and sensible reasons, to impose greater top-down strategy on the state's investment in research, the underlying cultural assumption has been to follow the Columbus model, that is, to rely substantially on the instincts and interests of the research community and on a rigorous peer-review system to determine where investment should take place. The statutory independence of the separate research councils, their membership drawn from academic leaders in their fields, offered a guarantee that scientific and scholarly principles, not political or short-term economic argument, would determine their direction of travel. This has not prevented arguments against the research council system on the grounds that it was too protective of individual disciplines and insufficiently flexible in encouraging interdisciplinarity. In a period of austerity the cost implications of reducing administrative duplication have also played a part in removing their statutory independence through the agency of the Higher Education and Research Act (HERA), which has brought them under a new powerful central body, United Kingdom Research and Innovation (UKRI). There were few public criticisms of the change.

More controversial, however, has been the transfer of the Research Excellence Framework (REF) function, the other half of the dual funding system, from the Higher Education Funding Council for England (HEFCE) to a new body, Research England, which is part of UKRI, so that the institutional funding element of the dual funding system, the quality research (QR) funding, is now to be administered under the same authority as project funding. Unless the research community is able to sustain the separation of the two approaches, the danger is that the diversity of funding sources, both in respect to the needs of the research system and organizationally, will be lost. It is, of course, too early to assess the future of this reorganization but it does conform to the current model of opening the door to greater state intervention in England – the distribution of QR funds remains with the funding councils in Wales and Scotland. (It would only be a short administrative step in England to integrate the two funding processes.) This is particularly important because it has the potential to overweight the top-down strategic direction of research funding in the delicate balance of responding to the bottom-up interests of individual researchers, which, prima facie, are intrinsically more likely to produce a higher level of creativity and innovation. The danger is heightened if one believes, with Baumberg, that centralized research systems are more likely to commit themselves in the present over-competitive climate to bandwagon research ideas with essentially short-term instrumentalist objectives, rather than more speculative projects that could lead to the field being changed (Baumberg 2018). It would be ironic if a government that has put so much effort into developing a market for students has created machinery that could have the effect of restricting investment in a market for research ideas.

A more immediate problem is the separation of government departmental responsibilities for research on the one hand and teaching on the other, with research being the responsibility of Business, Energy and Industrial Strategy (BEIS) and UKRI and teaching of the Department for Education (DfE) and Office for Students (OfS). The appointment of a minister of higher education and science, with responsibilities spanning both departments, represents a fig leaf in the light of the record of the average tenure of such ministers. Neither department appears to have responsibility for higher education as a system or for higher education institutions as institutions, yet historically higher education institutions, and particularly universities, have played an important public role in society. Universities are responsible for about 90 per cent of the national effort in fundamental (pure) research in science and the shape of that contribution is determined, in large part, by the student market for undergraduate places, because that provides the resource to fund the expansion or contraction of permanent posts in academic departments. Within universities, critical decisions about buildings, infrastructure or league table ranking embody both research and teaching considerations. The disconnect at government departmental level means that there is no body responsible in England for thinking about institutions in the round – whether they encourage good academic work, how they impact on their local and regional economies, or how their individual performance matches the needs of the system. The OfS, without a single scientist on its board, is certainly not qualified for this, nor is it charged with such a role, and UKRI's concentration is so closely directed towards research that its interests will always be in research policy and in the major research institutions, rather than in wider sectoral issues. Higher education institutions seem to be seen as service providers, either in research or in teaching, and not as institutions that play an important role in the cultural and economic life of society.

Research and institutional differentiation

Research excellence and intensity represent the foremost drivers for institutional differentiation and are more important than previous intuitive rankings based essentially on the age of the institution: Oxbridge, the civic universities, the 1960s new universities, the ex-polytechnics and so forth. A number of the post-1992 universities have overtaken some pre-1992s in the recognized ranking lists. Institutional research standing in the UK is generally recognized as being defined by membership of the Russell Group (although membership of the Group does not cohere fully with rankings defined simply by results in the REF). A comparison of how differently ranked institutions describe their attitudes to research tells us a great deal about the way research determines their strategies. Thus two Russell Group vice chancellors, separately, but typically, described to us the fundamental aims of their institutions in Humboldtian terms:

> You can describe what universities do as creating knowledge and disseminating knowledge. So that seems to me [that] the bedrock of what we do hasn't changed and won't change. (4)

> We are really here to deepen and broaden the fund of human knowledge and pass the benefits on to others. But in order to do that I have to go out to the money markets. (5)

By contrast, an urban, post-1992 vice chancellor offered a quite different vision of the aims of his institution, which, again, is perhaps typical of its genre:

> The majority of our business is about students, it's not research. We are not research-intensive, students are at the heart of everything we do. (6)

A very different vision emerges from the CEO of our alternative provider case study:

> So [the private equity owner]'s strategy is that they have invested a significant amount of money in [the institution] and they've done that via a fund and the fund has a fixed term, albeit there are ways of extending the term, but ultimately they want to exit and they want to exit on a massive multiple and make lots of money. (7)

(It should be added that the institution's academic community saw its aims and objectives in much more positive educational terms.)

The differentiation between research-intensive, research-active and teaching-intensive universities has historically, and intentionally, been greatly increased by the effects of the Research Assessment Exercise (RAE)/REF. With the competition for research funding that these pressures have exerted, it has become increasingly difficult for academics from research-active and teaching-intensive universities to break into the more established patterns of funding enjoyed by the larger research communities: they lack the research infrastructure, the depth of referee support and the context of a research environment, which the research-intensive universities provide. The concentration of research funding in twenty-five or so institutions has had a negative impact on universities seeking to grow their research performance from a narrow base. Nevertheless, the growth of these institutions over the last fifteen years and the turnover of retiring staff has considerably increased their research strength because they have been able to draw on a pool of PhDs and postdoctoral researchers unable to find posts in the restricted number of research-intensive universities. There is thus a much more research-active community in some post-1992 universities than previously, developing research interests often very different from those in the established research-intensive institutions because of the different institutional context. It is absolutely important that these new research hubs are encouraged in the interests, not only of the intellectual life of their institutions but also of the future diversification of national research themes and approaches.

These new research growth points have difficulty in obtaining access to research council funding, outgunned by well-established research groups working in well-established research areas in the well-resourced environments of well-recognized research-intensive universities. The decision to remove the cap on student numbers has allowed the research-intensive universities to hoover up students who would otherwise have accepted places at other universities, giving the former the freedom to expand at the expense of newer institutions, and to grow their staffing of departments in established research areas. Meanwhile, many of the research-active universities are fighting shortfalls in student numbers and the loss of tuition fee income, and having to embark on staff redundancy programmes. Institutional commitments to support growing research potential in selected areas are in danger of being overtaken by concerns about long-term survival; and investment in expensive subject areas is being sacrificed for subjects that can generate a financial surplus. The dangers implicit in too great a commitment to research concentration are being compounded by the disadvantaging of many universities where the green shoots of promising new research developments are facing a critical change of climate that could challenge their survival, let alone the prospect of breaking into the magic circle of research council or QR support. The disequilibrium of the new student market is in danger of snuffing out new research thinking springing out of new research environments.

Research and the academic autonomy of the individual

Organizationally, one of the important characteristics of research is that it presupposes that academics have the individual autonomy to pursue their interests freely and that they are given time to do so. A committed researcher in a post-1992 university saw his success in research as providing a trade-off for attendance at meetings and undertaking administrative duties (8), while, in a Russell Group university, a lecturer of about the same age believed that in her institution

> there is a very strong consensus that research is important; this has to be protected and everyone is entitled to it. (9)

The impact of the research element in academic work in a research-intensive university is, automatically, to give academics a greater sense of autonomy than their colleagues in institutions where research is given lower priority. Unfortunately, most research is structured around the demands of the REF. Initially, when the first research selectivity exercise was launched in 1985, at a time when the UGC was criticized by the Treasury for funding all universities on a common unit of resource, it was primarily a mechanism to switch resources from the least research-active to the most research-intensive universities. Later, in the 1990s, it became a mechanism to protect the position of research-intensive universities when university unit costs, based on student numbers, were in sharp decline. By 2000, when tuition fees were first introduced to reverse this decline, the need for the concentration of research in a broadly based higher education system was so embedded that it is arguable that the RAE, as it had become, was no longer necessary to preserve a research elite. Its continuance now has become much more an instrument of accountability for the differential funding involved.

In terms of system governance the REF has become the most prominent intervention into the national development of institutions until the introduction of the Teaching Excellence Framework (TEF), itself a product of concern that performance in the REF was taking too high a priority over teaching. It is undoubtedly the case that the REF and its RAE predecessor have had a profound impact on the culture of the British university system, on internal governance and management structures and on the practice of academic work. No one would argue that this impact has been entirely prejudicial but the downsides for the research process itself are often not recognized. Complaints are common, of course, about the constraints of publishing according to the dates of REF submissions and the expected rate of publication, the influence it exercises on the form of publication, the need to accumulate research grants and PhD students to assist ranking in REF assessments, and the destructive effect of academic headhunting to improve a REF submission. But the real damage to research and good governance lies in the administrative structures that universities choose to maximize their REF return: the creation of new administrative hierarchies, the restructuring of faculties and departments, and the categorization of staff as 'un-REF-able'. (An entirely plausible account of the brutal pressure applied to staff in a Russell Group university not considered suitable for submission in the REF is quoted anonymously in the *Times Higher Education* 2019: 27.) This creates instability and introduces hierarchical power relationships that undermine collegiality and free discussion of academic ventures. There has always been competition in academic life between institutions and between departments and individuals, but the RAE/REF has institutionalized it within a new market framework, which, because success or failure can have a serious financial impact on the fortunes of the institution, encourages a resort to outright managerialism and various forms of top-down compulsion. Success in the REF may have considerable financial and reputational benefits; failure may lead to staff losses, a drop in reputation, staff restructuring programmes and, in the longer term, shortfalls in student recruitment. Nowhere is this more obvious than in institutions ambitious to rise up the ranking lists, institutions on the fringe of the Russell Group or even a member of the group concerned to keep up with its more successful members. These are institutions where competition can become counterproductive because of the pressure exerted from the top for higher and higher achievement in activities that will contribute to higher rankings. Thus, in one such university, the university imposed targets for research income that

> were all set at corporate level and at faculty level and at school level but they were brought down to an individual level. As a simple sort of disaggregation, if a school had a target of X million pounds that was simply divided by the number of staff in the school, taking account of position and everyone was given an individual target ... it was much too pressured, without recognising the realities of academic performance. (10)

At another university an academic said:

> I just feel that we are constantly ... maximising our research outputs and our league table standings at the expense of optimising what it is to be an academic. (11)

Asked whether academics had the opportunity to challenge his institution's policy the reply was:

> Academics are frightened, academics are frightened for their jobs, and they are scared to say, I don't think this is right. (11)

Another academic at a third university argued that the pressure on accumulating grants for REF reporting, and the competition for grants, produced a safety-first mentality: when you know that only one in five research applications is likely to be funded you bid for safe projects and 'play the percentages and submit far more applications than you know will be funded' (12).

A wider question relates to the extent to which the current research-funding regime is less open to new research ideas than previously. A professor at a Russell Group university told us:

> I'm not a romantic about blue skies research but the sense of academic freedom of us knowing better than them [the funders] what the direction of travel in research ought to be, where the interesting questions are, what we don't already know, and the sense that we can pursue these and make policy proposals which are independent of what the customer wants, the customer being whichever government department it happens to be, that's all come under a lot of pressure ... [it]is not so much that we only answer the questions which we are told to answer, it's more like we are trying to second guess what funders and policy-makers want to hear ... making one feel like a kind of intellectual 'subordinate'. (13)

The narrowing of research evaluative principles to basically 'REF criteria' and industry/business priorities – with the resulting centralization of research interests and funding focused towards a narrow group of universities – can lead to the loss of autonomy, innovation and creativity within the academic community, as well as within the whole of the higher education system. As Stark's research indicates, innovative action is 'facilitated not by convergence or agreement on a principle of justification but ... by the collision of evaluative principles. It is when things do not fit together comfortably that novel recombinations become thinkable. ... Disagreement about what's valuable can make for new value propositions' (2017: 388). Organizations facilitate innovation and creativity, not when they exclude conflicting evaluative criteria and build consensus by adhering to a single set of values, but rather by supporting dissonant principles of worth and putting lateral governance structures in place that allow for such principles to be openly explored and played out, both within the walls of the university and beyond.

However, what we have currently is a system for the governance of research activity, which in many ways has been very successful, but which has also encouraged top-down governance and management styles and the adoption of performance management approaches that not only cause tension and resentment but can be counterproductive in imposing pressures on how academics publish their research, and in what form. The market framework appears designed to increase stress and difficulty for institutions but it also acts as a powerful incentive to academics, perhaps particularly in less research-intensive universities, to engage in research and realize the additional personal autonomy within the institution that research success brings. It is clear, nevertheless, that the REF no longer fulfils its original purpose and that its value as an accountability mechanism is outweighed by its costs, even though it has become an integral part of university life. If, as our interviews suggest, it also encourages a safety-first response and a sense that academics are no more than 'intellectual subordinates' instead of intellectual leaders in the creation of new ideas and new ways of thinking, then it represents an inhibition to innovation and creativity, the characteristics on which the reputation of the UK's research has rested. In the 1980s and 1990s, the RAE performed the valuable task of establishing and legitimizing a subset of research-intensive institutions, but later RAE and REF exercises have confirmed a stability in the membership of this institutional subset that obviates the need to retest it for that purpose. The Stern Review (2016) offers some amelioration of the ill effects of the REF but it remains hard to conclude that its benefits outweigh its hidden costs.

Academic priorities, teaching and the market

One of the ways in which innovation and creativity are injected into the national skills base is through challenging and academically demanding university teaching; teaching that is based on the interest and intellectual curiosity of the teacher seems intrinsically more likely to be innovative and creative than teaching that is simply driven by market needs, although, as Gibbs (2010) points out, such distinctions are difficult to measure. In our data, there was a clear division between universities that felt they were being driven by the market and those by academic priorities, albeit no university claimed that it utterly ignored the market. Thus, one senior professor in a research-intensive university in responding to staff coming forward with new ideas said:

I want them to make a business case at the back of their minds, so [I want them to] describe why this idea is fascinating intellectually and how we will not lose money achieving it. (14)

But it was a common theme among research-intensive universities that, in creating new programmes, academic priorities took precedence:

The academic priority ought to drive everything. We are not here to make money, we don't have shareholders, we are here to do teaching, research and public engagement. That's what we are here for. And all the other stuff is just the means by which we do it. (15)

However, adopting academic priorities involves risk. As one vice chancellor put it:

So what has changed fundamentally in the last 10 years, and absolutely must be reflected in the strategy and tactics is the fact that there is nothing in the centre of what might be called a stability diagram anymore. Everything is risky … even the core activity of educating undergraduate students … but the old policy of saying well let's make sure we minimise risk [is] no longer a sensible strategy. (16)

By accepting risk, financial or reputational, when you are a strong, research-intensive university is one thing, but accepting it and going ahead when you are a post-1992 university with recruitment problems, is another: student recruitment, as the chair of one post-1992 university told us, is the 'killer risk' (17). As the chair of another post-1992 university expressed it:

You can have as many academic priorities as you might wish … and all the things the university has prided itself on over the years but you can't achieve any of those things without having a real understanding of the current state of the market. … That's the lifeblood of the institutions isn't it? No recruitment, no institution. (18)

His vice chancellor corroborated this view: 'We are more than halfway, I think, to being much more driven by market rather than driven by … just individual academic interest' (19).

For many universities concern about recruitment determines the nature of the academic programme. Shortfalls in enrolment bring down instructions from central management to change the curriculum, university marketing departments begin to dictate the curriculum and academic staff have imposed on them teaching requirements that are influenced by their own employment prospects. Professional marketing departments played a significant role in the teaching programmes in three of the four post-1992 case study universities that suffered recruitment difficulties. Thus, in one university, which also employed an external company to assist in recruitment, the marketing director condemned an academic programme as 'messy' and the senior lecturer in charge met the marketing director approximately weekly to recalibrate it (20). Another senior lecturer in the same university explained how the analysis of student choices for course options was left to the marketing department, which would then assess what additional options were necessary to attract students (21). At another university, a senior academic openly resented the power of the marketing department in controlling course publicity:

> Sometimes you'll see a poster of a student that we didn't pick ... and we wouldn't have put it on the side of a bus, and we wouldn't have phrased it in that way, but we weren't allowed, or we were discouraged or they just ignored us and went ahead anyway. (22)

In a third university, academics complained that the centralization of the marketing department in a multi-campus institution deprived academics of the freedom to market, promote and recruit to a course in the way they thought best (23).

The involvement of marketing departments in curriculum construction, and the authority that they apparently wield as part of central management, strikes a blow against the traditional autonomy of the academic community in designing and teaching the programmes that it has itself conceived. It is clear that this is a particular problem in universities that have recruitment problems, where, inevitably, authority shifts to the centre because institutional survival is potentially at risk. However, even in strong pre-1992 universities, the process seems to be hardening:

> Until now [University X had] a relatively benign bureaucratic environment, in the sense that if you wanted to introduce a new programme, yes, there were internal blockages you had to get through, but I haven't seen too many things blocked because of central [University] bureaucratic or political issues or financial issues. ... But this is changing, I think, with the more financial pressure you have, and the fact that you need to run a School like a small business so [one] becomes almost like a middle manager, without being properly equipped as a middle manager, and with more financial pressure exercised on [the University central management]. (24)

Formulating academic programmes according to the best 'business case' limits the scale and scope of innovation and creativity within institutions while also limiting the exposure of students to new and innovative ideas. Gearing academic programmes to an assumed student recruitment market discounts the fact that students may be attracted by more innovative course offerings. Attempts to reduce short-term risks in the 'market' may thus increase the long-term risks an institution incurs, by limiting the opportunity of its academic workforce for intellectual renewal and by limiting its students' exposure to new ideas and critical thinking, spreading the 'risks' beyond the walls of the institution into the employment market. Misreading the external environment and mistaking 'uncertainty' for 'risk(s)', universities may become too risk averse. Stark argues that 'in circumstances of risk, chances are calculable; that is, the distribution of outcomes can be expressed in some probabilistic terms. Uncertainty, however, lacks calculation: (…) the question is not what we do not know, but what cannot be known' (2009: 15).

Translating this into the particularities of the British higher education system, it is not risks – for example fluctuating student numbers – but uncertainty surrounding current operations that should be the key focus of organizational thinking and governance. 'Organizations that keep multiple evaluative principles in play,' suggests Stark, 'foster a generative friction that disrupts received categories of business as usual and makes possible an ongoing recombination of resources.' This is important because, in Stark's view, 'the most innovative ideas are not "out there" in the environment. … Instead of waiting to be found, they must be generated' and 'Creative friction yields an organizational reflexivity' (2009: 15–18). Heterarchy, as a form of governance, is thus strongly linked to operational reflexivity rather than to an attachment to managerial and bureaucratic hierarchies. We have seen evidence of this characteristic at different levels in the operational models of many of our case study universities, but the overall tendency of the sector is towards a more top-down hierarchical mode of governance. This has implications for the sector's resilience.

Bureaucracy and regulation

One might have expected that with the move to a full-blown higher education market, financed by tuition fees, and the removal of constraints on student numbers, bureaucracy and regulation would be reduced. But, as Chapter 2 makes clear, the contrary has been the case and each new apparent freedom has been accompanied by a new example of control or centralized data collection. The planned development of a metrics-based, programme-by-programme, TEF system, apart from representing almost the ultimate in state micro-management, will impose yet further demands for data on universities. Inevitably the demands of this bureaucracy not only requires increased manpower at the centre of an institution but penetrates down to faculties, schools and departments, imposing administrative and other burdens that stifle the ability to make time for new academic ventures. The following quotations are typical of the academic response:

> When I first started I had really a lot of autonomy about how many pieces of coursework I wanted to ask students to do [for a module]. These days it's much more likely that there'll be a university norm or there'll be some kind of regulation about it: there are regulations about how many hours a programme is supposed to cover, so you have to work out this much is lectures, this much is student work, this much is assessment. (25)

> The summer period is the main period where you can do research ... as regulation increased what I've noticed is that this is massive now, that the summer is completely booked with meetings and with tasks that need to be fulfilled ... and this is especially pronounced from where I sit, but then I pass that down to colleagues. When I first started the summer was basically research time, and now there's all this kind of stuff where you need to tick boxes and fill in forms .... (26)

> Administration and e-mail is just never-ending ... and also you keep getting asked for nonsense information you know is never going to be used. So you get someone in a position of power be it a head of faculty or PVC or whatever who came up with an idea, they want this information, they want it yesterday, and it just filters down, and you know full well that they've changed their mind by the time the information goes up and they don't need it any more but you've had to spend a lot of time putting that together. That drives you absolutely nuts. (27)

> In the UK the system of [course] accreditation is incredible, and I don't think it ends up with better results at all. ... The threshold for the substance that would trigger a revalidation ... [is very low] ... [and the] internal review process through the quality assurance committee really is like, you know, the Stasi, at least at our university. ... It really discouraged the faculty from doing any changes, and then why should they if it really [is so difficult]. For me I could never teach a module the same way twice, I always wanted to change things, it was a very useful way to fold my own research in and my own intellectual journey in with the course, and I think it always worked for the better. ... [So, I

only taught one class] and in part I was discouraged by that process from [taking on more teaching], but I think I would have just had to not make many changes. And I don't see that there were many changes made, I didn't see many people taking their course at the end of the year back to revalidate for the next year. (28)

These complaints could be written off as simply the grumbles of individuals but they are widespread from all types of university and levels of academic staff. Thus a senior academic in a Russell Group university says:

I think there is still a lot of freedom on what to teach, what to do research on but the type of outcomes which are acceptable have become more closely defined, more narrowly defined, and the processes are also more scrutinised and managed, controlled, regulated so there is more surveillance, there is more management control. (29)

The consequences are serious for the long-term success of the British university. The accretion of top-down management, mostly arising from increased demands for accountability, is in danger of stifling individual initiative and originality. This is summed up in the following quotation, again from a Russell Group university:

I think my perception is that higher education has become more business-like and that it is more of a top-down system now, rather than an academically-driven system. So I guess by that I mean that I think in the past academics have set the trajectory of the university, of schools and departments, within schools, for better or for worse and now I think my perception is that certain roles that historically would have been led by academics have become led by administrative or [in this university] we call them professional services staff. I think my feeling is over the last six years there has been erosion of the autonomy of academics. (30)

The power of the executive

Chapter 4 gives an account of the rise of the executive and of the dominant role it can achieve in a university environment. When Clark (1998) wrote about 'a central steering core' he was concerned about how 'Traditional European universities ... exhibited a notoriously weak capacity to steer themselves'. He argued that as complexity and the pace of change accelerated, the weakness 'became more debilitating, deepening the need for a greater managerial capacity'. But he emphasized that, while this steering core could take different shapes, 'it must embrace central managerial groups *and* [Clark's italics] academic departments. It must operationally reconcile managerial values with traditional academic ones' (Clark 1998: 5–6). Clark deliberately talked about 'steering' rather than 'directing' and envisaged a body that coordinated university business, encouraged approaches to decision-making and acted as a policy forum that considered and reconciled different points of view and recommended ways forward to decision-making bodies.

What is apparent is that under pressures from governors or from the external environment recruitment, financial and physical constraints – and especially in institutions that see themselves as being at risk, the central steering core has become a central directing body, acting very much as if it was the executive of a large company and bypassing senates and academic boards and their committee structures. Its membership is ex officio and is made up largely of people appointed from outside the institution, backed up by an army of professional staff who owe their primary allegiance to the executive rather than to the institution as a whole. Such bodies can become inured to arbitrary decision-making. Which departments, research groupings and in what combination should it submit for the REF? Which staff should be included or excluded to get the best result? How should the institution react to a perceived recruitment crisis? Which academic programmes should be run down? How many redundancies should be sought? Where should new academic investment take place? Such decisions, integral to the well-being of the institution and debatable as to the evidence, are often taken outside the framework of academic decision-taking and reported directly to the lay governing body.

An example can be drawn from a post-1992 university facing recruitment issues. Here, the executive, through the agency of a deputy vice chancellor, produced an academic blueprint that aimed to impose uniformity across all degree programmes, with each module requiring no more than two pieces of assessment (31). The effect was to ignore previous disciplinary-based differences in favour of a bureaucratically tidy and regulated system that provided an apparently equitable basis for determining staff teaching loads and a potential platform for declaring redundancies. The blueprint was put out to consultation, received a predictable response and was summarily implemented. On the one hand, it represented a triumph of managerial rationality but, on the other, the subordination of disciplinary individuality and creativity to an institutional management agenda.

Our interviews imply that in universities hierarchy is now preferred to the more collegial, heterarchical modes of governance, partly because it is assumed that only this form of governance allows for proper accountability within the organization and to the public. But, as Stark argues, it should not be taken for granted that 'hierarchy resolves problems of accountability', especially as 'the principle of hierarchical accountability too often stops at the bottom' (2009: 202). As our data indicate, this seems to be the case in universities. In recent years, it has been exclusively the executive that initiated organizational restructuring and made decisions about venturing into new research areas and large campus developments, often generating levels of (possibly) unmanageable and unsustainable. However, when financial strains on an institution become evident, it is not inadequate management and financial miscalculation at the very top, but research 'productivity' and recruitment numbers that take centre stage, and it is often the academic community and other 'front-line staff' who suffer:

> What they are saying is that it's mainly senior management who are being got rid of, and it's not ... I'm struggling to find a single senior manager who is going to lose their job in what's happening at the moment ... they are calling it streamlining ... the argument is that we are not recruiting enough students, so they need to streamline the department, so they need to reduce the number of staff. (32)

By its nature, arbitrary decision-making in academic life is a product of authority structures that dispense with debate and academic argument where the clash of ideas creates the sparks of innovation and new thinking, and, ultimately, it drives them underground; it is inimical to the conditions that produce good academic work.

Authority structures in higher education

It can reasonably be argued that the doubling of the age participation rate to nearly 50 per cent justifies a larger role for the state in the governance of the higher education system than in the past. But whether it justifies governing it as if it was a utilities industry (see Chapter 2, p. 33) is much more questionable. There has been no single decision that has created the situation where a senior academic in a pre-1992 university can say:

> I think the academic community, in a way, has come to accept that this is how higher education in the UK operates in the contemporary context: that it's regulated, managerialised, centralised, that it would be possible to change that, but it would be so much of an effort would it be worth it? (33)

The Higher Education and Research Act of 2017 was no more than a step on a road that began, if not in 1992, then certainly in the Dearing Report of 1997. But two decisions have pushed the English system decisively in its present direction: the first was to remove the cap on student numbers (coupled with the OfS's statement that it would not offer a lifeline to institutions threatened with market failure); and the second was to require governing bodies to accept formal responsibility for the quality of the degrees their institutions were offering.

Both have strongly reinforced authority structures within universities. The removal of the cap, as it was intended to do, has strengthened the position of universities with good recruitment profiles and that want to expand, at the expense of universities that are already facing recruitment difficulties. But, more importantly, it has imbued traditional methods of university marketing throughout the English (and Welsh) sector with an acute sense of risk and uncertainty as the effects of expansion at the top of the market cascade down to the more vulnerable institutions. This has had two academically undesirable effects. The first has been to put a premium on those parts of the programme that are favoured by the markets (and to threaten those that are not), encouraging the domination of markets over academic priorities, legitimizing the intervention of marketing professionals over academic recruitment and eliminating the possibility of new, exciting and innovative programmes because of the risks they might generate. The second has been the impact on the vulnerable institutions. Such universities know they are at risk, employ agents to assist with recruitment (sometimes even paying them per student recruited, with all the academic risks that that entails), create employment concerns among their staff and may force economies on academic infrastructure. The institutional consequences become the subject of pessimistic rumour-mongering, a characteristic that makes for unstable teaching for the probably weaker students the institution is able to attract. The policy is prejudicial to the interests of the students who, through no fault of their own, find themselves attending 'at risk' institutions and being taught by staff uncertain of their futures. So, whereas the market strengthens strong institutions, it weakens vulnerable ones, most especially when it is emphasized that there will be no serious attempt to reverse market failure. If there is a way of delivering a second-rate student experience, this is it, and one that is in direct conflict with the claims of the OfS, which are to support the needs of the student consumer. We need to think much more about maintaining a high-quality British higher education system than adopting policies that favour the successful and seem to want to shake out the more vulnerable.

The reification of a market philosophy has inevitably strengthened centralized decision-making within institutions and the authority structures that accompany the REF and the TEF. These are further reinforced by the implicit mirroring of governing bodies as boards of directors and the senior management teams as executive groups answerable to them. The HEFCE recognition of the board as responsible for maintaining academic standards not only legitimized lay interventions into senate/academic board business, but further weakened academic authority by giving the executive a role in interpreting board interests to the academic community. The academic inappropriateness of some lay views on the academic programmes can be judged by the comment from the chair of one pre-1992 university, that the bulk of the academic business of his university's senate 'is a back-breaking tedium, grinding through academic courses, things that are of no interest whatsoever to council' (34). If typical, such remarks do not make a strong case for the value of the guarantees about academic quality that governing bodies are required to give, and they reinforce the doubts that almost all respondents had of the competence of lay bodies to carry out the new responsibilities effectively.

It is tempting to accept these developments as simply part of the contemporary and future world of British higher education, an inevitable consequence of mass higher education and the application of new public management and market principles, and it is easy to forget that the Oxbridge universities represent a standing rejection of all these principles and yet still contrive to dominate all national ranking lists for academic achievement. As one senior academic told us:

> We essentially have a governance structure which is self-governing. There is no external chair and external board that can hold a vice-chancellor or deans to account. So we are holding ourselves to account; so the only way to make that work is by rallying the confidence and effectively making good arguments with people that challenge what you're trying to do. (35)

Academic departments are self-governing with complete power over their own budgets and strategies with divisional reviews of performance every six years. If a department gets into difficulty, it can rely on the university to support it. The essential principle is to give academics freedom to follow their own path so decision-making is essentially bottom-up:

> This university will always be carried by the voices of scholars, wanting to attract students, faculty and access to the resources they need. It is my job to make sure they listen and in the end suggest to the council of the university what I think people want and it's for the university council [made up entirely of academics

and chaired by the vice-chancellor] to adopt those recommendations and to defend those decisions back to the faculty. (36)

It can be argued that Oxbridge has special advantages not available to other institutions: history and tradition, reputation, a college system, a unique physical environment and inherited resources. But the governance principles on which the two universities are run are so diametrically opposed to national policies developed from the Dearing Report onwards, and have so successfully resisted the adoption of any of the post-Dearing mantras, that it is surprising that the evidence of their continued academic success has not apparently had any influence on national policymaking.

A conclusion to be reached from our study is that the more research active a university is, the more likely it is to have a higher level of academic participation in governance and the more likely it is to be innovative, to teach and research creatively and to rely more on the individual professionalism of the academic community than on management authority and an enormous burden of regulation. The British higher education system needs to be trusted more to govern itself in the best interests of its core business of teaching and research or it will lose those qualities that have given it such success. It is evident that collegiality, freedom of discussion over academic matters and intellectual exchange about teaching and research continue to flourish 'below stairs' at faculty, school and departmental meetings, but the picture that emerges is that this does not penetrate the higher reaches of institutional governance. The business model of governance does not work because it imposes strict hierarchy on decision-making and creates a system that is over-regulated towards prioritizing accountability and caution over risk-taking. Both are bad for the future vitality of British higher education.

Chapter 6

Globalization and Higher Education Governance*

Pressures on institutional governance arising out of globalization are of relatively recent origin. If you had asked the authors of *Power and Authority in British Universities* back in 1974 whether the international world of higher education exercised any influence over the style or mechanics of the governance of British universities they might have conceded, probably reluctantly, growing pressure from models from the United States, but they would have asserted the leadership of the British university system over higher education in the Commonwealth. They would not have taken seriously the proposition that there might be useful ideas or applicable models emanating from international bodies or from continental European systems, and they would have ignored completely any suggestion that higher education in China, or anywhere else in Asia, could one day represent a threat to British and US academic hegemony. An important new development occurred in 1980 when the Thatcher government took the decision that henceforward tuition fees for international students would no longer be subsidized by the government through universities' recurrent grant; universities would in consequence be required to charge the full cost of their courses. The effect of this was a saving of £100m from the government's budget for higher education.[1] The government then followed this decision by imposing a financial cut of 8.3 per cent on the universities. It did not take long for the universities to realize that charging international students full cost, or 'full cost plus', tuition fees could represent a route to replacing the income lost from their recurrent grant. The competitive recruitment of international students and, later, the opening of satellite overseas campuses were the result. The recruitment of international students paying high fees rapidly became a priority for British universities, a decision widely copied by universities in other countries. British

---

* This chapter represents a joint contribution from Ellen Hazelkorn (Emeritus Professor, Dublin Technological University) and Dr Aniko Horvath.

universities approached the task with unbridled laissez-faire enthusiasm and a semi-commercial enterprise which led to internal organizational and governance change. It also led to British universities adopting a global perspective on student recruitment very different from their previous passive acceptance of students primarily from Commonwealth countries.

The evolving global architecture

Meanwhile, and quite separately, a supranational governance and informational structure in higher education was in the process of being formed, comprising a loose superstructure developing out of coordination by international agencies, national collaboration agreements, demands for comparative data and institutional networking. These developments rapidly came to have implications for governance both at national and institutional levels. Indeed, global factors today have become increasingly influential, to the point that they frame and underpin national policy across most countries and sectors (Hazelkorn 2018). Despite the fact that nations invest heavily in their own education and science systems – as a source of economic empowerment as well as for competitive advantage – higher education institutions are no longer simply part of their national systems. In fact, the biggest change over recent decades is the extent to which universities and colleges are no longer simply local institutions. Rather, higher education R&D systems are open systems (van Damme and van der Wende 2018) dependent on highly internationalized knowledge and research networks and collaborations. As Marginson and Rhoades (2002) argue, higher education institutions are 'imperfectly integrated' within this complex and dynamic landscape, which sees them operating as global actors but bound within national systems and defined by their individual institutional missions and circumstances. The components of this complex landscape vary according to country, socio-economic and political circumstance, including geopolitical position and institutional mission. Nonetheless, there is, it is argued, a strong convergence around common principles and rules (van Damme 2018).

The interdependence of the major political players and economies became imperative in the years and decades following the aftermath of the Second World War. The interconnectedness of the global economy, political systems and labour markets may be challenged by the rise of nationalism in various guises but it is nonetheless clear that, as 'national economies have become ever more closely integrated', this 'openness is not confined to trade flows, investment flows and financial flows' (Nayyar 2002: 3, 7) but includes higher education and research, and their outcomes such as graduates and knowledge. The signature characteristic has been the establishment of mechanisms of interstate relations, fostering the rise of rule-making systems and processes capable of responding to issues of multilateral cooperation and the provision of global public goods, including financial stability, peace and security, human rights, environmental protection, etc. (Held and McGrew 2002: 8). The result has been an assemblage of active and inclusive governance arrangements that overarch individual states and societies and intervene when necessary. Multilateralism lies at the heart of the European Union, and other such common higher education areas that are emerging in Asia, Africa and South America (Ligami 2017). The UK is part of this complex multi-layered, multi-dimensional and multi-modal architecture, whether it recognizes it or not.

Critics often view the growing role and authority of international organizations as a process of 'ceding authority and sovereignty' (Robertson et al. 2016: 1) or of denationalization whereby global outlooks and norms influence and/or overtake thinking, decisions and processes at the national level. As Held and McGrew (2002: 10) explain, the 'reconfiguration of authority between various layers and infrastructures of governance' exposes tensions around autonomy and sovereignty, international and regional alignment, and priorities. Others have characterized international organizations as vehicles for marketization, neo-liberalism and imperialism as part of a wider discussion about globalization, its effects and discontents (Cerny 2000; Stiglitz 2017). An alternative perspective is that these developments are a response to increasing interdependence, regulatory deficiencies, limitations of bilateral agreements, and overall complexities associated with globalization and the internationalization of knowledge. The objective is, as one chief officer of an international organization put it, 'to connect [with] institutions globally to provide a common language, common metrics, common accreditation frameworks that put institutions on a level playing field ...' (1). In this context, multilateral and transnational structures and coordinating frameworks serve a growing need. The result is a complex and overlapping set of multi-layered, multi-level and multi-modal relations.

Multilateral organizations are well-established players in the higher education arena, and are formative in the construction of a global agenda, with implications for nations and institutions. The foundation of the United Nations (UN), the International Monetary Fund (IMF), the World Trade Organization (WTO), the United Nations Educational, Scientific and Cultural Organization

(UNESCO), etc. laid the ground work for the growing prominence of higher education regulations, formal and informal, with intergovernmental networks and academic collaborations providing the underpinning architecture and essential enablers to access resources and talent (Wagner, Park, and Leydesdorff 2015). Despite the fact that education was not a core component of their foundation, by 1960 the Organisation for Economic Co-operation and Development (OECD) and the World Bank had both added education to their portfolio of activities. The inclusion of education by the WTO within the General Agreement in Trade and Services (GATS) negotiations furthered this process, although it simply acknowledged higher education's position as an internationally traded service.

Historically, higher education has been a key component of European policymaking since the early days of the European Coal and Steel Community and the decision to establish the European University Institute in Florence in 1955 (Corbett 2003). In the 1990s, the benefits of the 'information society' and then the 'knowledge economy' began to dominate policy discourse across Europe, following the publication of *Europe and the Global Information Society* (Bangemann 1994).[2] The Lisbon Strategy[3] followed with the aim 'to make the European Union the most competitive and dynamic knowledge-based economy in the world by 2010' (Europa 2000). These developments coincided with publication of *The Knowledge-Based Economy* (OECD 1996), which emphasized the centrality of higher education as the engine of growth. Greater prominence was placed on the production of new knowledge and knowledge management as vital for economic growth rather than simply accessing technology. Since then, and in response to challenges associated with geopolitical and competitive positioning, and amplified by global rankings, higher education and university-based research have become central to the European Union (EU) – and British – policymaking in dramatic and significant ways (Department of Trade and Industry 1999). In turn, these developments have had a significant impact on institutional governance, strategy and organizational structures.

The EU modernization and research agenda

The Sorbonne Declaration of 1998,[4] with its focus on the 'harmonisation of the architecture of the European higher education system', was an initiative of four education ministers – from the UK, France, Germany and Italy. It proclaimed that 'the Europe we are building is not only that of the Euro, the banks and the economy, it must be a Europe of knowledge as well' (Witte 2006: 124). That view was formalized with the Bologna Declaration[5] of 1999, which anticipated the need for enhanced convergence across national systems to create a coherent system of higher education able to compete internationally (van Damme 2009: 40–1). It emphasized student learning outcomes, free movement of students and faculty across national boundaries, and comparability in standards and quality through curriculum and quality assurance changes. The Copenhagen Process sought to do similarly for vocational education and training (VET). The vision was outward-looking and foreshadowed the European Research Area (ERA)[6] in 2002, which was significantly strengthened in 2012 (Europa 2012), and the European Higher Education Area (EHEA)[7] in 2010.

The themes of consolidation, excellence and 'modernisation' were intrinsic to these developments, to which the EU returned again and again. The Lisbon Strategy marked a significant policy direction:

> Given the significant role played by research and development in generating economic growth, employment and social cohesion … Research activities at national and Union level must be better integrated and coordinated to make them as efficient and innovative as possible, and to ensure that Europe offers attractive prospects to its best brains. (Europa 2000)

In *Delivering on the Modernisation Agenda for Universities: Education, Research and Innovation* (Europa 2006: 3), the EU urged greater professionalization, greater accountability and improved university governance 'if Europe is not to lose out in the global competition in education, research and innovation' (Europa 2006: 11; see also Europa 2003, 2007, 2010). Three main concerns were highlighted in subsequent high-level communications (Hazelkorn and Ryan 2013):

- Europe has too many universities seeking to 'compete in too many areas, while comparatively few have the capacity to excel across the board' (Europa 2011: 2);
- European universities suffer from poor governance, insufficient autonomy and often perverse incentives due to traditional decentralized organizational structures and civil service-type governance arrangements and academic contracts;
- Public policy supported too many universities of similar quality rather than investing in those with the best potential for excellence; as a result, public funding is spread too thinly.

The Communication, *On a renewed EU agenda for higher education* (2017), urged the higher education sector to be more attuned to meeting EU objectives. It called for strengthening collaboration with business, supporting talent and strengthening capacity and capability in research, development and innovation. These priorities presupposed stronger alignment across EU boundaries, most notably with respect to the promotion of Networks of European Universities (Myklebust and O'Malley 2018), the automatic mutual recognition of diplomas and the creation of a European Student Card.

Education is not an EU competence.[8] Rather, the EU gains authority through the principle of the 'open method of co-ordination', a non-binding tool that seeks to progress change without infringing national rights. In contrast, research and technological development is a shared competence, and here the EU's influence has strengthened in line with large increases to its research budget. The Framework Programme, which began in 1984, followed by the European Research Council (ERC) in 2007, shifted from encouraging the growth of research to consolidating and concentrating research in centres of excellence. In this way, 'research in Europe' was effectively recast as 'European research'. EU influence is manifest also in national and institutional decisions around research infrastructure, faculty and student mobility, open science and international collaboration, the impact agenda and the reorientation of priorities towards global societal challenges. EU strategies for research excellence have spurred consolidation and concentration of resources and expertise (Myklebust 2018; Technopolis 2017) albeit they have led to concerns about regional disparities, uneven growth and social exclusion, both within countries and across Europe.

The complexities associated especially with (basic) science and large-scale research infrastructure means, as asserted by a president of an EU agency, 'there's nothing that's done on a national basis purely in research any more, it's almost impossible … to achieve the scale on a national basis' (2). As the EU moves towards mandating Open Access (OA), this is likely to have further implications for all nations, and national agencies, such as JISC (formerly the Joint Information Systems Committee) or the Scottish Higher Education Digital Library (SHEDL), with respect to reconfiguring their e-resources models and funding. Compliance undoubtedly throws up many complexities associated with internalized rules and guidelines, but so does operating in a global science community (Europa 2016; Schiltz 2018). Plan S, which commits all 'research funded by public grants provided by national and European research councils and funding bodies … [to] be published in compliant Open Access Journals or on compliant Open Access Platforms' by 1 January 2020, has been endorsed by a coalition of research-funding agencies known as cOAlition S, which includes UK Research and Innovation (UKRI).[9] Likewise, to successfully position a university for Horizon 2020, or subsequently for Framework 9,[10] requires embedding characteristics of those programmes within a university's research governance and management system.

Finally, higher education has been brought directly into debates around skills, competences and employability, and regional development. The role of universities as anchor institutions and drivers of growth has come to the fore (Goddard 2011). The EU's Research and Innovation Strategies for Smart Specialisation (referred to as RIS3) have sought to maximize collaboration by leveraging expertise across enterprise, local and regional government, and civil society, based upon identification of place-based strengths and economic potential;[11] the UK has been part of the process not least because having an RIS3 strategy is conditional for structural funds.[12] University research has been central to this strategy (EUA 2016), albeit attention is beginning to focus on human capital development and, in particular, VET and technical and vocational education and training (TVET) (Edwards et al. 2017; Hazelkorn and Edwards 2019).

International organizations and the accountability agenda

OECD and UNESCO

International agencies have played a major role pushing the accountability agenda forward with implications for university and system governance. Almost everywhere, as one former CEO of an international higher education organization put it, there is a 'preoccupation with quality and quality assurance and accountability as a way to steer the system' (3). Before global rankings began to be published, comparing and benchmarking performance – using a preponderance of quantitative indicators across a variety of 'governance indices' – had been a growing part of public policy across many sectors in order to drive, monitor and evaluate behaviour and outcomes (Erkkila and Piironen 2009; Sauder and Espeland 2009: 64). The OECD began compiling statistical information shortly after it superseded the Organisation for European Economic Co-operation (OEEC) in 1961, 'collecting cross-national data to identify long-term labour market needs, especially in the areas of science and technology' (Henry et al. 2001: 85). Country and thematic reviews served a similar purpose. The *Frascati Manual*, first developed in 1963, became the international standard for R&D statistics across OECD countries and around the world (OECD 1980), and laid the basis for the OECD *Main Science and Technology Indicators*, biannually published since 1981, which drew on the Science Citation Index and the Social Sciences Citation Index (Jacso 2010). The OECD *International Indicators and Evaluation of Educational Systems* (INES) project paved the way for *Education at a Glance*,[13] one of the OECD's premier publications, published annually from 1991.

In 2000, the *Programme for International Student Assessment* (PISA)[14] was launched. Its success, alongside growing criticism of global rankings during the mid-2000s, spurred a desire to develop more appropriate instruments for higher education. In 2008, the Programme for the International Assessment of Adult Competencies (PIAACC) began conducting a survey of adult skills. In 2005, the first phase of the EU-sponsored U-Map project began as a profiling tool, following the publication of *Institutional Profiles – Towards a Typology of Higher Education Institutions in Europe* (van Vught et al. 2005, 2010). The aim was to highlight the diversity of European higher education institutions. It paved the way for the EU-sponsored U-Multirank (UMR) (CHERPA-Network 2010), a user-driven multi-dimensional ranking system (Hazelkorn 2012), which was developed simultaneously with the OECD's Assessment of Learning Outcomes in Higher Education (AHELO) initiative. Both UMR and AHELO were conceived as alternatives to rankings (OECD 2013), which focused disproportionately on research. AHELO was controversial from the start because it aimed to compare learning outcomes across countries, similarly to PISA; hence it was often derogatively known as 'PISA for higher education'. Opposition from university organizations, along with methodological challenges and rising costs, led to its eventual abandonment in 2015. The UK was one of the countries that decided not to sign up to further implementation testing (Morgan 2015). The OECD is currently developing a system benchmarking project (OECD 2017); however the UK is not participating in the current phase.[15] By focusing on 'systems' rather than 'institutions', the OECD hopes to overcome objections to AHELO while replicating the policy value of PISA.

The EU has also been expanding its role and capacity in this area. In addition to U-Map and UMR, there is an alphabet-soup of projects, inter alia: ETER, the European Tertiary Education Register[16] (Bonaccorsi et al. 2010); DEQAR, Database of External Quality Assurance Reports;[17] EUROGRADUATE, a graduate survey;[18] and EURITO, EU Relevant, Inclusive, Timely, Trusted, and Open Research Innovation Indicators[19] (EHEA Ministerial Conference Paris

Communiqué 2018). Together they form the basis of an EU-wide quality assurance and information framework.

UNESCO has also been pivotal in this space. The International Standard Classification of Education (ISCED) framework (1976) has formed the backbone of national qualifications frameworks. It has also been active in identifying appropriate indicators (Martin and Sauvageot 2011), and a driving force behind promoting a global conversation around quality. The 2002 and 2004 Global Forums on International Quality Assurance, Accreditation and Recognition of Qualifications in Higher Education coincided with WTO and GATS discussions (Eaton 2003; UNESCO 2005). The regional meetings, leading up to the Global Convention on the Recognition of Higher Education Qualifications planned for 2020, is being held against the backdrop of growing internationalization and student mobility, but also against its nationalist antithesis (UNESCO 2018).

As one senior official put it, the intention is to provide

> fair, transparent, non-discriminatory recognition of foreign qualifications ... and requiring ultimately, after it's adopted and ratified, member states to apply those common principles to every foreign qualification regardless of where it comes from. (4)

This is hugely influential work, not least due to an increasing realization of the need for a framework, structure and mechanism(s) to uphold the quality of higher education in the international sphere, and to produce transparency for transnational provision and cross-border mobility (Sharma 2018).

UK higher education and its national agencies are deeply embedded in these developments, despite some reluctance on their part. Although a signatory, the Bologna Process has had relatively little impact on the daily life of UK universities, because the UK system differed considerably from its continental counterparts, especially with respect to governance and institutional autonomy. Its qualifications were already demarcated between BA, MA and PhD; hence, as the CEO of a European higher education organization described it, there was little interest: 'at the beginning of Bologna ... they said "oh we've all done it before thank you very much"' (5). Nonetheless, the Quality Assurance Agency for Higher Education (QAA), is a member of the European Association for Quality Assurance in Higher Education (ENQA), and is included on the European Quality Assurance Register for Higher Education (EQAR). The latter is the official register of validated quality assurance (QA) agencies, an accreditation required by most governments. Compliance with the principles of the European Standards and Guidelines (ESG), which provide criteria for reviews, is a requirement for all agencies and universities.

Whatever the lack of interest in the UK, the Bologna Process is being copied around the world (Adelman 2009), with initiatives at different stages of development, for example, the Association of South East Asian Nations (ASEAN) Qualifications Reference Framework (AQRF) Task Force in Asia, the African Quality Assurance Network (AfriQAN), the francophone Le Conseil Africain et Malgache pour l'Enseignement Supérieur (CAMES) and South America's MercoSur-Educativo. The desire for greater international coordination around matters of quality assurance, mobility, qualification recognition and cross-border regulation has not simply been a call by governments. It has also come from higher education and its representative associations, such as the International Association of Universities (IAU) and the European University Association (EUA), as well as the European Association for Quality Assurance in Higher Education (ENQA), the Council for Higher Education Accreditation (CHEA), the International Network for Quality Assurance Agencies (INQAAHE) and the CHEA International Quality Group (CIQG).[20]

The OECD's influence has also extended beyond data collection and analysis. In education, it has been important in raising policy issues, stimulating governments to review and rethink policies by comparing performance against policy choices, using techniques of benchmarking and peer learning as well as peer pressure. A senior official suggested that the process seeks to 'give countries a mirror where they can see themselves in light of other institutions, what other countries are doing, achieving' (6): PISA and *Education at a Glance* are good examples, with results being news headlines, prompting discussion across all media formats. The UK has been an active participant, receiving and commissioning reports on all aspects of tertiary education,[21] including a thematic review of UK tertiary education in 2006 (Clark 2006).

The OECD also created the programme for the Institutional Management of Higher Education (IMHE) in the late 1990s as a forum for educational leaders to address key issues.[22] Hosted by the Directorate of Education, IMHE was a unique institutional, membership-based unit, with an associated fee. Its biennial general conferences attracted ministers and policymakers, senior university leaders and academics from around the world, thereby providing one of the few venues for cross-dialogue. UK civil servants, higher education leaders and the Higher Education Funding Council for England (HEFCE) were regular attendees and participants on IMHE committees and projects. Governance was a consistent theme, with the OECD discussing the importance of balancing the authority of the state and the power of the markets in ways that enhanced, rather than compromised, institutional autonomy (OECD 2003: chapter 3). IMHE conference themes explored various aspects, and like the EU 'Modernisation' agenda, promoted professionalization and strategic capacity building as a necessary response to an increasingly massified and globally competitive landscape. Such topics were included in *Higher Education Management and Policy*, a refereed international journal published by IMHE from 1997 to 2012. In January 2010, IMHE proposed the development of a learning outcomes test for global use, the AHELO initiative, which, if successful, would have had considerable implications for university governance in terms of establishing an externally validated quality assessment instrument. Several factors converged, and the programme's mandate expired on 31 December 2016. Since then, the OECD has prioritized skills and competences and re-energized discussion around conceptualizing a post-secondary or tertiary system rather than focusing only on higher education,[23] under the remit of the Skills Beyond School (SBS) division,[24] a theme also reflected in the reform of Welsh higher education (see Chapter 3).

The European University Association

Governance has also been a key theme of the EUA,[25] which was established in 2001 from the merger of the Association of European Universities and the Confederation of EU Rectors' Conference; it now comprises over 850 members, including 33 national rectors' conferences. It is the primary university network, acknowledged as the official stakeholder organization with the EU institutions, the Council of Europe and the Bologna Follow-Up Group (BFUG).[26] UK universities are members of the EUA and have been members of its executive and various initiatives over the years, including its involvement in data collection with respect to governance. Most notably, this includes the *Autonomy Scorecard* project, which monitors the degree of autonomy according to four characteristics: organizational, financial, staffing, and academic (Pruvot and Estermann 2018, 2017);[27] and the Universities for Strategic, Efficient and Autonomous Management (USTREAM) project, which looks comparatively at matters of effectiveness, efficiency and value for money which was inspired by British experience (Estermann and Kupriyanova 2018).

Global rankings and the internationalization of British higher education

Global university rankings have been an important feature of this evolving architecture, filling the space left by what Nayyar terms the 'missing institutions' of globalization (Nayyar 2002: 375). The emergence of global rankings followed almost a century of national rankings, most prominently in the United States. Their appearance was recognition that higher education was indeed a global enterprise, and that national reputation was no longer sufficient. It is argued that their methodology and choice of indicators is controversial, the data used often unreliable and they foster 'mimetic behaviour and shared notions of excellence' (van Damme 2018). But by holding up a mirror to universities and nations, rankings have filled a recognizable gap, providing information about the nature and quality of research and higher education, and, correspondingly, about national competitiveness. The shock created by the publication of Shanghai Jiao Tong's *Academic Rankings of World Universities* (2004), followed swiftly by the *Times Higher Education*, QS World University Ranking and Webometrics rankings, created an immediate response across Europe and elsewhere.

Initially, the EU highlighted the diversity of European higher education institutions, arguing this was a characteristic to be celebrated. This led to the U-Map and UMR approaches to ranking. However, as concerns about global competition rose, the EU took an increasingly more interventionist position. A 2007 resolution urged European higher education to respond to 'challenges posed by globalisation' (Europa 2007: 2). It acknowledged that both national and European standards were no longer sufficient, saying there was a need to enhance the international attractiveness and competitiveness of European higher education (Europa 2011). National responses varied: France and Germany in particular sought to make sweeping structural changes. The German *Exzellenzinitiative*, launched in 2007 and starting its third phase in 2018,[28] sought to create a German Ivy League in order to reclaim the country's historic leadership position (Hazelkorn 2015: 181–8); France, beginning in 2007, embarked on a series of legislative changes promoting greater institutional autonomy in order to encourage stronger management and better planning as well as consolidation for critical mass. Today there are at least fifty excellence initiatives around the world (Salmi 2017).

Global rankings are a controversial measure, but they display an underlying 'epiphenomenon' about scientific and academic prowess. Given that they record performance in terms of investment in talent and scientific papers that has already occurred, they are a 'lag'-indicator. The ability versus inability to compete at this level is amplifying global divisions between economic regions, as well as between universities, and shaping institutional strategies. The exact nature of the relationship between global rankings and institutional governance and strategic decision-making can be difficult to pin down, but there is solid evidence to show that rankings have been a significant influence on strategic decision-making at all levels of the organization. While many university leaders claim they do not overemphasize rankings, there is plenty of evidence to the contrary, with references to rankings in policy statements, in conversations or speeches to students or key stakeholders, or in the media including in the UK (Hazelkorn 2015; Locke et al. 2008). How high a university is ranked can be so significant that a university may use rankings as a 'bragging tool' (Busby 2018) and/or misrepresent ranking results to students, the public or other stakeholders (Weale 2017; ASA/CAP 2017). Governments and politicians are also sensitive to rankings and if university performance has slipped, may be sympathetic to arguments as to how increased funding would help avert further negative consequences.

The UK has traditionally performed well in global rankings, nonetheless there is a keen desire to perform better, especially in comparison with the United States and now vis-à-vis China, and in the context of Brexit. In 2004, when the Shanghai Jiao Tong University's *Academic Ranking of World Universities* (ARWU) was first published, the United States and Europe dominated, with 179 universities listed among the top 200; by 2018, however, the United States and Europe held only 159 places. China had two universities in the top 200 compared with 19 for the United Kingdom and 90 for the United States. By 2018, China had 15 universities in the top 200 compared with the UK's 21 and the US's 69 (*Academic Rankings of World Universities* 2018).[29] Despite criticizing global rankings, UK universities have been reluctant to participate in the EU alternative, UMR. Most witnesses to a parliamentary committee 'were unconvinced by the merits of yet another league table' until the deficiencies were overcome; a clearer preference was shown for the *Times Higher Education World University Rankings* but arguably the UK has benefitted from its English-language bias (European Union Committee 2012; Hazelkorn 2013; van Raan, van Leeuwen and Visser 2011).

Universities have generally felt relatively safe within national boundaries and national legislation. Indeed, many of the fundamental structures for higher education remain unchanged at the national level. The role of international organizations, including the EU, is naturally constrained by national laws and regulations, sentiment and the fact that undergraduate students are predominantly domestic. But the internationalization of higher education and research as well as geopolitical shifts are challenging this. Countries, like individual universities, are developing strategies to secure national interests, while learning to compete with others previously unknown or considered. The pursuit of global strategies is necessarily overdetermined by international standards and guidelines that frame the underpinning architecture and smooths the process. Participation in international organizations, and membership of the proliferating number of university networks[30] is now vital, and involves a series of soft and hard relationships that act simultaneously as defensive and offensive instruments. They serve to strengthen capacity and capability, quality, reputation and global reach – enabling access to talent and resources beyond the scope of individual, nation-bound, institutions.

Bilateral relations are seen to be inadequate in this increasingly complex international landscape. A senior official of an international organization suggested that:

> higher education needs some global regulation because you cannot leave this too completely to be a wild west market type of reality, so you have to have some elementary forms of consumer protection, you have to have some basic agreements on recognition of qualifications. (7)

Perceptions of global and European influences on British higher education

In the light of the above, and the British higher education sector's role and embeddedness within global and European structures, it has been one of our most surprising findings that – when asked about global or European influences on British higher education governance – the most frequent reply we received from our interviewees was that 'there's nothing [global or European] that fundamentally drives a different governance model' (8) for the UK higher education sector. This perception, with slight variations, was widespread across mission groups, government policymakers and institutional leadership. Such opinions were particularly puzzling because they frequently emerged in contexts where even smaller regional universities were referred to as 'global businesses', while the everyday practices of teaching, research and civic engagement, as described in most of our interviews, painted an image of a sector that was deeply linked to, influenced by and aligned with global trends, networks and processes. Nevertheless, if one looked only at the discursive level and at perceptions of key actors in the sector, it often seemed that time had indeed stopped at a point when it was still possible for the authors of *Power and Authority in British Universities* to describe British higher education as a nation-state-bound matter where British universities – wishing to be engaged abroad – believed they were destined to lead the world of higher education, rather than follow or adopt the practices of international organizations or other European models.

To untangle the contradictions in our data between perceptions and practice, in the remaining parts of this chapter we will explore the sector's attitudes towards and understandings of global and European influences, as they emerged from our interviews. Simultaneously, we will also explore how far the British system of higher education and its institutions are influenced by global bodies and 'governance technologies' (such as league tables) relative to their own governance. Throughout, our analysis is focused on 'governance', not on the more general issues of globalization at the institutional, national and international levels.

Discrepancies between perceptions of global influences and practice

Some of the most typical answers we received from British policymakers were the ones that, although expressing some regrets for the insularity of their approaches, acknowledged that they do not pay particular attention to global and European influences, nor do they see them as having much impact on the British higher education system or on their universities' organizational models. For example, one of our English policymaker interviewees, when prompted about global and/or European influences, responded:

> Well, we, I think, wrongly, are quite kind of complacent here, so there is a picture that British universities, English universities, are of a high standard, ... and we have this problem that we are very insular and our students don't go abroad, so ... I'm trying to think, it must be ... um ... but no, I can't claim there was a big EU or global influence, because I don't think there are even any global institutions involved, are there? (9)

This was no different from the way policymakers interviewed in Scotland and Northern Ireland replied to questions about paying attention to global organizations and/or governance models:

> To be honest, and to my shame, not really ... The closest I would say, and it's still pretty parochial, is we occasionally have had interaction with our colleagues in jurisdictions that are quite similar to us, i.e. Australia, New Zealand, Hong Kong ... I didn't say it was right, just [the] nature of common language, common background in history ... [and] we have had some interaction with Ireland. (10)

> I think to be frank [laughs] yes [laughter] caught up within the ... [laughter]. Yeah, we would be caught up in day-to-day problems. There would be a bit of sort of horizon scanning around, you know, what [are] the next big things, like data analytics and that sort of thing ... but a lot of it is day-to-day, I have to say. (11)

It was only in Wales that policymakers talked about having a global focus and conducting an active search for other relevant system-level models to be applied to their higher education sector:

> I would say that the standard point of reference in Wales for policy-making for many years had been England. ... Now, about four or five years ago, a number of people across the Welsh government began to start talking about, well if Wales was really going to do anything significant it needed to raise its sights beyond that comparison with England ... [and so a few years ago] a number of us went to Scotland for two weeks and went and visited everybody and sought to gain lessons from that experience, and Scotland has been very influential, not only in education but [in] a range of other ways. ... In higher education policy ... increasingly the points of reference are moving beyond the British Isles ... to somewhat further geographically ... [so we look at] Finland, there will be certain provinces in Canada, there will be ... the Netherlands, Scotland, New Zealand ... small states that are post-industrial that have been heavily influenced by large near neighbours and are trying to get a more independent sense [of] themselves. (12)

Within universities, like the views of English, Scottish and Northern Irish policymakers, most chairs of governing bodies claimed that there were no international dimensions to their jobs and they could not think of any global models that impacted on their thinking on how to organize or run their universities:

> I think the short answer is no, I'm not particularly conscious of there being a global model ... in terms of structures, governance structures, I can't think that I am particularly, or our court, is particularly attuned to other models. (13)

No, no, none. It didn't, no it hasn't impinged at all. There's been no overseas aspect to my job at all, apart from last summer going over with our VC for the graduation ceremonies at our partner university in China. (14)

However, in many cases, just as in this latter statement there was a puzzling discrepancy in the ways senior university officials reflected on and understood global 'impacts'. While in their replies they were claiming that they could not think of any global trends that influenced their strategies or overall thinking, often in the same sentence they also referenced international partnerships, global rankings, international or European quality assurance as everyday practices for their institutions that had significant impact on their work:

No, [there are no global influences]. I mean the only thing that does come to my mind … [is that] there's growing recognition that we need to pay some attention to our global reputation, and a sense that our ranking in terms of reputation … doesn't actually match the hard evidence behind it. … And we are therefore at the early stages of thinking about what that means. So, I think that's probably the best answer I can give you in terms of that sense of global organisations. (15)

Certainly, European Quality Assurance, in terms of … what we are required to do through the Quality Assurance Agency, and that's very much within a European framework, but I would be lying if I said that, you know, there were global influences. … It's probably a regrettable thing but there are so many national … regulatory requirements that it's very difficult to lift your head up and look at best practice in another country. (16)

Another typical answer we received from senior university officials, especially in post-1992 universities, was that while they were aware of global and international trends and organizations, they did not see them as particularly relevant to or impacting on their own practices and operations:

One of the dangers, you know … is not to know your place within a very differentiated sector. I think that's been one of the things that has impeded the development of post-92 universities, they sort of set themselves up as global players. Some have succeeded to a limited extent … [but] if you try and just transplant that … and say we are going to be a global university … you can't do that from a standing start, it takes a long time, and I suppose one of the lessons it taught me was each university has to play to its distinctive strengths, and for me we are in the [global] world and that's important, but we are an anchor institution, we are a local institution really when all is said and done, and if you begin to get confused about that identity, [that becomes problematic]. Now that means [that] some of the stakeholder connections that are far more important to me are the Mayor [and its office] ... than what's happening at the European Universities Association. (17)

University officials in some other universities argued that while global organizations impacted on their own institutions to only a limited degree, they used the research conducted by such organizations in an instrumental way to influence and steer national-level policymaking:

> When the HE Bill ... came out for consultation, I personally used a lot of the European University Association [research] ... so we looked at a number of [their] studies as well, to see what we could learn, because the governance group [for the HE Bill] ... said that it was going to use international material and it didn't, and I delivered all the evidence that I found, and that I was aware of, and it was not referred. So, I was a bit angry about that. (18)

In contrast, when individual academics were asked about international engagement, the picture that emerged was much more nuanced and complex than the answers that emerged from institutional leadership and policymakers. Academic interviews, across all four nations, painted a picture of a higher education system that was linked to and deeply impacted by international processes and networking, at the level of *teaching* (overseas campuses and partnerships, large numbers of international and EU students, Erasmus student and staff exchange programmes, internationalization of the curriculum, global placement schemes, etc.), *research* (participation in European and global research networks and funding schemes, co-authorships, university–industry collaborations, etc.), and *civic engagement* (e.g. collaborations with global organizations, such as the World Health Organization, the UN Human Rights Council, UNESCO, etc.). This, academics argued, significantly influenced the everyday running of their universities, including institutional governance. The following three quotations from senior and mid-career academics exemplify the discrepancy that often exists between the perceptions of senior university officials and the experience of academic staff. A mid-career academic in a Welsh university argued that external pressures caused him to drop his productive research and teaching career to identify:

> business opportunities [in terms of new courses] that would provide additional student recruitment markets, that would balance the [financial] deficit that we are suffering here. Hence this [overseas] project, where we are looking at attracting a new market, a market that may be difficult [to bring] to the UK but [where they] study similar degrees to what we offer here but in a different part

of the world. So, there is no doubt I've changed direction, and probably it's not something of choice, but something in terms of impacting upon the changes that surround me. (19)

A senior academic from a large London-based English university, who was running projects in four European countries as well as China and Singapore, argued that over the past decade he has seen a huge increase in the number of boards and committees that approved European and global partnerships. He felt this changed their university fundamentally; while the influence of such bodies has been increasing, the 'old' structures were struggling to accommodate new units:

> [So, there are more bodies than there used to be and] I think they are trying to exercise influence, and sometimes there's a clash between their perspective and the strategic perspective of the university, but at this stage I see this as growing pains rather than something that becomes part of the ideology of the board or the ideology of the university. I think [these new bodies] are trying to understand themselves, where they are sitting and what they are doing, but increasingly you have a university that is very international, with a bureaucracy that does not necessarily recognise that international character, and the way boards work is influenced by the bureaucracy, so you can see a little bit of tension there. (20)

Another senior academic in a medium-size, research-intensive, regional English university argued that a consequence of the intense marketization in the higher education environment was that universities now had greater autonomy in shaping their growth and expansion strategies, including global engagement. This led to the internal restructuring of their institutions:

> A good example of that is our university [is] now starting to change its profile. … And I guess one of the reasons we want to do that … is that we can grow our revenue, so we can expand, we can internationalise. … [So we] work collaboratively with our professional services, and joining up and aligning, and this is a big part of what we are doing at the moment, the kind of work that goes on at departments, faculty, and also the centre of the university … I have a team of associate Deans, undergraduate, postgraduate, research, and one that does international and engagement together, so they are very involved in trying to do this coordination work. (21)

The approaches and strategies of the two British higher education unions clearly reflected this deeper global engagement of academic staff and student members.

Thus, union officials were very engaged with international and European organizations, often coordinating their actions across countries. As a senior official from the staff union argued, global engagement had to be an important part of their work, because the sector was highly internationalized both in terms of its staff and students, and in terms of

> some of the policy drivers, like the rankings and the desire to create world class universities. So, we are affiliated with international mission groups and we work quite closely with them and [with] organizations from other countries doing similar work. And you mentioned the OECD for example, it's through [such partnerships] that we challenged their projects on learning outcomes. ... So, some of it is sharing strategies, some of it is [challenging] international bodies, which have an impact on policy in the UK, like the OECD for example. (22)

However, the National Union of Students – working closely with the European Students' Union as well as students' unions from Australia, New Zealand and Canada – argued that because of the different regulations that were in place across countries such collaborations could be limited in forcing change at the national level:

> [Joining forces] has a benefit more in terms of what the student movement can do for wider political issues, for instance ... dealing with problems that are global, so dealing with things like climate change, ... open borders, and immigration. These are problems which the student movement can unite and deal with, but because of the kind of specificities of the educational issues in each country I think it's more difficult for an internationalised student movement to have effects in each state on their education systems. (23)

Mission groups, on the other hand, seemed to be less actively and systematically engaged internationally than the two unions. While Universities UK said that they had personnel specifically focusing on global engagement most mission groups argued that they had no resources to engage in depth at the European or global level. Instead, it seemed, many focused on incorporating international and global research evidence to steer national policymaking. For example, one member of a mission group argued that

> I did use a report from the World Bank actually, for my own purposes ... because [it] was talking about the importance of ... building on excellence, and ... saying don't try and spread your funds too thinly, concentrate on building a few strong institutions. Go for quality as opposed to quantity. ... So we certainly used that and shoved it in the face of British policy-makers. (24)

Other mission groups – strikingly, and in contrast to what we learned in many of our case study universities – argued that they did not need to engage internationally because their members were individually networked both at global and European levels:

> As a mission group we don't [engage], we just aren't resourced to have a whole lot of engagement with EU institutions. … Having said that, all of my institutions will have their own relationships, a couple of them have offices in Brussels and many of them will have partnerships of different kinds with universities based in Europe, but I don't. I don't engage with the EU or people there. (25)

Finally, when our interviews moved beyond the lack of impact that global and European processes had on system-level and institutional governance, all our interviewees made strong arguments about the importance of the creation and maintenance of international research networks and the value of these networks in the development of research. The following remark by the vice chancellor of a Russell Group university about their European research collaborations was fairly typical of the opinions we encountered:

> Being part of a community of five hundred million citizens really makes a difference. I mean scale and diversity matter for universities, because it's through the diversity that innovation and fresh thinking thrives, and that's how you get the best education. If you understand other people's points of view, learn about other parts of the world, [and] can travel freely in a much bigger area it takes you out of the confines of what otherwise might be limited thinking. (26)

There is no doubt that being part of these European and global research networks imposed governance in academic practice and, if pursued at an institutional level – e.g. via the Consortium of European Research Universities – also influenced the governance of institutions in its broadest sense. However, while the importance of international research networks was highly rated, their impact on governance was rarely acknowledged. The following response by a vice chancellor of an English university reflects this duality in perception:

> I don't think the EU has had a significant impact on the way we are run. Absolutely, [the EU] has an impact on the way we operate and our success, … a huge influence on the way we work, and what we can achieve academically, but I can't think of any influence that the EU has had on the way we run ourselves as an organisation. … You could, I suppose, argue on that basis that if we have been part of those networks on the research side primarily then we have somewhat missed a trick in not trying to learn more within those networks about how universities are organised. But rightly or wrongly I don't think there has been much effect. (27)

Heterogeneity of strategies, outreach and reference points within a single institution

Part of the explanation for the perception that British higher education institutions were not influenced by and would be unlikely to consider other models of governance might be that, in relation to global impacts, senior university officials understood 'governance' only in its narrower meanings. Thus, 'governance' was often exclusively to be the binary power-sharing between the executive and the governing body, with neither systemic issues nor diverse institutional practices seen to be part of 'governance'. The mushrooming of specialist committees and back offices – such as international and European research support offices, global recruitment offices, international student support offices and legal and business committees securing the smooth running of overseas operations – were apparently not considered to be part of institutional 'governance'. Similarly, the impact on university governance of changing academic practice that emerged from the internationalization of the curriculum, international work placements for students, the non-UK quality assurance for university degrees and being part of international research networks were usually ignored by most of our institutional executive respondents as being a sort of 'add on' to the central functions of a university.

From our data, it was also clear that often the chair of the governing body, vice chancellor, academics and support staff/administration had different strategies (and interpretations of such strategies) within the same institution in terms of research, teaching, outreach, management of academic affairs, networking and collaborations/competition. This meant that, although institutional mission and governance practice were presented to the external world as homogenous, in practice, a multiplicity of strategies and models were to be found, even within the same institution. If there were any 'global reference points', there was often a discrepancy between points of emphasis for the chair of the governing body, the vice chancellor, academics and professional services. On the one hand, vice chancellors and governing bodies most commonly focused on performance indicators, quality assurance and rankings. On the other, academics and professional services – as they had to manage the day-to-day business of shared projects with global partner institutions – were more likely to be interested in legal frameworks, organizational governance and academic teaching and research practice than they were in performance indicators and rankings. In a best-case scenario, and where there was good top-to-bottom communication between the different layers of the institution, more complex understanding of the global field by the top echelons of the university existed that strengthened the global positioning of the institution. In a worst-case scenario this led to rifts between management, the academic body and professional services, resulting in 'messy' institutional governance.

Finally, our findings show that these internationalization and globalization processes – at least when it comes to the priorities of institutional leadership – are mainly driven by financial considerations, rather than by a wish to be integrated within emerging global higher education structures and networks. Thus, while universities were often ready to condemn the government's marketization of higher education, they were enthusiastic about the market for international students. On the one hand, this might have had to do with the decentralization of decision-making to faculties/colleges, which saw their share of the income from fees as a way of cushioning shortfalls in other income. On the other, international markets were attractive for central university management because they were much less subject to regulation from above, by the state. As a result, one could often see 'split personalities' in senior university officers who were at one and the same time cautious bureaucrats in terms of the basic running of their institution and eager entrepreneurs in sending missions to far-off countries to try to recruit international students, without any evidence that they would turn out to be successful markets. Giving priority to the recruitment of international students often impacted negatively on the governance of universities, bringing pro-vice chancellors for international affairs into privileged positions in relation to other pro-vice chancellors, adopting different standards of management control over overseas activities, the argument being that different standards apply overseas, and the increased demands on central management staff of managing overseas campuses decreasing the time and thought they can expend on their core British operations.

Governance, its conceptualization and globalization

Our evidence suggests that the concept of governance is broadly defined within British higher education, in that it stretches from institutional governance mechanisms, to policy intrusions by the state, to the more indirect modes of regulation and coordination provided by international agencies as well as by partnerships and collaborations initiated by the institutions themselves.

As the first half of this chapter describes, British universities are subject to a network of direct and indirect governance conditions because they are part of an increasingly globalized system but, in practice, their focus is dictated much more by their own immediate operational instincts, which give priority to regarding the international scene as a market to be exploited rather than as an extended global academic community to which they are contributors.

National-level policymakers seem rarely, if ever, to think of and act on governance as a complex and comprehensive issue that comprises both systemic and institutional 'governance', as well as the practices of academic work. So, while scholarly concepts of 'governance' offer broad definitions that can simultaneously reflect on and analyse multiple processes at different levels, practitioners often use narrower and more flexible descriptors for what 'governance' means. Thus, national policymakers usually restrict talk of 'governance' to system-level considerations, claiming that their focus is not on what happens at the institutional or academic practice level. For example, three answers from our interview with a government policymaker, highlight how – depending on context – multiple meanings of 'governance' are implied, mobilized and drawn upon, even by the same person within a brief interview. Our interviewee, when asked to explain his department's use of the term 'landscape' in relation to higher education – a passive word that masked the fact that his department was among the key agents of change that had initiated deep institutional reform – replied with an all-encompassing definition:

> [Our perception of the sector includes] primarily the public bodies that straddle the higher education sector, though I would also probably include, though we have a different relationship with those other bodies that are sector owned, but in a sense you've kind of got universities and colleges, providers, and then sitting across that the landscape is the public bodies, be it the Higher Education Funding Council, the Office for Fair Access what will be the Office for Students, but then also the sector-owned bodies, the Quality Assurance Agency, the Higher Education Statistics Agency, the Universities and Colleges Admissions Service, the Leadership Foundation. And so, the landscape term, in Whitehall language, is describing the interplay and interaction between those various bodies, what their roles and responsibilities are, what their accountability is, what their governance is, how they interact with the sector at large. (28)

Later in the interview, he gave a detailed account of what his department saw as good institutional governance – 'strong leadership in the VC and PVCs ... active engagement with staff, students, academics and the wider university community and the wider community in the locality of the university, and a ... university council that is holding them to account' (29) – but at the same time he also argued that they sought to stay clear of institutional governance as 'we are trying to avoid any kind of description of this is what good looks like' (30). Then, when asked about global and European influences, the interviewee once again took an exclusively system-level perspective and argued that global and European processes had no impact on UK system governance, maintaining this view even though making it clear that the department closely followed key global issues, such as rankings and how they affect: 'the way UK universities ... play into ... wider, global markets'; international quality assurance and how 'degrees hold currency internationally'; and research collaborations across borders and 'the free movement of labour' (31).

Finally, the following statement, from the same interviewee, shows how government policymakers envisaged their intervention in higher education regulatory processes as a routine exercise of decision-making and not at all as an intrusion into the 'governance' of the sector:

> I think there is a longer standing kind of policy recognition that innovation, science, research ... is innately a good thing, is a kind of real strength of the UK's economy, is something that we are starting from a strong base on, and so I don't think that ... the reforms [in the last twenty years] ... changed the direction. What they've done is tweaked, and so moving from the RAE to the REF was a chance to put impact higher up, or moving, kind of giving some more funding here and bit less there, ... trying to get more business collaboration with universities ... but all of that is under the same overall objective, which is science research and innovation is good for the economy, we need more of it, we'd like to be globally more competitive. (32)

This quotation reflects the contradiction between perception and practice: when global competitiveness within the sector is a key concern for the government (and it is prepared to act to maintain and/or improve such competitiveness), it is clear that global processes do impact upon and steer national-level policymaking. This remains the case even if, at the discursive level, this is not acknowledged as influencing governance.

It is important to understand that the way the meanings of 'governance' are used flexibly and interchangeably by national-level policymakers to support their arguments – as shown above – do not necessarily reflect the way state actors think about higher education. Rather, they reflect the way policymakers conceptualize the state's role – and especially its autonomy and authority to act – within the national and international arenas. If observed from this angle, it is easier to see that the *all-encompassing* definition ('landscape') that the policymaker used to describe their involvement within the 'borders' of the nation state created broader possibilities for intervention for the state, while it made the extent of such interventions less visible and direct. On the other hand, when the policymaker used a narrow meaning for governance – implying that governance was exclusively to do with regulatory and legislative processes, not 'steering' or 'soft governance' – he depicted the state as being in control of higher education processes in the international arena. This framing implied that state bodies enjoyed greater sovereignty than they might actually have in transferring global trends into the national arena, or in disrupting their impacts on the higher education system. At the same time, at the level of discourse, such representations also helped frame other actors – for example, mission groups and individual universities – to seem more disempowered than they were, underplaying their role in shaping the international higher education field and the complex multi-layered relationships within it.

Neither British policymakers nor British universities appear to recognize the full extent to which global processes and governance structures impact on their operations and influence their institutions' day-to-day work. And, while British academics are highly efficient in maintaining global research networks and in winning competitive European and international research monies, in many universities the emerging new governance structures and the resulting institutional hierarchies do not support such engagement. So, while at the level of discourse, those in the top echelons of universities argue that they highly value international engagement, when it comes to creating governance structures that could effectively facilitate such global work and outreach, universities often fall short of putting adequate institutional infrastructures behind academics and students. This is so even when the main drivers of these processes are not academic but financial, such as capitalizing on international student fees and winning well-funded research grants. Of more concern, however, is that senior university officials also seem not to be particularly knowledgeable about or connected to the emerging global higher education governance architecture. This puts them at risk for the future because other higher education systems that work with the grain of global regulation and play an active role in its formulation will be better adapted to the world of global competition that is developing.

This chapter set out to describe the complex mix of international regulation and coordination that, in combination, comprises the global governance of higher education. Some commentators argue that current political conditions imply an unwinding of globalization in areas like finance, but our expectation is that it will increase in higher education as the movement of students and collaboration in research across national boundaries increases. This may exercise some constraint on national policymaking, but it will certainly constitute a factor that the nation state and individual universities will need, increasingly, to take account of when formulating policy options.

Notes

1   Until 1967, home and international students were charged the same tuition fees, but the fees for home students were paid by their local education authorities. In 1967 the Treasury persuaded the then secretary of state for education to arbitrarily raise fees for international students to £250. This prompted an explosion of protest and two universities voted not to implement the increase though both fell into line later. It was Treasury pressure again that led to the move to full-cost fees in 1980. Mrs Thatcher was roundly criticized by prime ministers from developing countries at the Commonwealth Prime Ministers Conference in Kuala Lumpur in 1981 for the decision.

2   *Europe and the Global Information Society*, otherwise known as the Bangemann Report, was produced by the European Commission in response to the rapidly changing needs of society in the 'information age'. This was one of the seminal documents of its era, hugely influential for anticipating the knowledge economy paradigm. It made recommendations for implementing and maintaining information infrastructure across Europe: European Commission (1996). *Europe and the Global Information Society – Recommendations to the European Council.* Brussels: European Commission; www.europarl.europa.eu/sides/getDoc.do?pubRef =-//EP//TEXT+REPORT+A4-1996-0244+0+DOC+XML+V0//EN

3   The Lisbon Strategy was the development plan for the European Union's economy, covering 2000–2010. The necessity for change in response to globalization and the increasing ubiquity of a knowledge-driven economy was acknowledged as the impetus for the strategy.

4   The 1998 Sorbonne Declaration, signed in Paris by the education ministers of France, Germany, Italy and the UK, signified a commitment to enhancing mobility and cooperation between European higher education institutions while also promoting mutual recognition of qualifications throughout Europe. It was a precursor to important developments in the internationalization of higher education, such as the Bologna Declaration, the subsequent EHEA, *Sorbonne Joint Declaration – Joint Declaration on Harmonisation of the Architecture of the European Higher Education System*; www.ehea.info/cid100203/sorbonne-declaration-1998.html

5   The Bologna Declaration of 19 June 1999 was a voluntary joint declaration of the
    European ministers of education. It is the formative document of the Bologna
    Process, with 29 initial members, which aimed to establish a EHEA, along with
    a standardized two-cycle system of undergraduate and postgraduate studies,
    comparable terminology and standards and easily transferable qualifications. This
    action has been extremely influential across European higher education, with
    the structure of bachelor, master and doctorate programmes, not to mention the
    European Credit Transfer System (ECTS), being a direct result of this process.

6   The ERA, was established in 2000, and refined and reinforced in the policy
    communication of 2012. It is an initiative of the European Commission and,
    through a network of integrated resources and research programmes, forms a
    research area that is intended to be the research counterpart of the European
    common market. Further expansion and solidification of the ERA is central to the
    Horizon 2020 initiative (see note 7).

7   The establishment of the EHEA in 2010 marked the achievement of the main goal
    of the Bologna Process. Today, the EHEA consists of 48 countries that form an area
    with comparable and transferable higher education systems and qualifications,
    where mobility of staff and students is integral. It should be noted that the EHEA is
    not a product of, or delimited by, membership of the European Union. It consists
    of voluntary member states who are not bound by legal mandates but rather a
    commitment to implement reforms based on common values. Membership is also
    open to organizations, for example, the EUA and ENQA, which act as 'consultative
    members' that help to implement the Bologna Process.

8   'Competence' refers to areas where the EU has authority conferred on it by treaties.
    Under this principle, the EU may only act within the limits of the competences
    conferred upon it by the EU countries in treaties to attain the objectives provided
    therein. Competences not conferred upon the EU in treaties remain with the EU
    countries.

9   Science Europe, 'What is cOALition S?', https://www.coalition-s.org/about/

10 *Horizon 2020*, alternatively referred to as H2020, is the current EU research
    and innovation programme spanning 2014–2020. It is part of the sequence of
    Framework Programmes for Research and Technological Development, often
    referred to as Framework Programmes, or abbreviated as FP1 to FP7, with 'FP8'
    being named 'Horizon 2020'. First introduced in 1984, Framework Programmes
    were created to support and foster research across the ERA, with specific objectives
    and actions varying between funding periods. The scale of H2020 is unprecedented,
    with public funding of nearly €80 billion made available for research and
    innovation, to promote mobility and to further enhance and refine the ERA as a
    single knowledge market. An interim report on *Horizon 2020*, its successes and
    shortfalls, was made available in 2017: European Commission (2018),

Horizon 2020 Interim Evaluation – Maximising the Impact of EU Research and Innovation; https://ec.europa.eu/research/evaluations/index.cfm?pg=h2020evaluation. Work has already begun on Framework 9, otherwise known as Horizon Europe, with an estimated budget of €100 billion: European Commission (2018). *The Commission's proposal for Horizon Europe;* https://ec.europa.eu/info/node/71880

11 European Commission (2018). Smart Specialisation Platform; http://s3platform.jrc. ec.europa.eu; http://s3platform.jrc.ec.europa.eu/what-is-smart-specialisation-

12 Department for Business, Innovation and Skills (2015). *Smart Specialisation – Submission to the European Commission;* www.gov.uk/government/publications/ smart-specialisation-in-england

13 *Education at a Glance* is an annual OECD publication, focusing on the OECD and partner countries. It provides in-depth data and statistics and analysis about education systems, taking into account various indices, for example, performance, output, resources, finances, etc.

14 PISA is an OECD international survey. A test is administered every three years and evaluates over eighty education systems globally by assessing the scientific, mathematical, reading, collaborative problem-solving and financial literacy skills of 15-year-olds.

15 OECD (2017). *Enhancing Higher Education System Performance: Benchmarking Higher Education System Performance;* www.oecd.org/education/skills-beyond-sch ool/benchmarking-higher-education-systems-performance.htm

16 European Commission (2018). European Commission Memo – Q&A: European Tertiary Education Register; http://europa.eu/rapid/press-release_MEMO-14-447_ en.htm; http://risis.eu/data/eter-dataset/

17 EQAR (2018). Database of External Quality Assurance Results – DEQAR; www. eqar.eu/qa-results/deqar-project/

18 www.eurograduate.eu

19 CORDIS (2018). *Fact Sheet – EURITO;* https://cordis.europa.eu/project/rcn/211 945_en.html

20 The IAU, originally created by UNESCO in the 1950s, is a global, membership-based organization involved in trend analysis, publication and advisory services, peer-to-peer learning and global advocacy. The ENQA represents the higher education quality assurance organizations from the members of the EHEA. Its mission is to promote and maintain quality assurance of higher education qualification accreditation. The CHEA is an association of US-based degree-granting higher education institutions. It is an advocate for accreditation and quality assurance at a national level, while also promoting US accreditation internationally through the CIQG. The INQAAHE works with HE organizations involved in quality assurance, including ENQA and CHEA, to promote and advance quality assurance globally.

21 www.oecd.org/unitedkingdom/

22 www.oecd.org/education/imhe/

23 OECD (2015). AHELO Main Study; www.oecd.org/education/skills-beyond-school/ahelo-main-study.htm

24 www.oecd.org/education/skills-beyond-school/ahelo-main-study.htm

25 The EUA represents and supports more than 850 higher education institutions in 48 countries. It serves as forum for European higher education institutions, enabling the dissemination of knowledge regarding best practice and policies. Members include European universities involved in teaching and research, national associations of rectors/presidents and other organizations active in higher education and research. The EUA was formed from a merger between the Association of European Universities and the Confederation of European Union Rectors' Conferences in 2001.

26 Bologna Process Secretariat (2018). EHEA – Consultative Members; www.ehea.info/pid34251/consultative-members.html

27 www.university-autonomy.eu/countries/united-kingdom/; www.university-autonomy.eu/

28 Federal Ministry of Education and Research (2017). Excellence Strategy; www.bmbf.de/en/excellence-strategy-5425.html

29 Shanghai Ranking (2018). *Academic Ranking of World Universities 2018 – Statistics*; www.shanghairanking.com/ARWU-Statistics-2018.html; Shanghai Ranking (2005). *Academic Ranking of World Universities 2005 – Statistics*; www.shanghairanking.com/ARWU-Statistics-2005.html

30 The number of university network organizations is expanding. The following are among the most well-known: League of European Research Universities, Coimbra Group, Universitas 21, World University Network, Compostela Group of Universities, World Cities or the WC2 University Network, and the ASEAN University Network. Evidence of how much the world order is shifting can be illustrated by the recent formation of the Asian Universities Alliance (AUA) (Sharma 2017) (Chao 2017; ACE 2011).

The Strategic Implications of the Changing Governance Structures in British Higher Education

The role of the state

Perhaps the greatest change in the governance of British higher education from the system described by Moodie and Eustace has been in the role of the state. As we said in Chapter 1, in 1974 the position of the state was one of hands-off detachment, respect – even reverence – for university autonomy and a belief, even as the oil crisis struck government finances, that stability should be preserved in the funding of the university system. Forty-five years later the state occupies a dominant position, controlling machinery to monitor performance in research (the Research Excellence Framework (REF) and UK Research and Innovation (UKRI)) and teaching (the Teaching Excellence Framework (TEF)) and dictating tuition fee policy. In England, ministers are easily tempted to intervene over popular issues such as student mental health or grade creep instead of leaving them to university authorities to sort out. Over this period, and particularly since 1992, the state has become a powerful overlord of higher education, while leaving the institutions with only the trappings of their former autonomy. Universities retain operational autonomy (though in Scotland the legislation in respect to membership of university courts might represent a significant exception to this) but substantive autonomy has passed, to a very great extent, to the state or to agencies of the state like the Office for Students (OfS). It is no longer possible to write about governance at the institutional level, as Moodie and Eustace could do, without bringing extensively into play governance at the state level, because the policies of the state are, to a large extent, the determinants of change at the institutional level.

The question must be asked as to whether the state has exercised its new role beneficially towards higher education. The state, after all, especially when some

49.5 per cent of the relevant age group enter higher education, has a legitimate interest in its effectiveness, in its management and in the extent to which its strategic directions accord with the state's needs. The state could also, however, be said to have a duty of care towards higher education and its institutions. The record over the last decade on this seems to be very mixed. For example, on funding, vital for maintaining institutional stability and an ability to plan ahead, the system in England has faced the recommendations of the Browne Review in 2010, which suggested a rise in tuition fees from £3,000 to £12,000, the decision later in the same year, to raise fees to £9,000 (and then to £9,250) followed, only five years after implementation, by the appointment of a new review of the funding system, chaired by Philip Augar. The Parliamentary Select Committee on Education had urged the Augar Committee to be 'brave' in its recommendations, by implication to seek to overturn the funding structure established in 2010 (House of Commons Education Committee 2018: para 16). In practice the published report (for the main recommendations on higher education see pages 28–9) is timid not brave, attempting to meet criticisms of the student contribution by tinkering with the details of the scheme that are likely to please some but spark dissent in others. Of more interest from a governance standpoint are the extent to which – if implemented – it would reintroduce direct state control over the sector in respect to guarantees over the teaching grant, the variations in its size depending on subject cost, and the possibility of imposing restrictions on access to higher education on grounds of low qualifications – all issues of acute financial and academic interest within higher education. If a major responsibility of government is to create the stable conditions in which good academic work can be done, these changes of heart over funding policy undermine the ability of institutions to plan their futures and encourage hand-to-mouth short-termism.

This sense of instability has increased with the decision to remove institutional limits on home student numbers, leaving some institutions exposed to shortfalls that threaten their financial security. The statement by the chair of OfS, in line with the remit given to the OfS by the government, shows no sympathy for these institutions' position:

> This kind of thinking – not unlike the 'too big to fail' idea among the banks – will lead to poor decision-making and a lack of financial discipline, is inconsistent with the principle of university autonomy and is not in students' long term interests. ... We expect universities to develop realistic plans for the future which reflect likely student demand for their courses and how best they can meet that demand. Should a university or other higher education provider find themselves at risk of closure our role will be to protect students' interests and we

will not hesitate to intervene to do so. We will not step in to prop up a failing provider. (Adams 2018b)

The overall impact of such statements, and of interventions from ministers, is to convey a sense of hostility towards the university system rather than of understanding and support.

There is also a sense in England, though not in Wales or Northern Ireland and only spasmodically in Scotland, that party politics and political ideology have explicitly driven state policy in a way that has not happened before. When Keith Joseph launched his Green Paper, *The Development of Higher Education into the 1990s*, in 1985, it was almost universally excoriated for its forecasts on student numbers and its apparent subordination of the universities to economic interests, but it was not generally viewed as a political but as a Treasury-driven document. When Ken Clarke abolished the binary line and upgraded the polytechnics to universities, many critics were uncomfortable with the implications, but the majority's feeling was that it was an egalitarian, modernizing, policy that rectified past government mistakes. When the Blair government brought forward its proposals to raise tuition fees to up to £3,000 in 2003, opposition was based on the principle of charging higher fees and the government's case was made on the benefit to the higher education system. But the inclusion of the precursor ideas for the TEF in the Tory Party Manifesto, the appointment of a 'free schools' advocate to the membership of the OfS, the radical loosening of the regulations governing the establishment of alternative providers and, above all, the explicit adoption of a neo-liberal market policy for the management and control of higher education, reflected a partisan politicization of policy that sets precedents that other governments may be tempted to follow. Whereas the state in England was previously politically neutral and largely Treasury driven in its policies towards higher education, we now have policies that are ideologically charged, which can be seen seeping down into the governance of university institutions so that both students and staff, in some universities, are put into a position of moral hazard. The elimination of an independent intermediary body, a 'buffer' like the University Grants Committee (UGC) or even the Higher Education Funding Council for England (HEFCE), makes this all the more threatening for the longer-term future of the higher education system.

Whether or not there was a need for a teaching counterweight to the REF that could not be achieved by reforming the Quality Assurance Agency (QAA) and the external examiner system, the creation of the TEF and the removal of the REF to the UKRI puts the two key levers of academic work in universities potentially within reach of any government willing to use them. Strategically this offers a threat to the future vitality of the university system and should encourage the system to create stronger machinery than it presently has in order to maintain its independence, much as Scotland has sought to do through Universities Scotland (see Chapter 3).

The fact of devolution gives one the opportunity to compare four different systems, all governed under the same authority in 1992. The fees issue presents an obvious example of the fragmentation of a unified system, but a more interesting comparison lies in the contrasting academic cultures that have resulted. Wales and Scotland, the latter in spite of the Scottish government's intervention over the constitution of the university court, seem to have maintained academic morale in a way that England, definitely the outlier in policy of the four, has not. Where market forces are driving greater institutional inequality in England, the combination of apparently greater cultural affinities between institutions in Scotland, the refusal to accept the concept of 'teaching only' universities and the absence of a divisive tuition fee system has produced a more collegial style of governance. The contrasts are less clear-cut in Wales, which is more integrated with its much larger neighbour across the border, but even here the closer relationship between ministers, civil servants and the institutions themselves seems to make for a much less abrasive and more mutually supportive set of relationships than can be found in England. England has, perhaps, something to learn from its devolved siblings.

Higher education and the market

David Willetts, in his book *A University Education*, argues that a higher education system should 'rest on competition and choice' and goes on to state his belief 'that greater market competition leads universities to focus more on the classic quality of the academic experience' (Willetts 2017: 277). As minister, he saw 'taking most of higher education out of public spending' (that is, creating a tuition fee-funded higher education system in England) and removing 'direct controls set by government on student numbers university by university' (removing the cap) as 'the prize' in establishing a marketized system (Willetts 2017: 85). Both legs of the policy are controversial. With regard to the former, the government itself, or perhaps just the Treasury, seems to have lost confidence in the funding system adopted in 2010, while the latter appears to be destabilizing a substantial part of the English higher education provision. The problem with the arbitrary removal of the cap – 'these absurd controls' as Willetts calls them (Willetts 2017: 86) – is that no one foresaw the rate and the scale of the student number realignments that would occur or the extent to which it would benefit one type of institution, the large, research-intensive universities that had historic advantages in reputation and location, and would penalize newer institutions, those less research active, and those that served largely local catchment areas. Conspiracy theorists might find it difficult to believe that no one anticipated this result. The consequence is that nearly all universities' governing bodies have developed a close and, in some vulnerable institutions, an obsessive interest, in recruitment statistics to the exclusion of other important issues. Even in well-established and secure institutions, recruitment now engages attention right up through the governance structure because, in uncertain times, shortfalls in a given department may lead to immediate demands for the axe to fall to protect the costs being attributed to a whole school or faculty. In universities where numbers have fallen substantially, the consequences have mostly been to increase the concentration of power in the executive but also to make them more vulnerable to cross-examination and intervention by the governing body. All too often such institutions have compounded their difficulties by borrowing to pay for new buildings to improve their recruitment image only to find themselves falling squarely in the group of institutions defined in the OfS chairman's description, above.

Chapter 5 reports some of the academic consequences: the dominance of marketing departments in programme design, and the imposition from the top of new course structures aimed at capitalizing on modular course menus. Academic standards become at risk. But these are probably less significant than the loss of staff morale and the climate of concern that can percolate through institutions that struggle with recruitment problems. There is no research evidence in higher education that market competition on its own raises standards, as Browne claims in his 2010 Report and Willetts in his book. On the contrary, market forces may not necessarily actually shake out individual weak institutions but could have the effect of weakening a whole category of institutions that are heavily dependent on the student market and could not have been expected to forecast the impact that the removal of the cap would make. The risk is that recruitment becomes the major priority for governing bodies, to the exclusion of the protection of promising lines of research, to the establishment of a climate that deflects attention from the need to invest in academic innovation and that concentrates on institutional survival rather than on progress and development. In all this the sufferers will be the students whose interests the OfS is pledged to protect.

The creation of a market implies the existence of customers and the OfS, in spite of the strictures of the National Audit Office (NAO 2017b), has embraced this definition of the student component of it. But the problem is that the student body does not think or behave like this. Our evidence (see Chapter 4) suggests overwhelmingly that students see themselves largely as participants in a learning environment and generally only revert to consumer-driven language when they have real grievances they wish to articulate. Indeed, the only student leader who spoke the unadulterated language of the market, did so in circumstances where the objections to the power of a market philosophy are most obvious, where an institution that had been severely weakened by recruitment problems, arising essentially from the removal of the cap, was forced to concede an academic issue for fear of losing students to other local institutions. Partly, perhaps, as a result of pressure exerted by the National Student Survey, students are now deeply embedded in institutional course committee structures and can have a decisive voice in curricular matters. If this does not bear fruit, their officers have regular direct access to senior officers of the university. In most universities, teaching has become very much a partnership between the teachers and the taught, rather than a matter of the application of market principles. In practice, there has been a quasi-market for admissions since the Universities Central Council for Admissions (UCCA) became operational in 1964, giving applicants up to five choices of university listed in order of preference, with the universities having freedom of selection constrained only by the overall student number target for which they were funded. The Tory government's higher education market, on the other hand, represents a neo-liberal artificial construct that extends the idea of an admissions market to an enveloping market philosophy. Even at the admissions stage the concept of a pure market is confused by the very different aspirations of applicants – fear of debt through living away from home, trust in the student grapevine, preference for individual university locations including proximity to home, commitment to a particular discipline or ambition to attend a particular kind of university. (The Sutton Trust calculates that 25 per cent of students live at home and commute to their university (Donnelly and Gamsu 2018).) On the other side, institutions differ in their size, their history, their range of degrees, their locations, their reputations and league table ranking, as well as in their social and economic importance to their region or locality. Decisions on the shape of higher education and institutional futures should not be taken simply on the basis of the happenstance of market forces deriving from an ill-constructed market, but on the basis of mature judgements formed by a reconstructed OfS, working in close concert with Research England to ensure that teaching and research factors are considered together, and working, as necessary, with the funding councils in Wales and Scotland to ensure that regional issues and border overlaps are taken into account. The resulting conclusions should be transmitted in published form to the appropriate minister so that the policy issues are available for public scrutiny. Students, staff, governing bodies and regional interests deserve no less.

For-profit higher education

A further example of the Tory government's explicitly political approach to the governance of higher education can be found in the facilitation it provided for the entry of the alternative providers into the higher education market. The arguments for the policy were three-fold: the first was that, in an expanding market, the extension of private higher education would take some of the burden off public higher education institutions; the second was that, by making a condition that the eligibility of home students in private higher education depended on tuition fees charged at no more than £6,000, it automatically brought down the average total debt arising out of the student loans policy and also provided a useful benchmark against which the more expensive tuition fees for public universities could be compared; the third was more political: that there were significant numbers of financial groups keen to generate profits from an expanding higher education sector and there was a need to provide a 'level playing field' for them to enter the field. As we have seen in Chapter 2, two different types of private higher education institution emerged, one type operated as a charity (the long-standing Buckingham and the newer Regent's University), but the more common type was the for-profit, private equity-financed institutions (BPP University, the University of Law and the Greenwich School of Management being examples).

We noted in Chapter 2, that the removal of the cap on student numbers in the public institutions may have been influenced by the near impossibility of persuading the government's coalition partners to allow any expansion of numbers of home students in private institutions to make them financially viable. It is clear from the regulations that the OfS intends to encourage an increasing number of alternative providers by relaxing the norms that have previously applied in the sector. Thus, an institution may be given powers to award its own degrees on a probationary basis as soon as it is registered; institutions are not required to have a track record of delivering higher education to be registered but can qualify by demonstrating financial viability and sound business plans; institutions do not need to have 1,000 higher education students to achieve a university title; new providers do not have to meet the requirements of the Committee of University Chairmen's (CUC's) code of governance, which are said to be designed for larger universities, but must only demonstrate compliance with its main principles; new providers' registration fees may be subsidized by the OfS for a limited period; if there is difficulty in finding a validating partner for a degree programme the OfS could enter into a validation contract with an established institution on behalf of the provider or even, if authorized by the secretary of state, act as the validator itself.

What can have prompted such a blatant disregard of basic caution in creating these exemptions? Was it internal political pressures or simply naivety? David Willetts sees the new alternative providers as parallels of the 1960s new universities and writes: 'I believe that they will be recognised as the next wave of creation of new universities in the great English tradition' (Willetts 2017: 285). It is hard to account for such a delusion. It is difficult to believe that the government was not aware of the warning provided in the report, *For Profit Higher Education: The Failure to Safeguard the Federal Investment and Ensure Student Success* submitted to the US Senate in 2012 (Committee on Health Education, Labour and Pensions 2012), with its scathing criticism of the lack of regulation of the growth of US for-profit higher education. The US openness to for-profit providers was, after all, one of the models for the British higher education market. (One of the owners most criticized by the independent inspectors despatched by the Obama administration to review the institutions was also the owner of one of the British alternative providers granted a university title.) In 2017 the NAO reported that the wastage rate at thirty reviewed British alternative providers at 25 per cent was 15 per cent higher than the HEFCE average for the sector, and that the institutions concerned had lower rates of progression into employment and lower salaries than the average for graduates from HEFCE institutions (NAO 2017b). None has pretensions to be described as research active. The sector as a whole, with the exception of institutions based very clearly on pre-established professional qualifications, looks destined to constitute the lowest tier in the British higher education hierarchy.

The encouragement for the development of for-profit higher education institutions can be questioned on a number of grounds. The first is that the monitoring process imposed on the OfS to ensure that the exemptions to its regulatory regime quoted above are defensible and justifiable is out of all proportion to the contribution that the institutions themselves make to home student numbers and is open to backstairs pressure. A second is that for-profit higher education involves a financial risk in a less calculable way than for public higher education. Most for-profit institutions are financed through private equity investment, which generates its profit through adding financial value to the institution and then selling it on, normally after a period of four or five years. The private equity industry, which has grown very considerably over the last two decades, has benefitted from the low interest rates that have been a feature of the period of austerity since 2007, because in targeting growth rates – in some cases of at least three times the original investment – it has attracted substantial investment from pension funds seeking higher returns than are available elsewhere in the market. These conditions may not persist. Already, according to the *Financial Times* (Espinoza 2018a and b). the proportion of 'winning deals' is in sharp decline and the record of the University of Phoenix, owned by Apollo, and the reputation of the British for-profit institutions may make higher education projects more difficult to sell as investment vehicles. The financial performance of the Greenwich School of Management, which reported a £9 million deficit for 2016–17 represents a case in point (Morgan 2018). Moreover, the disruption when ownership changes occur, even though potentially mitigated by a requirement, imposed by HEFCE, that this should be followed by an external governance review, can interrupt business planning and set back institutional progress.

But a third ground for questioning is whether teaching and awarding degrees for financial profit is ever justifiable in the British higher education context. Primarily this is because the ultimate financial priority imposed by the fiscal conditions on which the governance of the institution is inescapably based may not be consistent with the academic and pedagogic priorities that are integral to university value systems. All universities, whether public or private, must balance financial constraints with academic priorities, but to make profitability the dominant institutional concern, as it must be in a private equity context, however much it is hedged around with academic caveats, is to threaten the academic integrity of the operation. It is no accident that one of the many criticisms of the for-profit higher education sector made by the US Senate Report is that the admission of students had become 'a sales process' in which the staff's salaries were tied to enrolment performance (US Senate Committee 2012: 4), precisely the finding of the BBC Panorama programme on one of the British for-profit universities (BBC News 2017) (and paralleled by one of our case study public universities facing shortfalls in the student market). Our research shows that for-profit institutions have very small governing bodies that are closely linked to the board of the private equity investor, with no internal academic representation, and that academic participation in governance even at an academic board level is minimal. Policy is handled between a chief executive officer of the private investor board and the vice chancellor, and external academics are often engaged to offer guarantees of academic standards and to advise on QAA and other processes. A very low proportion of teachers hold full-time academic posts. Governance structures bear token resemblance to those of well-established public universities, but are, in practice, much more aligned to business. Our conclusion is that there should be an extended pause in the further establishment of for-profit higher education institutions while the performance of the present group can be assimilated and for lessons to be learned. OfS review mechanisms should be alert to difficulties and swift to act if evidence of malpractice emerges in order to protect the reputation of the university system as a whole.

Is university governance fit for purpose?

This was a question asked of every university chair and vice chancellor or principal we interviewed, and we were surprised, bearing in mind the significant changes in the higher education environment, that only one, a chair, responded with a positive proposal for change. Mostly the responses were that, although not altogether satisfactory, the current arrangements were best left unchanged. This could be interpreted as a reluctance born of a concern as to who might institute change – probably the government or some government-appointed commission, an expectation entirely understandable looked at from a Scottish perspective – or as the result of a lack of much serious thinking about the direction of change in the external environment. This does not mean that governance structures have not evolved – the variety is striking within a broadly common model – but the evidence suggests that most changes resulted, not from extensive review, but for adventitious or short-term reasons. Thus, in the past, and certainly before 1992, it was a cardinal principle of the bicameral structure that senates were represented on university governing bodies, with academic representation amounting to up to a third of the total membership. The argument for this was that, in the event of the prospect of a lay governing body being tempted to reject a recommendation from the senate, it was necessary to ensure that the vice chancellor, as chair of the senate, was well supported in defending the senate's recommendation. Nowadays the position is reversed, with moves to reduce or weaken academic representation in order not to have potentially discordant voices confusing the message that the vice chancellor and his/her executive wish to deliver to the governing body.

As one of our interviewees, an experienced practitioner of governing body effectiveness reviews, told us, in some universities academic representation had descended to 'a form of tokenism' (1). In others, subtle adjustments had been made in the constitutional arrangements to reduce academic influence. At one pre-1992 university, where there were four academics elected onto the governing body from different constituencies within the institution, three were senior lecturers not necessarily familiar with the detail of university business and were, therefore, not effective in representing academic opinions on complex issues. At another, senior professors were identified by the governing body's nominations committee, but were not subject to nomination by the senate. At a post-1992 university, which had two places on its governing body reserved for academic representation to be filled by election by and from the academic staff as a whole, the governing body acted to avoid this representation being dominated by trade-union interests by inviting applications for the positions for the nominations committee to interview and select the successful candidates. All these examples, and many others, contribute to the distancing of senates and academic boards from the headline decision-making that defines a university's future, often leaving it to take place essentially between the vice chancellor, the executive and a governing body, the latter meeting only infrequently during the year.

While the post-1992 universities have always had unicameral constitutions, it looks very much as if there is a common effort to neutralize, if not eliminate, the bicameral structure from the pre-1992 universities and to reduce the academic input accordingly. This raises the important question as to whether governing bodies have sufficient expertise, understanding of higher education and background institutional knowledge either to control and direct the executive or to reach informed decisions of their own. There is not much evidence that they have. In the one area where one might have expected external professional experience to have made an essential contribution, the control of executive salaries, their decision-making has been at best limp and ineffective, and has damaged the sector's reputation in Whitehall and with the public. A more recent concern of the OfS about grade inflation now falls under their responsibility for maintaining academic standards, but it is a measure of the way they are regarded, and particularly as to their competence in academic areas, that nobody has suggested that they should be called upon to act on the issue. A question at interview about institutional European or international strategies received responses from chairs such as 'not my forte' or 'not on my radar', effectively washing their hands of involvement in such issues. Yet overseas campuses, inter-institutional partnerships and the market for international students represent one of the highest long-term risks on which governing bodies might reasonably have been expected to exercise a critical scrutiny of executive forecasts.

Most governing bodies meet four or five times a year, the fifth meeting being sometimes a special strategy meeting, with committee meetings occurring in between or sometimes on the day of the main meeting if governors do not live locally. Many members, coming with a PLC corporate governance background, naturally expect to play a more hands-on role than they are permitted to do and are surprised to find business carried out by an executive separately from the board. Indeed, they quickly realize that they are dependent on the executive team as their major source of information and advice. A further weakness is the ambiguity, outlined in Chapter 4, in the roles of an assertive chair and an ambitious chief executive. The old assumption, current in the early 1990s, that one difference between the pre- and post-1992 universities was that where, in a pre-1992 university, the chair and the vice chancellor could not get on the chair resigned, but where the chair and the vice chancellor of a post-1992 could not get on, the vice chancellor had to go, is no longer valid (2). In this, as in other matters of governance, the two sides of the former binary line have drawn much closer together, and the increased pressures of accountability, financial, academic and from governance requirements, bear equally heavily on both sides.

The chairs of governing bodies have a representative body, the Committee of University Chairmen, but this is a body for mutual encouragement that sees itself primarily as providing support for its chief executives and their representative body, Universities UK (UUK). Their public or political impact has been negligible, even during the period when outrage at vice chancellors' salaries was at its height. The idea that governing bodies can act as the real strategic and controlling organ of a university is a pipe-dream born of misunderstood analogies with corporate governance in business and the government's fond hope that lay governors might prove to be more supportive of, or malleable towards, its own policies than the academic community might be.

This leads directly to the one proposal we encountered for an alternative form of governance. It should be added that the proposer was an energetic public figure with an academic and government background. His starting point was 'whether the governance system of British universities has adjusted to the changes in the market situation facing universities … it's much more like running a business than it used to be' (3). His concern was that the governing body was not constructed, and did not behave like, a board and his proposition was that it should be replaced by a smaller body made up of the vice chancellor and selected senior executives, with a limited number of laymen serving as non-executives, in other words a body operating like a corporate board with the executive team of pro-vice chancellors serving as its executive members and lay members providing the challenge as non-execs. Under pressure, he agreed, he would retain the senate. One effect, of course, would be that much of the business conducted now by the executive would become board business and the board would need to meet more frequently than the governing body does at present.

Our view is that while the proposed structure addresses one of the current weaknesses, the need for quick decision-making in market conditions, it opens up the possibility of serious downsides: pro-vice chancellors with an academic background might soon be replaced by professional officers responsible for finance or estates, so that an academic input into governance at the highest levels could be reduced or lost altogether; lay non-executives would almost certainly have to become fee-based posts because of the time and responsibility involved, just as they are in PLC corporate governance; consideration would need to be given to how student and academic staff interests could be represented and to the implications for the retention of charitable status; the role of the senate would inevitably change and the academic voice of teachers and researchers in governance would be seriously reduced.

The 'business model' favoured by successive governments and by civil servants does not work for universities and is under challenge in corporate governance in commerce and industry as being too simplistic (Mayer 2018). Universities' corporate purpose is not to enhance shareholder value; they do not have shareholders in the fiduciary sense but they do have stakeholders in the shape of students, employers, industry, government and the public services. Governing bodies are not the 'owners' nor can they be described as the 'principal agents'. In practice they exercise a role not unlike that of non-executive directors, except that their boards are made up of only a minority – in some governing bodies a tiny minority – of executive member equivalents (the vice chancellor, selected members of the executive group or representatives of senate). The boards also contain students, for whom no analogy exists with company boards, and, in post-1992 universities, elected staff members. The theme of Mayer's disagreement with Milton Friedman's thesis – that the prime purpose of a company is to make profits for the shareholder – is that companies have wider purposes, social, economic or simply enhancing the business. By the same token a university set of purposes would not primarily be to make a financial surplus, though that might represent an important component, but would relate variously to excellence in teaching and research, widening participation, local economic regeneration, international collaboration and so forth. The 'business model' of university governance excludes or minimizes the role of decision-making of just those whose responsibility is to develop and deliver on these purposes in favour of external non-executive board members meeting only four or five times a year. Because company purposes are so diverse, Mayer argues that uniform corporate governance codes may inhibit company performance and 'exacerbate rather than mitigate risks of failures spreading across countries and companies' (Mayer 2018: 115). The same argument may be applied to the CUC's Higher Education Governance Code, the accepted model for university governance, which prioritizes the role of governing bodies at the expense of senates and academic boards, to whose statutory responsibilities it makes only a single reference. It conveniently forgets to mention that Britain's two most successful universities in world league table terms are entirely academically self-governed and have no lay governing bodies at all.

In assessing whether university governance structures are fit for purpose, our preference would be not to dismantle the bicameral structure, which represents the traditional model for universities in the UK, but to recognize it as a sui generis form of governance appropriate to institutions of higher learning whose core business is teaching and research and to make it work better. In the current conditions of the increased size of institutions and of competition and financial instability, the rise of an executive group within each university is an inevitable development and the issue is not to constrain it but how to make it accountable, not just to the governing body, but to the academic community. We would reverse the recent trend to make appointments to senior academic/managerial posts almost automatically to people from outside the institution, but draw more, as in industry, on talent within so that the post-holders are firmly embedded in the organizational culture of the institution, going outside for an appointment only when the culture was somehow dysfunctional. And we would require the executive to report to the senate or academic board as well as to the governing body. This would help senates and academic boards to re-engage with institutional policymaking. A major step, in the post-1992 universities, would be to restore the power of academic boards, which they lost in the 1988 legislation, to take part in planning and strategy on the grounds that these institutions are now mature bodies that would be improved by the provision of greater formal academic input into policy. We would want to reinforce the academic voice in both senates and academic boards both to rekindle the sense of academic citizenship that may have been partly lost in the developments of the last two decades and to give space to creativity and innovation even at the cost of, as some would think, some short-term inefficiencies, in order to stimulate academic performance.

The academic community

It cannot be said too often that the prime business of a university is teaching and research, and that a university's reputation is dependent on its academic performance in one or in both of those activities. It follows that the most important task of governance, among many, is to provide the conditions in which good academic work can thrive. For this to be achieved, academics need to be at the heart of university governance, not, as in some institutions, at the periphery. This calls for a revival of the role of senates and academic boards and the incorporation of their ideas into strategic decision-making; the subordination of advice from the executive to the governing body to scrutiny and comment by the senate or academic board; and the strengthening of the representation of senate or academic boards on the governing body. For this to be effective, senates in some universities would need to be reduced in size for manageable discussions and responses to take place. The directive from HEFCE, that henceforward governing bodies should be responsible for the quality of education in their institutions, should be rescinded so that accountability is returned to where it de facto belongs, with senates and academic boards. At best the present situation encourages unnecessary bureaucracy, but at worst it extends the nominal responsibilities of governing bodies far beyond their capacity to meet them. Machinery for approving salary increases for vice chancellors and other senior academic officers should always include some senior academic colleagues who, it can be anticipated, will be much more realistic in their opinions than their lay colleagues. The last two decades have seen a downgrading of the perception of senior academics' capabilities in management and decision-making, forgetting the demands made on their skills in running multimillion-pound departmental enterprises, managing major research grants or advising industry or government on significant policy initiatives, and in being required to make fine-grained, objective, professional judgements over colleagues of national or international distinction. This is not in any way to disparage what laymen bring to the table as is well described by the chair of a Scottish university court in Chapter 3 (see p. 58). They may be summarized as giving technical and professional advice, acting as a critical friend, refereeing internal arguments, representing the public interest, reading the external environment, taking the long view and, most important, appointing the vice chancellor. As our interviewer, quoted above in this chapter, told us:

> I think universities are extraordinarily lucky in being able to get people to do this sort of role without huge difficulty … generally you can get people of high distinction with a great variety of experience that are willing to give up their time to do it. (4)

Indeed, what it emphasizes is the value of 'shared governance' where external lay thinking can be brought together with high-level expertise in the best interests of the university.

Over the last decade two changes to the university environment have brought with them sharp changes to institutional governance, which have had severe impacts on internal academic cultures and on the conduct of academic work. Neither is easy to roll back. The first is the climate of uncertainty, which has particularly infected higher education in England, but which has also affected higher education in Wales, Scotland and Northern Ireland. Partly, this is related to policies on tuition fees, but in England it has been accentuated by an explicit imposition of a market structure, through tuition fees and the removal of the cap on numbers, onto a higher education system that had previously been essentially centrally managed. This has led to a hardening of hierarchies in institutions, an overwhelming centralization of decision-making and the substitution of a regime of top-down directives in place of consultation and discussion, which is changing the character of academic life. Moreover, in spite of the apparent affluence of many universities, fuelled by the tuition fee regime, the proportion of teaching given by staff hired on short-term casual bases or by postgraduates and postdoctoral researchers is growing at an unhealthy rate creating a subclass of university teachers who are not enfranchised to play a part in institutional governance. There is a need to restore academic governance at intermediary levels between senates/academic boards and departments/schools of study, that have often been swept aside to reinforce the powers of executive deans, so that professional authority is restored to the academic community for the conduct of the academic programme. These actions would do much to restore the morale of the academic community even in the circumstances of a reduction of tuition fee income and a resumption of austerity. They would also help to ensure that a greater balance was restored between top-down and bottom-up governance, that the bureaucracy that invariably accompanies governance by directives would be reduced, and that the open climate of internal consultation and debate, which is an essential requirement for the encouragement of new approaches to teaching and new avenues of research, would be reinforced. Levels of autonomy at the individual pedagogical and research levels have slipped considerably in many universities and must be restored if British universities are to maintain their reputation for creativity and innovation.

The student voice

The kind of academic culture outlined above offers a great deal more to the student experience than formal meetings because it encourages students to take part in the debate. A senate or academic board that is actively considering institutional policy issues is much more stimulating to take part in than one that is restricted to approving curriculum changes and routine amendments to academic administration. The procedure we found in some universities, where the students' union president wrote a report for each meeting of the governing body, appears to be an effective way of ensuring that institutional issues between the students' union and the university are identified at an early stage. The regular meetings between university officers, including the vice chancellor, and union officers, which seem to take place in all institutions, provide an admirable framework for working in partnership, as do the parallel arrangements for close consultation at the academic programme level described in Chapter 4. These arrangements do not speak to the concept of students as customers but to students as engaged participants and as co-learners in the world of higher education. This does not mean they do not have rights, does not mean that a student does not have entitlements, but reflects that students are now intimately involved in what is taught, how it is taught and what the outcomes might be. UCAS procedures may imply the existence of a market but once an applicant enrols as a student they become, as provided for in the statutes of many pre-1992 universities, a member of the corporation. The student has become accepted as an important and routine component of university governance.

The global environment

Research conducted by Ellen Hazelkorn, and reported on in Chapter 6, emphasizes the extent to which European, international and global agencies and networks regulate or influence British higher education. Such forces have in many ways reshaped our institutions involving building many more student residences, the creation of international partnerships, the development of overseas campuses, the establishment of large international offices, the designation of senior academics as pro-vice chancellors (international) and the dependence on international students' tuition fees to support institutional development. At the same time our research has made us aware of the extent to which British universities, at the senior levels of their governance, appear to be disconnected from participation or even from basic understanding of the contexts that these regulations and influences provide. This is much less true of the academic community, particularly those heavily involved in research, who are very well informed and sensitive to the regimes laid down by international, especially the EU, agencies in respect to research collaboration and how it is funded. Major research groups carefully monitor policy changes, position themselves to take advantage of them and make it their business to be involved in the relevant decision-making processes. This disconnect at the top of university governance structures is dangerous. It is fuelled by a strong sense of Britain's historic high standing in world higher education rankings without recognizing that other countries are engaged in reform programmes that will challenge that position. Complacency and insularity are reinforced by the worldwide growth in the international student market, of which Britain has been a prime beneficiary. Indeed, the attraction of globalization for some higher levels of university governance and management has not been the academic value of networking, the research partnerships and collaborations, the engagements with a wider intellectual community, but the commercial benefits of franchising degree programmes to foreign institutions, contracts with overseas recruitment agents, the fact that international students can be charged tuition fees of up to 50 per cent more than British students, and the entrepreneurial enterprise in establishing outposts or campuses overseas, all fuelled by competition for resources at home.

It is time to redress the imbalance. The increasing development of global regulation in higher education, the growing reform of the governance of continental European university systems to give institutions greater operational autonomy, and the substantial investment in selected groups of institutions around the world, all spell a continued escalation of international competition. If British higher education is to retain its brand it needs to play an altogether larger role in this global architecture. Institutions that nourish global ambitions, whether in teaching or research, or both, need to engage in professionally well-informed strategizing about their international ambitions and how they integrate them with their long-term aims and objectives. Regarding international students' tuition fees simply as the cash cow that keeps the university out of financial difficulty will not be sufficient to maintain league table positions in the future.

Policymaking

Present national governance arrangements for higher education are defective in that they provide too much rein to pronouncements by ministers, which often reflect short-term pressures and the need to create a political profile in departments, which do not immediately command much public interest. They are also flawed because the two key functions of the institutions that deliver higher education, research and teaching, are split between two government organizations, the UKRI and the OfS. In England the minister is expected to play a coordinating role, and holds appointments in both departments, but the spread of those functions and the rapid turnover of ministers combine to make it more likely that the minister will concentrate on short-term issues rather than longer-term concerns about the viability or well-being of institutions or of the higher education system. They are also at the mercy of the Treasury and the Public Expenditure Survey (Shattock 2016). In Wales and Scotland, while ministers have close relations with the institutions, responsibility for research is essentially subject to UKRI control. We believe it is dangerous to rely on a single minister in England to knit together the two aspects of higher education for this purpose and we suggest that cross-membership between the OfS and Research England, as well as formal arrangements for close administrative relationships between the staff of the two bodies, would give greater security. Where issues about individual institutions arise, particularly where the future of an institution is in question, we think that decisions should be taken jointly. Advocates of a pure market philosophy will argue that the sector would learn from the OfS conducting an entirely hands-off policy in relation to an institution that had grossly under-recruited or which was unable to meet borrowing requirements, but its care for the student interest is bound to involve it in the interstices of the institution's management plight. Such an institution might, however, have small peaks of research where it would be in Research England's interest for them to be maintained, whether by propping the institution up, or by advising a merger where comparable research interests are followed or by simply funding the transfer of the research to a more congenial environment.

The most difficult problem for higher education over the last decade has been the instability of the political and funding environment and the uncertainty that this has caused within institutions. There seems to be little sign that this will change in the short term. Bringing the OfS and Research England closer together would make some contribution to greater stability and might help to ensure that there is an institutional as well as a 'provider' focus in national decision-taking, but it would only be one step.

A further step would be for the representative bodies of the different mission groups to collaborate more closely in addressing government. It is generally acknowledged that UUK has lost its standing in Westminster and Whitehall, as the mission groups, particularly the Russell Group, have developed individual policy networks and policies that reflect their own particular interests. But this has weakened their policy clout. There will always be issues of individual mission group concern that justify separate approaches to government, but these groups' interests are mostly more connected than they might first seem and a pooling of representation of the four groups with UUK itself might provide a more effective representation to government on broader higher education interests. On many issues they would also benefit from joining forces with the National Union of Students (NUS).

The net effect of establishing, through the fees policy and the removal of the cap, that the governance of the sector was to be determined by the market should have in theory removed the government from a policy-formation role except in relation to research. In practice, however, ministers continued to seek to influence the market with, for example, the introduction of the TEF at institutional and now disciplinary levels. What this also achieved was a fundamental break with the past where government saw itself as having, in addition to a policy-formation role, a responsibility for the support and the future of higher education, what we called earlier in this chapter a duty of care. Anyone reading John Major's autobiography, in respect to the granting of university status to the polytechnics (Major 1999: 212), or Tony Blair's account of his dinner with members of the Russell Group about the need to invest more in higher education in order to compete with foreign competition (Blair 2010: 483) must be impressed by the extent to which two successive prime ministers were concerned for higher education and its future well-being when compared with later governments' strategy of letting higher education sink or swim at the mercy of market forces.

Perhaps the most pressing issue of governance is to provide stability to the sector, relieve the recurrent sense of uncertainty that besets institutions and remove the concern that they are potentially 'at risk'. Good governance and good academic work require conditions of stability or, if the environment changes adversely, that a safety net exists to help institutions adapt and that the government will be sufficiently concerned to act on their behalf. British universities have shown their resilience over the years, but the instability of the governance regime, especially since 2010, can only prejudice their academic performance in an internationally competitive environment.

A century ago, at the end of the First World War, the universities and the government were wrestling with the problem of the role of the state in the funding of universities. There was a view that universities should not be over-dependent on tuition fees, as many were, and that the state should play a greater role in their funding. This appears to have been accepted both by the chancellor of the exchequer of the day, Bonar Law, and by the president of the Board of Education, Geoffrey Fisher. The latter, in his summing up speech at a meeting with all the universities, both supported the need for the state to make a solid contribution to universities' budgets but also emphasized the importance of maintaining university autonomy (Taylor 2018: 154). This set in place the essential architecture for the governance of British higher education until the funding reforms of 2010 and the legislation of 2017, although it remains still broadly in place in Wales, Scotland and Northern Ireland. It has undoubtedly been an enormously important factor in the comparative standing internationally of British higher education. We have, however, seen a clear loss of autonomy in system governance, a considerable narrowing of autonomy in institutional governance and a significant diminution of individual professional autonomy. Unless these losses are reversed, it will be surprising if they are not reflected over time in institutional rankings and the standing of the British system in the global world of higher education.

References

(References from anonymized interview transcripts)

Chapter 2

(1) A.10.1
(2) A.10.1
(3) A.5.4
(4) A.1.5
(5) A.1.10
(6) 8.6.3

Chapter 3

(1) A.14.1
(2) 10.2.2
(3) A.13.19
(4) A.14.2.2
(5) A.14.2.2
(6) A.14.12
(7) A.14.13
(8) A.14.10
(9) 2.4.7
(10) 10.7.8
(11) A.15.17
(12) A.16.2
(13) 11.4.13
(14) 11.1.3
(15) 7.1.3
(16) 7.2.10
(17) 7.1.1
(18) 7.1.1
(19) 7.2.3
(20) 7.1.1
(21) 7.2.2
(22) 11.1.2
(23) 11.1.3
(24) S.1.4.10
(25) S.1.7.11
(26) S.1.7.11
(27) A.15.20
(28) 9.1.4/5
(29) 9.2.2
(30) 13.2.3
(31) 9.2.4
(32) 9.2.4
(33) 11.5.12

Chapter 4

(1) 6.4.7-8
(2) 1.2.5
(3) 6.1.10
(4) 3.2.5

(5)	6.1.8	(33)	2.2.2
(6)	12.1.2-3	(34)	8.1.1
(7)	5.2.1	(35)	3.6.1
(8)	8.1.1	(36)	10.6.9-10
(9)	5.2.1	(37)	8.7.16
(10)	2.1.1	(38)	3.6.2
(11)	3.2.1	(39)	5.6.13
(12)	1.1.1	(40)	11.7.12
(13)	1.2.1	(41)	9.3.3
(14)	12.1.1	(42)	1.7.7
(15)	A.7.11	(43)	5.6.8-9
(16)	10.2.3	(44)	9.3.23
(17)	10.4.4	(45)	2.6.8
(18)	1.4.3	(46)	7.3.11
(19)	12.4.16	(47)	11.3.14
(20)	3.4.14	(48)	10.7.8
(21)	8.2.4	(49)	1.2.10
(22)	5.3.10-11	(50)	1.4.13
(23)	2.5.2	(51)	12.7.9
(24)	2.4.4	(52)	8.6.13
(25)	2.2.5	(53)	3.3.21
(26)	11.1.3	(54)	1.4.4
(27)	7.5.9	(55)	1.6.4
(28)	3.3.4	(56)	3.3.3
(29)	8.1.1	(57)	5.4.9
(30)	8.4.4	(58)	7.4.4-5
(31)	8.5.17	(59)	9.2.5
(32)	8.5.14	(60)	11.4.5

Chapter 5

(1)	12.2.3	(10)	9.2.2
(2)	3.3.13	(11)	5.5.10-11
(3)	10.4.1	(12)	11.5.6
(4)	8.2.6	(13)	8.5.9
(5)	2.2.1	(14)	8.4.5
(6)	1.2.9	(15)	2.2.2
(7)	4.2.5	(16)	8.2.7
(8)	1.6.2	(17)	1.1.12
(9)	8.6.6	(18)	10.1.3

(19) 10.2.3	(28) 12.4.5-6
(20) 12.4.6-7	(29) 2.4.2
(21) 12.6.17	(30) 2.6.1
(22) 3.4.15	(31) 10.4.2-4
(23) 10.6.7	(32) 10.4.7-8
(24) 8.4.2	(33) 2.4.5
(25) 7.4.6	(34) 8.1.3
(26) 7.5.10-11	(35) 6.1.9
(27) 7.6.19	(36) 6.1.8

Chapter 6

(1) B.9.10	(17) 12.2.15-16
(2) B.20.21	(18) 7.2.13-14
(3) B.13.4	(19) 10.5.3
(4) B.6.2–3	(20) 8.4.2-7
(5) B.1.31	(21) 5.3.1-6
(6) B.9.1	(22) A.3.6-17
(7) B.8.2	(23) A.2.16-17
(8) A.6.22	(24) A.9.14-15
(9) A.10.13-14	(25) A.4.15
(10) A.15.17	(26) 2.2.10
(11) A.17.29	(27) 8.2.13
(12) A.13.21-22	(28) A.1.2-3
(13) 7.1.17	(29) A.1.12
(14) 8.1.10	(30) A.1.12
(15) 8.3.11	(31) A.1.16
(16) 7.3.16	(32) A.1.6

Chapter 7

(1) A.11.6	(3) 5.1.1
(2) A.11.11-12	(4) A.11.4

Works Cited

ACE Blue Ribbon Panel on Global Engagement (2011) *Strength through Global Leadership and Engagement: US Higher Education in the 21st Century*, Washington DC: American Council of Education. Retrieved from www.acernet.edu/news-room/Documents/2011-CIGE-BRPReport.pdf

Adams, R. (2018a), 'Business leaders to head university watchdog', *The Guardian*, 1 January.

Adams, R. (2018b), 'Universities facing cash shortfalls will not be propped up – regulator', *The Guardian*, 7 November.

Adelman, C. (2009), *The Bologna Process for U.S. Eyes: Re-learning Higher Education in the Age of Convergence*, Washington DC: Institute for Higher Education Policy.

ASA/CAP (2017), *Universities: Comparative Claims: Advice*, London: Advertising Standards Authority and Committees of Advertising Practice. Retrieved from www.asa.org.uk/advice-online/universities-comparative-claims.html

Baumberg, J. J. (2018), *The Secret Life of Science*, Princeton: Princeton University Press.

BBC News (2017), 'Student loans fraud exposed by Panorama', 13 November. Retrieved from www.bbc.co.uk/news/uk-41966571

Bird, R. (1994), 'Reflections on the British Government and higher education in the 1980s', *Higher Education Quarterly*, 48(2): 73–85.

Blair, T. (2010), *A Journey*, London: Hutchinson.

Bolden R., Gosling, J., O'Brien, A., Peters K., with Longsworth, L., Davidovic, A. and Winklemann, K. (2012), *Academic Leadership: Changing Conceptions, Identities and Experiences in UK Higher Education*, London: Leadership Foundation for Higher Education.

Bonaccorsi, A., Brandt, T., Filippo, D. De, Lepori, B., Molinari, F., Niederl, A., … Slipersaeter, S. (2010), *Feasibility Study for Creating a European University Data Collection (EUMIDA): Final Study Report*. Brussels: European Commission.

Britton, I., Dearden, L., Shephard, N. and Vignoles, A. (2016), *How English Domiciled Graduate Earnings Vary with Gender, Institution Attended, Subject and Socio-economic Background*, Institute for Fiscal Studies, IFS Working Paper W16/06. Available online www.ifs.org.uk/uploads/publications/wps/wp201606.pdf

Browne, J. (Browne Review) (2010), *Securing a Sustainable Future for Higher Education*. https://assets.publishing.service.gov.uk/government/uploads/system/uploads/attachment_data/file/422565/bis-10-1208-securing-sustainable-higher-education-browne-report.pdf

Bryman, A. (2007), *Effective Leadership in Higher Education*, London: Leadership Foundation for Higher Education.

Busby, E. (2018), 'Universities make "misleading" marketing claims to students, report suggests', *The Independent*, 21 September. Retrieved from www.independent.co.uk/news/education/education-news/marketing-claims-students-which-university-rankings-advertising-standards-authority-a8547416.html

Cabinet Office (1987), *Civil Research and Development: Government Response to the First Report of the House of Lords Select Committee on Science and Technology, 1986-87 Session*, CM 185, London: HMSO.

Carswell, J. (1985), *Government and the Universities*, Cambridge: Cambridge University Press.

Cerny, P. G. (2000), 'Restructuring the political arena: Globalization and the paradoxes of the competition state', in R. D. Germain (ed.), *Globalization and Its Critics. Perspectives from Political Economy*, 117–38, Basingstoke: Palgrave.

Chao Jr, R. (2017), 'A new dawn for Asian higher education regionalization?' *University World News*. Retrieved from http://www.universityworldnews.com/article.php?story=2017050822311447

CHERPA-Network (2010), *U-Multirank: Project 'Design and Testing the Feasibility of a Multi-dimensional Global University Ranking'*, Twente: CHERPA-Network.

Clark, B. R. (1998), *Creating Entrepreneurial Universities: Organizational Pathways of Transformation*, Oxford: Pergamon.

Clark, T. (2006), *OECD Thematic Review of Tertiary Education: Country Report: United Kingdom*, Paris: OECD.

Committee on Higher Education (The Robbins Report) (1963), *Higher Education: A Report*, Cmnd 2154, London: Her Majesty's Stationery Office.

Committee of University Chairmen (CUC) (2014; Revised 2018), *The Higher Education Code of Governance*, London: CUC.

Committee of Vice-Chancellors and Principals (CVCP) (The Jarratt Report) (1985), *Report of the Steering Committee for Efficiency Studies in Universities*, London: CVCP.

Competition and Markets Authority (2015), *Advice to UK Higher Education Providers on Consumer Protection Law. CMA Response to the Consultation: 12 March 2015*, London: CMA.

Corbett, A. (2003), 'Ideas. Institutions and Policy Entrepreneurs: Towards a new history of higher education in the European Community', *European Journal of Education*, 38(3): 315–30.

Department of Business, Innovation and Skills (2011), *Higher Education: Students at the Heart of the System*, Cm 8122, London: Her Majesty's Stationery Office (HMSO).

Department of Business, Innovation and Skills (2016), *Success as a Knowledge Economy: Teaching Excellence, Social Mobility and Student Choice*, Cm 9258, London: Her Majesty's Stationery Office (HMSO).

Department for Education (2017), *Securing Student Success: Risk Base Regulation for Teaching Excellence, Social Mobility and Informed Choice in Higher Education: Government Consultation on Behalf of the Office for Students*, London: DfE.

Department of Education and Science (1985), *The Development of Higher Education into the 1990s*, Cmnd 9524, London: Her Majesty's Stationery Office.

Department of Education and Science (1991), *Higher Education: A New Framework*, Cmnd 1541, London: HMSO.

Department of Education and Science (2003), *The Future of Higher Education*, Cm 5735, London: HMSO.

Coates, D. and Warwick, K. (1999), 'The knowledge driven economy: Analysis and background', Paper presented at the 'Economics of the Knowledge Driven Economy' conference, DTI & CERP, London, 27 January.

Donnelly, M. and Gamsu, S. (2018), *'Home and Away': Social, Ethnic and Special Inequalities in Student Mobility*, Sutton. Available online: www.suttontrust.com/wp-content/uploads/2016/02/HomeTrust and away FINAL pdf

Doyle, S. (2017), 'Higher fees mooted for cash-strapped universities', interview of Professor Paddy Nixon, *The Irish News*, 25 September.

Eaton, J. S. (2003), 'The UNESCO Global Forum: Continuing Conversations About Quality Review and Higher Education', *International Higher Education*, 30: 14–15.

Edwards, J., Marinelli, E., Arregui-Pabollet, E. and Kempton, L. (2017), *Higher Education for Smart Specialisation, Towards Strategic Partnerships for Innovation* (S3 Policy Brief Series No. 23/2017), Luxembourg: Publications Office of the European Union.

EHEA (2018), *Paris Communiqué*, EHEA Ministerial Conference Paris, 24–25 May, Paris: EHEA.

Epstein, L. D. (1974), *Governing the University*, San Francisco: Jossey Bass.

Erkkilä, T. and Piironen, O. (2009), 'The Iron Cage of Governance Indicators', in R. W. Cox (ed.), *Ethics and Integrity in Public Administration: Concepts and Cases*, 125–45, Abingdon: Routledge.

Espinoza, J. (2018a), 'PE firms raise money at fastest pace since 2006', *Financial Times*, 18 July.

Espinoza, J. (2018b), 'Fewer winners: Private equity deals have lost some of their lustre since crisis', *Financial Times*, 19 October.

Estermann, T. and Kupriyanova, V. (2018), *Efficiency, Leadership and Governance: Closing the Gap between Strategy and Execution*, Brussels: European Universities Association.

Estermann, T., Nokkala, T. and Steinel, M. (2011), *University Autonomy in Europe II*, Brussels: European Universities Association.

Europa (2000), *Presidency Conclusions: Lisbon European Council*, Brussels: European Commission.

Europa (2003), *The Role of the Universities in the Europe of Knowledge* (Communication from the Commission No. COM (2003) 58 final), Brussels: European Commission.

Europa (2006), *Delivering on the Modernisation Agenda for Universities: Education, Research and Innovation* (Communication to the Council and the European Parliament No. (COM) 2006 208 final), Brussels: European Commission.

Europa (2007), *Modernising Universities for Europe's Competitiveness in a Global Knowledge Economy*, Brussels: European Commission.

Europa (2010), *Europe 2020 Flagship Initiative: Innovation Union* (Communication from the Commission to the European Parliament, the Council, the European Economic and Social Committee and the Committee of the Regions. No. COM(2010) 546 final), Brussels: European Commission.

Europa (2011), *Supporting Growth and Jobs – An Agenda for the Modernisation of Europe's Higher Education System* (No. COM(2011)567/2), Brussels: European Commission.

Europa (2012), *A Reinforced European Research Area Partnership for Excellence and Growth* (Communication from the Commission to the European Parliament, the Council, the European Economic and Social Committee and the Committee of the Regions. COM(2012) 392 final), Brussels: European Commission.

Europa (2016), *The Transition towards an Open Science System* (Proceedings of the Council of the European Union No. 9526/16), Brussels: European Commission.

Europa (2017), *On a Renewed EU Agenda for Higher Education* (No. COM (2017) 247 final), Brussels: European Commission.

European Universities Association (2017), *University Autonomy in Europe III*, Brussels: European University Association.

Gibbons, S. and Vignoles, A. (2013), 'Geography, choice and participation in higher education in England', *Regional Science and Urban Economics*, 42(1): 98–113.

Gibbs, G. (2010), *Divisions of Quality*, London: Higher Education Academy.

Goddard, J. and Kempton, L. (2011), *Connecting Universities to Regional Growth: A Practical Guide*, Brussels: European Commission.

Hazelkorn, E. (2011), *Rankings and the Reshaping of Higher Education*, London: Palgrave Macmillan.

Hazelkorn, E. (2012), 'European "transparency instruments": Driving the Modernisation of European Higher Education', in S. P. Scott, A. Curaj, L. Vlăsceanu and L. Wilson (eds), *European Higher Education at the Crossroads: Between the Bologna Process and National Reforms*, vol. 1, 339–60, Dordrecht: Springer.

Hazelkorn, E. (2013), 'Europe enters the college ranking game', *Washington Monthly*. Retrieved from http://washingtonmonthly.com/magazine/septoct-2013/europe-en ters-the-college-rankings-game/

Hazelkorn, E. (2015), *Rankings and the Reshaping of Higher Education: The Battle for world-class Excellence* (1st edn), Basingstoke: Palgrave Macmillan.

Hazelkorn, E. (2016), *Towards 2030—A Framework for Building a World Class Post-Compulsory Education System for Wales*, Cardiff: Welsh Government.

Hazelkorn, E. (2018), 'Reshaping the world order of higher education: The role and impact of rankings on national and global systems', *Policy Reviews in Higher Education*, 2(1): 4–31.

Hazelkorn, E. and Edwards, J. (forthcoming), *Skills and Smart Specialisation: The role of Vocational Education and Training and Adult Learning in Smart Specialisation*

Strategies, JRC Science for Policy Report, Luxembourg: Publications Office of the European Union.

Hazelkorn, E. and Ryan, M. (2013), 'The impact of university rankings on higher education policy in Europe: A challenge to perceived wisdom and a stimulus for change', in P. Zgaga, U. Teichler and J. Brennan (eds), *The Globalization Challenge for European Higher Education: Convergence and Diversity, Centres and Peripheries*, 79–101, Frankfurt: Peter Lang.

Held, D. and McGrew, A. (2002), 'Introduction', in D. Held and A. McGrew (eds), *Governing Globalization: Power, Authority and Global Governance*, 1–21, Malden: Polity Press.

Henry, M., Lingard, B., Rizvi, F. and Taylor, S. (2001), *The OECD, Globalisation and Education Policy*, Oxford: IAU Press/Pergamon/Elsevier.

Higher Education Funding Council for England (2015), *Annual Accountability Returns 2015: Request for Information*, HEFCE, September 2015/16.

Higher Education Funding Council for England (2016), *Financial Health of the Higher Education Sector: 2015-16 to 2018-19 Forecasts*, HEFCE, November 2016/34.

Higher Education Funding Council for England (2017), *Circular Letter re Assurance Statements about Quality and Standards from Accountable Officers for 2017–18*, HEFCE, October 2017/37.

House of Commons Education Committee (2018), *Value for Money in Higher Education*, London: House of Commons Seventh Report 2017–19, HC 343, 24 October.

House of Lords' European Union Committee (2012), *The Modernisation of Higher Education in Europe*, London. Stationery Office, 22 March.

Independent Panel Report (Augar Review) (2019), *Review of Post-18 Education and Funding*, London: HMSO CP 117.

Jacso, P. (2010), 'The impact of Eugene Garfield through the prism of Web of Science', *Annals of Library and Information Studies*, 57(September): 222–47.

Johnson, J. (2017), 'Emergency Debate Tuition Fees', *House of Commons Hansard*, Volume 627, Column 886, 19 July.

Lambert, R. (2003), *Lambert Review of Business-University Collaboration, Final Report*, London: HMSO.

Leadership Foundation for Higher Education (2017), *Reviewing Academic Governance in Higher Education: A Framework*, London: Leadership Foundation for Higher Education.

Ligami, C. (2017), 'Heads of state declare common higher education area', *University World News*, 19 May. Retrieved from www.universityworldnews.com/article.php?story=20170519145012846

Locke, W., Verbik, L., Richardson, J. T. E. and King, R. (2008), *Counting What is Measured or Measuring What Counts? League Tables and their Impact on Higher Education Institutions in England*, Bristol: Higher Education Funding Council for England.

McKie, A. (2019), 'Two-thirds of students think TEF based on Ofsted-style inspection', *Times Higher Education*, 31 January: 9.

Major, J. (1999), *The Autobiography*, London: Harper Collins.

Marginson, S. and Rhoades, G. (2002), 'Beyond national states, markets, and systems of higher education: A glonacal agency heuristic', *Higher Education*, 43(3): 281–309.

Martin, M. and Sauvageot, C. (2011), *Constructing an Indicator System or Scorecard for Higher Education: A Practical Guide*, Paris: International Institute for Educational Planning & UNESCO Institute for Statistics.

Mayer, C. (2018), *Prosperity*, Oxford: Oxford University Press.

McGettigan, A. (2015), *The Accounting and Budgeting of Student Loans*, HEPI Report 75, Oxford: Higher Education Policy Institute.

Moodie, G. C. and Eustace, R. B. (1974) *Power and Authority in British Universities*, London: Allen and Unwin.

Morgan, J. (2015), 'OECD's AHELO will fail to launch, says education director', *Times Higher Education*, 12 September. Retrieved from www.timeshighereducation.com/news/oecds-ahelo-will-fail-launch-says-education-director

Morgan, J. (2018), 'DfE "bends over backwards" to help for profit', *Times Higher Education*, 22 November. Retrieved from www.timeshighereducation.com/news/dfe-bends-over-backwards-help-englands-biggest-profit

Myklebust, J. P. (2018), 'H2020 failing to ease Europe's research funding divide', *University World News*, 17 February. Retrieved from www.universityworldnews.com/article.php?story=20180217050748749

Myklebust, J. P. and O'Malley, B. (2018), 'Macron's vision of universities networks moves forward', *University World News*, 5 May. Retrieved from www.universityworldnews.com/article.php?story=20180505051434124

National Audit Office (2017a), *Follow Up on Alternative Higher Education Providers*, HC 411 Session 2017–2019, 18 October.

National Audit Office (2017b), *The Higher Education Market*, Department for Education HC 629, Session 2017–2019, 8 December.

National Committee of Enquiry into Higher Education (The Dearing Report) (1997), *Higher Education in the Learning Society*, London: HMSO.

Nayyar, D. (2002), 'Towards global governance', in D. Nayyer (ed.), *Governing Globalization: Issues and Institutions*, 3–18, Oxford: Oxford University Press.

OECD (1980), *Measuring Science, Technology, and Innovation*, Paris: OECD.

OECD (1996), *The Knowledge-based Economy*, Paris: OECD.

OECD (2003), 'Education Policy Analysis 2003', in *Education Policy Analysis*, Paris: OECD.

OECD (2013), *Assessment of Higher Education Learning Outcomes (AHELO) Feasibility Study Report: Volume 1 – Design and Implementation: Executive Summary*, Paris: OECD.

OECD (2017), *Benchmarking Higher Education System Performance: Conceptual Framework and Data*, Enhancing Higher Education System Performance, Paris: OECD.

Pruvot, E. B. and Estermann, T. (2017), *University Autonomy in Europe III, The Scorecard 2017*, Brussels: European Universities Association.

Pruvot, E. B. and Estermann, T. (2018), 'University governance: Autonomy, structures and inclusiveness', in A. Curaj, L. Deca and R. Pricopie (eds), *European Higher Education Area: The Impact of Past and Future Policies*, 619–38, Dordrecht: Springer.

Raffe, D. (2016) 'Higher Education governance and institutional autonomy in the post-devolution UK', in S. Riddell, E. Weston and S. Minty (eds) *Higher Education in Scotland and the UK: Diverging or Converging Systems?*, 19–32, Edinburgh: Edinburgh University Press.

Riddell, S., Weston, E. and Minty S. (eds) (2016), *Higher Education in Scotland and the UK: Diverging or Converging Systems?*, Edinburgh: Edinburgh University Press.

Robertson, S., Olds, K., Dale, R. and Dang, Q. (2016), 'Introduction: Global regionalism and higher education', in *Global Regionalisms and Higher Education: Projects, Processes, Politics*, 1–23, Cheltenham: Edward Elgar Publishing.

Rowlands, J. (2017), *Academic Governance in the Contemporary University*, Singapore: Springer.

Salmi, J. (2017), 'Excellence strategies and world-class universities', in E. Hazelkorn (ed.), *Ranking and the Geopolitics of Higher Education: Understanding the Influence and Impact of Rankings on Higher Education, Policy and Society*, 216–43, Abingdon: Routledge.

Sauder, M. and Espeland, W. N. (2009), 'The discipline of rankings: Tight coupling and organizational change', *American Sociological Review*, 74 (1): 63–82.

Schiltz, M. (2018), *Science Without Publication Paywalls a Premable to: cOAlition S for the Realisation of Full and Immediate Open Access*, Brussels: Science Europe.

Science Europe (2018), *Plan S: Accelerating the Transition to Full and Immediate Open Access to Scientific Publications*, Brussels: European Commission. Retrieved from www.scienceeurope.org/wp-content/uploads/2018/09/Plan_S.pdf

Scottish Government (2007), *Principles and Priorities: The Government's Programme for Scotland*, Edinburgh: Scottish Government.

Scottish Government (2013), *Scotland's Future: Your Guide to an Independent Scotland*, Edinburgh: Scottish Government.

Sharma, Y. (2017), 'New Asian universities' alliance to increase mobility', *University World News*. Retrieved from http://www.universityworldnews.com/article.php?story=20170504205518718

Sharma, Y. (2018), 'UN convention on degree recognition comes into force', *University World News*, 13 January. Retrieved from www.universityworldnews.com/article.php?story=20180113050903364

Shattock, M. L. (1994), *The UGC and the Management of British Universities*, Buckingham: Open University Press.

Shattock, M. L. (2006), *Managing Good Governance in Higher Education*, Maidenhead: Open University Press.

Shattock, M. L. (2012), *Making Policy in British Higher Education: 1945–2011*, Maidenhead: Open University Press/McGraw-Hill Education.

Shattock, M. L. (2016), 'Financing British higher education: The triumph of process over policy', in R. Barnett, P. Temple and P. Scott (eds), *Valuing Higher Education*, 59–76, London: UCLIOE Press.

Shinn, C. H. (1986), *Paying the Piper, The Development of the University Grants Committee 1919–1946*, London: Falmer Press.

Sloman, A. (1963), *A University in the Making: The B.B.C. Reith Lectures*, London: BBC.

Stark, D., Beunza, D., Girard, M. and Lukacs, J. (2009), *The Sense of Dissonance*, Princeton: Princeton University Press.

Stern, Lord N. (2016), *Research Excellence Framework Review: Building on Success and Learning from Experience*, Department for Business, Energy and Industrial Strategy, Ind/16/9, London: BEIS.

Stiglitz, J. (2017), *Globalization and Its Discontents Revisited: Anti-Globalization in the Era of Trump*, London: Penguin.

Taggart, G. J. (2004), *A Critical Review of the Role of the English Funding Body for Higher Education in the Relationship between the State and Higher Education in the Period 1945-2003*, PhD thesis, University of Bristol, School of Education.

Taylor, J. (2018), *The Impact of the First World War on British Universities*, London: Palgrave Macmillan.

Technopolis (2017), *The Role of EU Funding in UK Research and Innovation* (Commissioned by the Academy of Medical Sciences, British Academy, Royal Academy of Engineering and the Royal Society), Brighton: Technopolis.

Times Higher Education (2018), 'Campus estate upgrades at risk from Brexit borrowing squeeze', *THE*, 1 February, no. 2: 342.

Times Higher Education (2019), 'The REF games are even more brutal this time around', *THE*, 3 January, no. 2: 389.

UGC (1984), *A Strategy for Higher Education into the 1990s*, London: UGC.

UNESCO (2005), *Second Global Forum on International Quality Assurance, Accreditation and the Recognition of Qualifications: Draft Final Report*, Paris: UNESCO.

UNESCO (2018), *Global Citizenship Education and the Rise of National Perspectives: Reflections and Possible Ways Forward*, Paris: UNESCO.

University of Oxford (The Franks Report) (1964), *Report of a Commission of Inquiry under the Chairmanship of Lord Franks*, Oxford: University of Oxford.

US Senate Committee on Health, Education, Labor and Pensions (2012), *For Profit Higher Education: The Failure to Safeguard the Federal Investment and Ensure Student Success*, Washington DC: US Senate, 30 July.

van Damme, D. (2009), 'The search for transparency: Convergence and diversity in the Bologna process', in F. van Vught (ed.), *Mapping the Higher Education Landscape: Towards a European Classification of Higher Education*, 39–55, Dordrecht: Springer Netherlands.

van Damme, D. (2018), 'Dynamics of inequality, convergence and differentiation', in *Keynote Presentation, Constructing Higher Education Evaluation Systems for the Global Era*, Tsinghua University, http//www.u-map.eu/U-Map_report.pdf

van Damme, D. and van der Wende, M. (2018), 'Global higher education governance', in B. Cantwell, H. Coates and R. King (eds), *Handbook on the Politics of Higher Education*, 91–113, Cheltenham: Edward Elgar Publishing.

van Raan, A. F. J., van Leeuwen, T. N. and Visser, M. S. (2011), 'Severe language effect in university rankings: Particularly Germany and France are wronged in citation-based rankings', *Scientometrics*, 88(2): 495–8.

van Vught, F., Bartelse, J., Burquel, N., Divis, J., Huisman, J. and Wende, M. van der (2005), *Institutional Profiles: Towards a Typology of Higher Education Institutions in Europe*, Twente: University of Twente.

van Vught, F. A. A., Kaiser, F., File, J. M. M., Gaethgens, C., Peter, R. and Westerheijden, D. F. (2010), *U-Map: The European Classification of Higher Education Institutions*, Enschede: Center for Higher Education Policy Studies (CHEPS).

Wagner, C. S., Park, H. W. and Leydesdorff, L. (2015), 'The continuing growth of global cooperation networks in research: A conundrum for national governments', *PLoS ONE*, 10(7): 1–15.

Weale, S. (2017), 'Advertising watchdog forces Reading University to ditch "top 1 %" claim', *The Guardian*, 8 June. Retrieved from www.theguardian.com/education/2017/jun/08/advertising-watchdog-forces-reading-university-to-ditch-top-1-claim

Willetts, D. (2017), *A University Education*, Oxford: Oxford University Press.

Witte, J. K. (2006), *Change of Degrees and Degrees of Change: Comparing Adaptations of European Higher Education Systems*. Submitted for doctoral dissertation, Twente: University of Twente. Retrieved from https://www.utwente.nl/en/bms/cheps/education/phd-page/cheps-alumni-and-their-theses/2006wittedissertation.pdf

Index

Note: Page numbers followed by 'n' refer to notes.

Lightning Source UK Ltd.
Milton Keynes UK
UKHW020046210221
379122UK00003B/99